THE TWO-PARENT PRIVILEGE

The Two-Parent Privilege

» «

HOW THE DECLINE IN MARRIAGE HAS INCREASED
INEQUALITY AND LOWERED SOCIAL MOBILITY,
AND WHAT WE CAN DO ABOUT IT

» «

Melissa S. Kearney

Swift

SWIFT PRESS

First published in the United States of America by
The University of Chicago Press 2023

First published in Great Britain by Swift Press 2023

1 3 5 7 9 8 6 4 2

Offset by Tetragon, London
Printed and bound in Great Britain by CPI Group (UK) Ltd, Croydon, CR0 4YY

A CIP catalogue record for this book is available from the British Library

ISBN: 9781800753747
eISBN: 9781800753754

FOR WILLIAM, SOPHIA, AND ADELAIDE

Contents

Preface

There are all kinds of families and all kinds of households. People make their families work in all different ways, with various arrangements. The ways in which all of our families are different—with their own personalities, quirks, routines, and traditions—are part of what makes them so special. And part of what makes family so deeply personal is that exactly how any one of them works (assuming nobody is being harmed) is really no one else's business.

It is a separate question, however, how the structures of different families can deliver different benefits to children—and, in the aggregate, to society. It is reasonable to argue, for example, that a household with two parents has a greater capacity to provide financial and nonfinancial resources to a child than a one-parent household does. To argue this is not to judge, blame, or diminish households with a single parent; it is simply to acknowledge that (1) kids require a lot of work and a lot of resources, and (2) having two parents in the household generally means having more resources to devote to the task of raising a family.

The dramatic increase in the prevalence of one-parent households in the US reflects a profound change in the way children are being raised in this country, with implications for children but also for society. As uncomfortable as it might be to discuss this shift and its implications, avoiding a direct examination of the issue—well-intentioned as that tendency might be—is ultimately counterproductive.

I have studied US poverty, inequality, and family structure for almost a quarter of a century. I approach these issues as a hardheaded—albeit softhearted—MIT-trained economist. Based on the overwhelming evidence at hand, I can say with the utmost confidence that the decline in marriage and the corresponding rise in the share of children being raised in one-parent homes has contributed to the economic insecurity of American families, has widened the gap in opportunities and outcomes for children from different backgrounds, and today poses economic and social challenges that we cannot afford to ignore—but may not be able to reverse.

When I have spoken with other scholars in recent years about my plans to write this book, the most common response I have gotten is along the lines of "I tend to agree with you about all this— but are you sure you want to be out there saying this publicly?" I have thought a lot about that. No, but yes. No, because it's much more comfortable to talk about these issues in academic conferences, where we all are looking at the same data and evidence and can rationally and (mostly) dispassionately talk about what they mean. But yes, because even if scholars know about these trends and actively debate appropriate policy or government responses, societal change doesn't happen in the pages of academic journals or around the tables at academic conferences. Societal change happens when the public engages with an issue and policy makers have the facts and evidence. I have been studying and debating these issues in academic settings long enough to feel like it's time to take this evidence and the surrounding conversation to a wider audience.

I am a mom and an economist, in that order. I care deeply about children, all children, and their well-being. I care about the opportunities people have to live their best lives and thrive in society. I am constantly thinking about how economic structures enrich or impede people's lives. I am concerned about widening inequality and eroding social mobility in the US. My research has me convinced that the decline in marriage and the corresponding rise in the share of children growing up with only one parent in their home is both a cause and a consequence of economic and social challenges facing our nation. The nature of these challenges is detailed and substantiated in this book. They are wide-ranging and deeply challenging.

I am the granddaughter of an Italian immigrant who came to the US in 1921 with an elementary-school education. I am the daughter of a woman who didn't have the educational or occupational opportunities that I have had. And I am the mother of three children who are extraordinarily lucky to have numerous resource advantages, including the opportunity to attend good schools in safe neighborhoods. I see the role of economics and of luck, and the dreams and fears of parents, everywhere I look. I see the promise of children and the ways in which forces beyond their control shape their lives. I see the world around me through the lens of my own life, but I look to data and rigorous studies for answers about what is happening on a widespread basis, why it is happening, and ultimately what can be done to make people's lives better.

I fully expect that there will be some people who merely read the title and form a strong opinion about what they presume fills the pages. But there are no easy-to-dismiss straw-man arguments or claims in this book. I am not blaming single mothers. I am not diminishing the pernicious effects of racism in the United States. I am not saying everyone should get married. I am not dismissing nonresident fathers as absent from their children's lives or uninterested in being good dads. I am not promoting a norm of a stay-at-home wife and a breadwinner husband. What I am doing is arguing, through an appeal to data and rigorous studies, that two parents tend to be able to provide their children with more resource advantages than one parent alone. And furthermore, that a two-parent family is increasingly becoming yet another privilege associated with more highly resourced groups in society. That argument leads me to ask why so many parents are now raising their children outside a marital union. What factors are behind the reduction in marriage and why are college-educated adults getting married at much higher rates than others? How does the presence of one versus two parents in a home affect children's educational and economic outcomes and why?

I ask and answer these questions as an economist, not as someone with a moral or value-laden proposition. It is really challenging to discuss the topics of marriage and family without it feeling like a conversation about values, but my hope and intention is that by taking a social science approach to these important issues, we can take them out of the intractable culture wars and acknowledge them, debate them, and collectively take steps to improve the lives of American families.

COLLEGE PARK, MARYLAND
December 2022

ONE

The Elephant
in the Room

"Some areas of unequal opportunity are clearly evident. And some
of these are amenable to remedial social action. The clearest cases
are those outside the orbit of family relationships."

ARTHUR M. OKUN, "Equality and Efficiency"

Some years ago, I was at a small two-day conference that brought
together people from the academic and policy communities to talk
about income inequality, economic mobility, and other related challenges facing the country. As is the case for many professions, being an academic economist involves going to lots of these types of
conferences: traveling to a different city, attending a day of presen-
tations and panels (often in windowless rooms), having a group dinner with other conference participants, and waking up early the next
day to participate in another full day of sessions focused on a particular topic. People share their most recent research, discuss and debate ideas and evidence, make plans for additional research, and (in
the best cases) inform the decisions of policy leaders with the kind
of real-world evidence that economic data can provide. Then we go
home, think about the new results we saw and the conversations we
had, work some more, follow up with people we talked with, and re-
peat the process over again.

During this particular conference, we talked about the decline in US employment and widening income inequality. We talked about how the growing economic gap between America's wealthy and poor was making it harder for Americans to achieve upward mobility—to live a life better than their parents did, economically speaking, and achieve the proverbial American dream. Over the course of the conference, the conversations focused on the usual topics that come up when economists talk about such things. We talked about gaps in pay between workers with and without college degrees. We talked about how technology and import competition disadvantaged certain groups of workers. We talked about the decline in union representation and the rise of CEO pay. We talked about the need for improved educational institutions and discussed ways to strengthen the safety net and reform the tax code.

During one of the later conference sessions, I raised my hand and asked a question that I'd been thinking about for a while: how should we think about the role of family and home environment in all this? If we are talking about how people perform in school and the labor market, isn't the kind of household they grew up in an important determinant of that performance? There was quiet. After a few beats I continued talking, rattling off a few statistics and facts about class gaps in marriage and family structure, then suggesting that these class gaps should probably be part of our conversations about inequality and mobility. I pointed out that college-educated adults are more likely than non-college-educated adults to get married and to raise kids in two-parent homes. The resources of these homes (including money, but also time and energy in the challenging work of parenting) separated them from less educated adults and their children, who lacked such resource luxuries. The data suggest that these difference across households produce large economic differences in the lives of children. Don't we need to contend with these facts? What should we make of them and what, if anything, should policy makers do about them?

This was not the first time I'd raised this issue of family structure among peers, but this was one of the largest audiences for it, and the group assembled extended beyond the usual group of scholars who study poverty, children, and families. My questions were received about as I expected them to be. As in earlier instances, this set of questions elicited a muted reaction—uncomfortable shifting in seats and facial expressions that conveyed reservations with this line of inquiry. The apparent consensus I took from the room, expressed through limited language and unencouraging gestures, was that family and marriage were personal matters and somewhat out of bounds for this type of discussion. While my colleagues were willing to grant the point that an increasing share of US children were living in single-parent homes and that this was much more common among less educated families—and that outcomes of children from single-parent homes tend to be worse than those of children from two-parent homes, for a variety of reasons—the implication was that we don't really know what to do about it as a matter of policy. In my experience, people in these types of scholarly, policy-oriented settings are much more comfortable talking about the need to improve schools, expand college access, and increase the Earned Income Tax Credit than they are talking about family structure and how kids are raised. Don't get me wrong; I think those other issues are important and I'm always up for talking about them. My point was simply that the absence of a discussion of family seemed conspicuous and counterproductive.

After the day's sessions, in the lobby of the hotel, a prominent economist approached me and asked a series of pointed questions about the role of family structure in shaping children's life outcomes. If kids are being taken care of, he asked, what did it matter if their parents were married? Did the evidence suggest that parental marriage per se mattered for how kids do in the world? Here I recounted some more of what I knew from the data and existing research, all of which seemed to point to a distinct social and economic advantage for kids who grew up with married parents, largely because "married parents" tends to mean a two-parent home and a two-parent home tends to mean more resources available to the child than in a one-parent home. That economist kept peppering me with specific questions. After a few minutes, he asked in a more pointed way: if parents are divorced but the dad contributes a lot financially, are the kids still at a relative disadvantage?

I cut him off, too quickly. "Look, I'm not really that worried about the kids of rich parents who get divorced," I said. "The kids I'm worried about are the ones growing up in single-parent homes with very limited resources; they don't have anything near the experiences and opportunities that kids from higher-income households have." I suspected (not knowing his personal family situation) that he might be thinking of his own kids, who were most likely going to do fine in life.

That night, and the next day and the day after that, I kept thinking about the muted reaction to my questions in the group session and the follow-up one-on-one conversation in the hotel lobby. The economist's questions hadn't been motivated by mere scholarly or policy curiosity; if they had been, he probably would have asked them in the conference room where dozens of other economists and policy experts were gathered. His questions seemed personal, like he was asking as a father who (I suspected) was divorced and wanted the best for his kids, like every parent does. But the fact that he sought me out and asked me these questions privately is reflective of a divide between what many of us worry about personally for our own children and what we are inclined to talk about publicly when it comes to the well-being of children more broadly in society.

I thought about a conversation I had recently had with a different economist in a different setting who reacted negatively when I mentioned the importance of family structure to children's outcomes. He bristled, suggesting to me that I sounded "socially conservative," in a way that implied "not academically serious." I countered, "You are always talking about the things you are doing for your kids and how much time their activities take up in your life. Why would you be offended by the suggestion that maybe other kids would also benefit from having the involvement of two parents, and in particular a father, in their lives?"

The existence of such a divide is predictable, even reasonable. Matters of households and families are inherently personal, and it's the nature of personal things that we don't talk about them with just anyone. Nor do most people like to sound judgmental about people's life choices. It seems that this discomfort and hesitancy have stifled public conversation on a critically important topic that has sweeping implications not just for the well-being of American children and families but for the country's well-being, too.

The more I reflected on these issues, the more I wanted to look at the data and existing research to figure out how changes in family structure over recent decades mattered (or not) for children's outcomes and for society. Much of the older social science research on family structure is narrowly focused on the issue of poverty, both as a cause and an effect. When single motherhood was closely linked in earlier generations to teen childbearing and poverty, it made sense to study how teen childbearing, nonmarital childbearing, and poverty reinforced each other. The question now was whether (and how) things had changed: How should we think about family structure now that single motherhood is so much more common and extends to so many? Why are so many adults forgoing marriage, even when they have children? How are these trends affecting children from different backgrounds?

The general approach economists take to studying the complicated issue of families and the "economics of the household," as it is often referred to, is to try to break this highly complex topic down into a limited set of key features so that we can study tendencies and trends. We hypothesize potential relationships among factors, in terms of both cause and effect. Then we look at data to see whether a hypothesis holds. If the data don't support the initial hypothesis, we revise the theoretical model or framework. Then we look at the data through that revised lens. The conceptual framework guides our empirical exploration of data and the interpretation of empirical patterns. We try to ascertain what is happening *in general*. In other words, we look for the patterns and the rules, not the oddities and exceptions, to tell a data-driven story.

A key factor that turns out to be relevant in a study of the economics of family today is the growing gap in family structure between the children of college-educated and non-college-educated adults. I focus on the factor of four-year college degree attainment as a marker of socioeconomic class divide. To be sure, a college degree is a crude measure of economic status, but it is a meaningful one nonetheless, and it is something that we observe in almost all national data sets. College-educated adults in the US today have higher earnings, on average, and they are more likely to be employed, on average. Their children are more likely to grow up to earn a college degree and have high earnings themselves. Of course, none of this accounts for whether someone is a good person or has a strong sense of self-worth or a fun sense of humor or finds love, or whether their child will be or do any of those things. But to the extent that a college degree is predictive of economic security and well-being, it is a useful marker of socioeconomic class distinction. It is also a driver of income inequality, which features prominently in the story I tell in this book.

The United States today is characterized by tremendously high rates of income inequality that exacerbate the country's cultural and institutional divides. As the income gaps between those with more and less education and those with higher and lower levels of income have widened, shared experiences and the promise of equal opportunity have eroded. Children growing up in these separate spheres do not have anything close to equal opportunities in life. Children born to highly educated, high-income parents are almost all being raised in highly resourced two-parent homes; they live in safe neighborhoods with well-funded schools, surrounded by high-test-scoring peers; most of them graduate from high school and then enroll in college; a majority of those who enroll in college graduate with a degree. In other words, they are predisposed by virtue of their family background to reaching the milestones that are likely to help them achieve an economically secure life. In contrast, children born to unmarried parents are more likely to grow up in a one-parent household and are statistically less likely to have these resources or advantages. This correlation is exacerbated by the social trappings of American inequality. Children in families with fewer resources (as compared to those who come from having two adults in the home) often live in low-income neighborhoods and attend inferior schools, because they have no other choice. They graduate high school and enroll in college at lower rates. Those who do enroll in college are much less likely to earn a degree.

Closing these class gaps will require many changes in society and vast improvements to a variety of institutions. Economic trends related to inequality will not just reverse themselves if left unchecked. When economic and social conditions reinforce class gaps, closing these gaps becomes increasingly difficult over time. Family structure perpetuates privilege and disadvantage across generations through its effects on the lives of children. While it is more comfortable to talk about elements of inequality, threats to social mobility, and policy interventions that are outside the orbit of family relationships, we need to discuss this metaphorical elephant in the room. This book aims to spotlight how an increasingly unequal economy has led to a class gap in family structure that perpetuates inequality and undermines economic mobility through its effect on children. This book puts a spotlight on the most fundamental institution to society: the family.

> **Over the past 40 years, there has been a dramatic decline in the share of children living with married parents; this shift has happened largely outside the college-educated class.**

In 2019, only 63% of children in the US lived with married parents, down from 77% in 1980. This decline has not been experienced equally across the population. There has been little change, for example, in the family structure of children whose mothers have a four-year college degree: In 2019, 84% of children whose mothers had four years of college lived with married parents, a decline of only 6 percentage points since 1980. Meanwhile, only 60% of children whose mothers had a high school degree or some college lived with married parents, a whopping 23 percentage point drop since 1980. A similarly large decline occurred among children of mothers

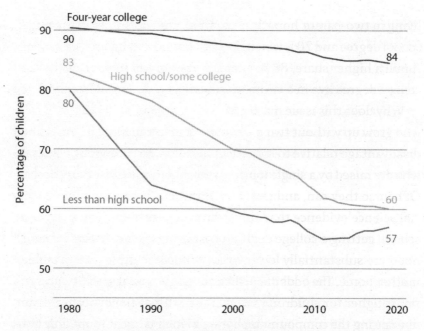

Figure 1.1 Percentage of children living with married parents, by maternal education level

SOURCE: *Author's calculations using 1980 and 1990 US decennial census and 2000–2019 US Census American Community Survey.*

NOTES: *Observations are weighted using child's survey weight.*

who didn't finish high school; the share of children in this group living with married parents fell from 80% in 1980 to 57% in 2019. Figure 1.1 plots these trends.[1]

Some might argue that placing marriage at the center of a conversation about children is antiquated and unhelpful: marriage is in many ways less fashionable than it was four decades ago. Marriage rates have fallen significantly in the US, including among adults who have children. It's important to recognize that these changes in marriage patterns are not without consequence for how children are being raised. Data show conclusively that parents are not cohabitating without marriage in a way that remotely accounts for the decrease in two-parent married households. These kids are more often living with one parent. What's more, data show that these trends are highly correlated with the parent's education: The share of children living in two-parent homes is 71% when the mother has only a high school degree and 70% when she does not have a high school degree. A much higher share, 88%, of children of mothers with a four-year college degree live in a two-parent home.

Why does this issue matter for kids' outcomes? Because children who grow up without two parents in their home are at a substantial disadvantage relative to kids who do. That is not to say that children who are raised by a single mother can't go on to achieve great things. Of course they can, and many do! But there are also mounds of social science evidence that shows how the odds of graduating high school, getting a college degree, and having high earnings in adulthood are substantially lower for children who grow up in a single-mother home. The odds of becoming a single parent are also substantially higher for children who grow up with a single mother, again illustrating the compounding nature of inequality. It is not only that lacking two parents makes it harder for some kids to go to college and lead a comfortable life; in the aggregate, it also undermines social mobility and perpetuates inequality across generations.

The forces that drive inequality are contributing to these demographic changes at the household level. Meanwhile, these household changes are exacerbating inequality. It is a vicious cycle. It has become increasingly difficult, for example, for someone without a high level of education or skill to achieve economic security and success in the US. Adults who have lower levels of education and earnings are less likely to get married and raise their children in two-parent homes. Their kids grow up with fewer resources and opportunities, and they don't do as well in school as their peers from married, higher-income families. Boys from disadvantaged homes are more likely to get in trouble in school and with the criminal justice system; girls from disadvantaged homes are more likely to become young, unmarried mothers. These children grow up to have children who are more likely to be born into disadvantaged situations. Social mobility is undermined, and inequality persists across generations. It is an economic imperative for the United States to break this cycle, and doing so will require coming at the problem from all dimensions.

**This is a book primarily about data,
interpreted through the lens of economics.**

This book draws heavily on data and empirical research, including the economic interpretation of statistics from public sources. The thesis of the book and the conclusions I draw are solidly grounded in evidence and in my professional expertise, which is analyzing and interpreting data. My training as an economist also leads me to approach data and evidence with a particular theoretical framework, one that thinks in terms of resources and the cause-and-effect relationships between factors and outcomes. In this book, I apply that approach to the complex issues of marriage, childbearing, and raising children.

I am keenly aware that behind every data point is a person or a family, people with their own unique stories and experiences. While economics is great for describing aggregate trends or identifying the cause and effect behind them (and indeed, this book will do both), such analysis can fall short when it comes to acknowledging exceptions, including the nuance—both wonderful and messy—of people's actual lives. As I write this book, I think of the mothers I met at a welfare-to-work program back in 1994; that was a job that animated my early interest in what has become a focus of my career as an academic economist. For a summer after my sophomore year in college, I worked as an intern at Bridgeport Jobs First, a job-training center in Bridgeport, Connecticut, that helped mothers on welfare train for and find employment. (At the time, most welfare recipients in the state—those without multiple, hard-to-overcome barriers to work—had to participate in job-training or job-hunting efforts in order to remain eligible for welfare benefits.) I taught math and computer classes and helped clients write their résumés. Working at that program gave me the opportunity to get to know, and in some instances truly love, economically struggling single moms whom I wouldn't otherwise have met. We'd go to McDonalds for lunch, or we'd grab food at the nearby pawn shop (where bagels and snacks were sold next to the guns) and eat together on a park bench. The women would tell me their stories; I would listen and both laugh and cry.

It was a stark lesson in how much more complicated and unpredictable people's lives are than policy conversations often assume. One of my coworkers at the center, who was a graduate of the center's program, was a person I remember for being cheerful, kind, funny, and bright, someone who seemed to face one major challenge after another with resilience and good humor. Even while her steady, well-paying job had stabilized some aspects of her life, it remained the case that some problems seemed unnavigable. One of her biggest worries that summer was what to do about her teenage son, who would begin high school the following year—a school where, she was sure, he would have to join a gang in order to survive. Together we researched scholarship options, to no avail. She was desperate to find a safe way for her son to attend high school, but given where she lived and her limited resources, she felt (and indeed seemed) trapped.

One of the people in my class that summer was a woman in her early twenties who had two children. By midsummer, she was visibly pregnant with her third. If she was worried about having another child, she didn't let on, seeming instead to take the development in stride. That same summer I read a news article about how the state of New Jersey, where I grew up, was experimenting with a welfare "family cap"—a policy that capped monthly household benefits based on the number of children a woman had at the time she enrolled in welfare, eliminating increases for additional children who might be born thereafter. The policy, motivated by the notion that women might be having additional children to qualify for more benefits, motivated some of my earliest research. A few years later, I investigated the policy as part of my dissertation research at MIT.[2] I found that policy makers' hunches were not supported by the data; specifically, births did not go down in response to family-cap policies. Instead, welfare recipients were having to make do with less income per child. When I wrote up the results of that analysis, I thought of that young woman in my class who had been pregnant with her third child, and I thought of all the other moms out there trying to provide for their children with increasingly stringent and less generous welfare assistance. Their lives were made more difficult by a public policy that was rooted in bad assumptions.

In the more than 25 years since my time in Bridgeport, I have conducted numerous studies that examine the economics of family formation, children's well-being, the effects of government safety-net programs, and the link between economic conditions and people's decisions about schooling, marriage, and having children. My summer at Bridgeport Jobs First was the first step in a research journey that ultimately led me to write this book about family formation in America and how it both reflects and reinforces economic structures and inequality.

Other people and experts are trained and experienced at eliciting the deeply personal stories of others through extensive interviews and relaying them through powerful vignettes. That is not my particular expertise. My training as an economist is about looking at complicated social phenomena and figuring out how to represent them with parsimonious mathematical models that can be empirically tested with data. My job is to look at vast amounts of data with nuance and precision and produce and interpret the resulting evidence. While this book will not contain mathematical equations or econometric specifications, it will present the findings of analyses that use them. As we say in econ-speak, that's my "comparative advantage." So, that's what I do in this book.

In addition to being an economist, I am a parent, and I have been shaped by my own family.

I have three children. I love being their mom more than anything in the world. But I will be the first to admit that parenting is hard—sometimes overwhelmingly so. Being a parent is at once wonderful and exhausting. There are plenty of occasions—more than I care to admit—when I don't parent the way I would like to or know I should. There are plenty of days when I feel like I just don't have the energy to deal with whatever kid stuff I have to deal with, whether that be cleaning yet another mess in the kitchen, making another meal, negotiating curfew time, helping with homework, driving one kid in one direction and another in another—this, despite the reality that I have a lot of resources to draw on, including a spouse who is a devoted dad to our children and partner to me. I think often about how much harder this would all be if I didn't have a partner to share the burdens of raising children or a steady income to reliably cover the bills.

I am also struck by how my own childhood experience and my family's trajectory of upward mobility would be almost impossible today. My grandfather arrived at Ellis Island from Italy with an elementary-school education and a trunk of personal belongings. He made a home on the Lower East Side of Manhattan, making a living selling ice (before the refrigerator was invented), then working various WPA jobs, and eventually selling used cars. He married my grandmother, also an Italian immigrant, and they lived in an apartment building with her brother and five sisters, raising my mom alongside her brothers and many cousins. My parents met at a street-corner dance when they were 15 and were married at 21. They raised four daughters in a New Jersey suburb, with my dad working odd jobs, including stints as a bus driver and an apprentice with an electrical union, before eventually starting a printing business that he ran out of our house. My mom did part-time secretarial work while she raised my three sisters and me. Later she enrolled at a local college and became an elementary-school teacher. All four of us went to college with the help of financial aid, scholarships, and loans.

As was reflected in my dad's favorite saying, "Sh*t will do for brains if you've got good luck," my family inhabited a specific time and place in American history when people could thrive on hard work and good fortune. That middle-class lifestyle and the upward mobility we experienced are harder to come by today. The demands and pressures of the modern economy, which delivers such unequal rewards to those at the upper and lower ends of the income distribution, would have likely made it impossible for a family like mine to experience the upward economic mobility we did.

I share this personal history because I know many readers will want to know where I'm coming from and what my experience is with the topic I am writing about. It also illustrates an essential point: just as I am a product of my family environment, my family was a product of our economic and social environment. The same is true today, albeit with an economy that is blisteringly unforgiving, a policy environment that doesn't sufficiently account for it, and a set of social norms where the separation of raising children from marriage is commonplace. In this setting, the disproportionate growth of single-parent households among America's non-college-educated population is both a reflection of and source of growing inequality—if left unchecked, these class divisions will deepen and perpetuate across generations.

I want to emphasize that I have no interest in waxing nostalgic for "simpler" times when the family construct meant married parents, defined by a male breadwinner and a stay-at-home mother. This convention does not describe my own marriage, nor would I wish it to, though I can easily see how it might work well for others. What marriage looks like for different people, and how various marital arrangements work better for different adults (including whether the marriage is between adults of the same or different genders), is not the topic of this book. This book is focused on how kids are raised, with an emphasis on whether a child has both a mother and father in the household or, more generally, two resident parent figures; on how these issues relate to broader economic trends and growing inequality in society; and on how policies and programs can shape these trends and their trajectories, for better or worse.

This book necessarily puts a spotlight on the role of marriage between parents.

This book necessarily puts a spotlight on the role of marriage between parents and the benefits that institution brings to children—not as a religious or cultural institution but as a practical and economic one that makes the challenging work of raising kids less impossible. Marriage is the most reliable institution for delivering a high level of resources and long-term stability to children. There is simply not currently a robust, widespread alternative to marriage in US society. Cohabitation, in theory, could deliver similar resources as marriage, but the data show that in the US, these partnerships are not, on average, as stable as marriages. (Another possible interpretation of these data: relationships are inherently difficult, and marriage provides an extra layer of institutional inertia that keeps them in place where simple cohabitation might not.) Over and over, study after study, empirical studies bear out the following reality: Children thrive in strong, stable families, and the breakdown of the two-parent married family for a large segment of the population—driven by a decline in marriage that has led to more children being born to unmarried parents—has generally not been good for children.

There is no doubt that marriage can be a terrible prison for some, and the argument of this book is not that such marriages should be maintained. But over the past 40-plus years, American society has engaged in a vast experiment of reshaping the most fundamental of social institutions—the family—and the resulting generations of data tell us in no uncertain terms how that has played out for children. The data present some uncomfortable realities:

- Two-parent families are beneficial for children.
- The class divide in marriage and family structure has exacerbated inequality and class gaps.
- Places that have more two-parent families have higher rates of upward mobility.
- Not talking about these facts is counterproductive.

Children's trajectories in life are also profoundly shaped by schools, and it is unquestionable that improving the life trajectories of children in this country will require improving those institutions. But that's not what this book is about. We already rely on schools to do too much in this country. Schools are tasked with equipping children with academic lessons and knowledge, as well as with the numerous cognitive and social skills they will need to ultimately be successful in today's demanding workforce. In addition, school faculty and staff are increasingly being tasked with addressing the non-academic or academic-adjacent needs of students. Schools hire social workers and mental health counselors and train teachers to notice the signs of family trauma. Our schools need more of these kinds of supports. But, realistically, schools can only do so much to make up for a disadvantaged family life and to close class gaps in children's outcomes. Children bring the consequences of their family environments (both good and bad) with them to their first day of school and every day thereafter.

Here, economic data tell a compelling story about where the United States is and where it needs to go in terms of arming families and children with what they need. But this conversation also requires honesty, even the difficult kind. It is precisely because of its importance that I have endeavored to take up this challenging topic—to bring the social science evidence on family structure from the obscurity of academic journals into the public conversation.

There is no easy answer to the challenges described in this book, but there are things that can be done. A strong, stable family life is the foundation upon which children find their surest footing in this difficult world. What can our society do to make sure that more children have that advantage in life? The answer is not nearly as straightforward as simply declaring that more parents should get married. We need to first understand why so many parents are not getting married and why so many dads are not living with their children. One important set of factors behind these trends are the same economic changes that have made it harder for people without a college degree, especially men, to be economically successful. These forces have contributed to the erosion of the two-parent family for a large segment of the population. For instance, the decline of manufacturing employment in recent decades has stripped many men—and the communities they live in—of jobs that have historically paid relatively high wages to workers without college degrees. Extensive factory closures in manufacturing towns across the country drove non-college-educated men into lower-paying, less secure jobs, or out of the workforce altogether. In affected communities, marriage rates fell, more children were born to unmarried mothers, and more children were living in poor households. These same communities also experienced increased rates of mortality from drug and alcohol abuse, or so-called deaths of despair.[3]

The fact that economic challenges have spilled over from the labor market and economic sphere into the sphere of family, with profound implications for children and society, heightens the imperative to address these economic challenges and promote policies and reforms that expand economic opportunity for all.

In addition to grappling with the economic challenges that have contributed to the erosion of the two-parent family, it is equally imperative to devise ways to strengthen families as they currently exist. Doing so means encouraging and supporting marriage among parents, but it also means working to promote strong and healthy family units in cases where parents cannot, should not, or do not want to be married. Policies are often made in a "second-best" world. If marriage won't work for some parents, then policies and programs should foster productive co-parenting and the healthy engagement of two parents in the lives of their children.

There is also the need to bolster the childhood experiences and opportunities of children who, through no fault of their own, find themselves in a disadvantaged family situation. This problem is not new, nor even specific to a landscape in which fewer people are marrying. But the challenge remains: how do we ameliorate childhood disadvantage through both government and community programs? Fortunately, the evidence-based policy movement has made great strides. Advances in data and scholarship mean there is now a lot of accessible evidence about what types of programs and policies help children succeed. Here, economists find some of their greatest value: producing rigorous studies of the causal effects of policies and programs. Those who design policies and programs should implement and expand policies and programs with evidence of success. Whatever choices adults make or barriers they face, children should not be left to suffer the consequences of an under-resourced or unstable home life.

As a social scientist, I am convinced that the two-parent family structure is, in general, advantageous for children and that we cannot ignore what the growing prevalence of one-parent households means for children and inequality in this country. We cannot throw up our hands and decide that family structure is a topic not to be discussed or an intractable issue that cannot be meaningfully addressed. For the sake of kids, we need to tackle this challenge head on, in a variety of ways.

A road map to this book

This book puts a conversation about family—and the evidence of its economic importance—at the center of the policy discussions about income inequality and eroding social mobility. The sources and arguments here come from a broad literature; what follows is a short road map to the chapters and their pieces of the argument.

Chapters 2 to 4 document the changing landscape of children's family structures in the US, why it matters, and what's behind it. In chapter 2, I show how the divergence in family structures has exacerbated income inequality across children's households. In chapter 3, I explain why marriage is such a relevant institution for children's economic well-being and life trajectories. I describe marriage as a long-term contract between two individuals to combine resources and share the responsibilities of keeping a household and raising children. The chapter describes theory and evidence showing that this more highly resourced arrangement leads to better outcomes for children. But the resource gain to marriage depends crucially on what both partners have to offer. If marriage has declined because fewer men are reliable partners or economic contributors, then the challenge is at least partially economic. Chapter 4 takes up this issue directly and describes the link between the economic struggles of non-college-educated men and their declining rates of marriage.

The next two chapters focus more directly on issues of parenting. In chapter 5, I describe how key parenting investments—namely, expenditures on children, time with children, and emotional engagement with children—differ across more and less highly resourced parents, specifically with respect to parental education level and marital status. Because single-mother households tend to be lower in resources, children growing up in such settings tend to receive fewer parental investments. The chapter considers a variety of potential explanations for the observed patterns and concludes that the most likely explanation for class gaps in parenting is that the luxury of resources—whether in the form of more income, a spouse or resident co-parent, or both—makes it easier for higher-income, more highly educated, and married parents to spend more money on, spend more time with, and have more emotional energy for their kids. In chapter 6, I discuss evidence showing that boys' outcomes are especially responsive to parental inputs, such that growing up with a single mother appears to disadvantage boys even more than girls. This finding is relevant to the broader fact that boys and young men appear to be falling behind girls and young women; they are now less likely to complete a college degree, for instance. The more boys struggle and fall behind, the less prepared they will be as adults to be reliable economic providers as husbands and dads. This creates a vicious cycle.

Chapter 7 looks at birth rates, complementing the discussion of marriage rates in chapter 4. I show that the rise in single-mother households has happened *despite* a reduction in childbearing overall, and specifically, among teen and younger women, who have typically had higher rates of nonmarital childbearing. Trends in childbearing would, all else equal, mean that children are being born into more advantageous situations than in the past. However, the share of births to unmarried mothers has climbed steadily over the past 40 years, and therein lies the issue. The rise in the share of children living with one parent reflects declines in marriages, not changes in childbearing patterns.

The final chapter, chapter 8, ties it all together with suggestions about what might be done to address the challenges described in this book and improve the family circumstances for children in America.

» «

Socially and economically, the US is at a crossroads. Millions of children are growing up in a disadvantaged family setting at the same time that global economic forces have raised the bar for economic success. If we do not take dedicated steps to address the relative disadvantages of children raised in a single-parent home, and to address the class gaps in family structure, millions of children will fail to reach their human potential, our class gaps will widen, social mobility will erode, and the social cohesion of our country will be further undermined. This outcome would be a travesty for affected children, as well as for our nation. We will not be able to meaningfully improve the lives of children in this country, nor address the vast and growing level of inequality between kids who are born into more highly educated, higher-income homes and those who are not without confronting the reality that family life is crucial and that divergent family structures are a key driver of widening class gaps.

TWO

Mother-Only Households

Families look different today than they did a few decades ago and a few decades before that. Household formations are numerous and varied and there are lots of ways we might classify and describe them: one parent or two; married or cohabitating; same-sex parents or different-sex parents; biological or adopted; one-generation or multigenerational; the list goes on. Every now and then I think about the first line of Leo Tolstoy's *Anna Karenina*: "Happy families are all alike; every unhappy family is unhappy in its own way." I take his point, but in reality, every family—happy or unhappy, small or large, married or unmarried—has its own way.

My husband's and my ways of parenting together are our own. Our ways are not quite like anyone else's, certainly not our own parents', nor even those of other couples who, like us, are married with three kids and both work full-time jobs. Each married couple shares the responsibilities, joys, and burdens of parenting in their own particular way—who brings in what share of income, who does which household chores, who drives the kids to school and puts them to bed, who tends to be the disciplinarian and who is more of the entertainer and nurturer. The same can be said for unmarried parents. An unmarried mother might never have had a meaningful relationship with her child's father and might have done everything on her own, or with the help of relatives or friends, from the beginning—attending prenatal doctors' appointments alone, figuring out how to install the car seat, taking her child to the first day of school, and eventually teaching her child how to drive a car. Some unmarried couples were married for some or even most of a child's life and, though now divorced and living apart, co-parent together actively—or not. Some unmarried parents were never in a committed relationship nor lived together, but have always been jointly committed to providing for their child. The set of precise circumstances is nearly boundless.

It is difficult to categorize families into only a few groups, based on a small set of variables, and draw general conclusions about what a particular family structure means. And yet, with full recognition of its limitations, this is precisely the data-driven approach I take in this book—to use a few variables to describe how the structure of families with children has changed in the US and draw general conclusions about what these changes tend to mean for children's lives.

Most Americans are loosely aware that the two-parent family is no longer as ubiquitous as it once was, but I want to set a couple facts straight about what that looks like. One notion that people might have about this general trend is that the decline in marriage between parents can be attributed to people who have a child together and choose to live in a committed partnership, but just not get married. This is generally not the case. Most unmarried parents today are not in relationships that are essentially marriage in all but name. Children whose parents are unmarried are much more likely to be living with just their mom than with both parents. In recent decades, more and more American children are growing up with only their mother in the home.

A second (mistaken) idea that people might have about this trend is that it is driven by economically successful women—women who make a great deal of money on their own and thus don't need a spouse to help. In fact, single mothers are disproportionately neither college educated nor high income. Of course, some single mothers and their families are economically very secure and have an abundance of resources. But in the societal aggregate, mothers who are raising their child or children without a second parent figure in the home face a multitude of hardships, from the readily observed (having to support the family financially while also being the primary caregiver) to the less visible (having nobody to pick up the slack when you're feeling tired or sick or to discuss the day's events with at night after the kids go to bed).

The economic story is more layered than the simple fact that raising children is more difficult for one parent than for two (though this is, again, on average, very much true). It's that the decline in marriage among US parents, and among adults more generally, has been most pronounced among the very groups that have been disadvantaged by recent changes in the economy: adults without a four-year college degree. The people forgoing marriage in large numbers are not economically successful, college-educated parents. Rather, the rise in one-parent families (and statistically they are almost always mother-only families) has happened for the groups for whom economic security has been weakened. The one-parent home is not, in general, associated with a position of economic privilege.

As college-educated adults have seen their earnings rise over recent decades, they have continued to get married and to marry one another. As they have had children, their children enjoy the heaping resources that two college-educated parents are able to shower on them. Meanwhile, as earnings have stagnated among those without a college degree, these adults have found marriage to be less of a value proposition than in past generations and have become more likely to set up separate households. As a result, their children are now more likely to have only one parent in their home. And because the share of children living with an unpartnered mother is more than twice as high among children whose mothers have only a high school degree compared to those whose mothers have a four-year college degree, there is now a sizable "college gap" in the family structure of children.

Understanding the divergence in family structures among US households is no simple statistical exercise. For all the richness of demographic data available to researchers today, the job of filtering, sorting, and comparing those data (which very often come from different sources, depending on what exact question you're researching) can be challenging. That challenge grows when you're trying to track outcomes over time; data sets and definitions change, along with the state of the world and what it all means.

In telling the story of US families with children over the last several decades, I draw on several observed patterns in available data, almost always relying on nationally representative data sets that include information on thousands (and sometimes millions) of US households. One pattern is how family structure has changed for children born to mothers of different education levels and racial and ethnic groups. Another is the extent to which alternative living arrangements have replaced marriage, including the role that divorce versus nonmarital childbearing plays in these trends. Data on each of these topics offer a rich, extensive statistical portrait of children's family structure in the United States.

Here are some of the key facts those data show:

- More than one in five children living in the US today live in a home with an unpartnered mother, meaning a mother who is neither married nor cohabiting. A majority of these households do not include another adult, such as a grandparent or other relative.
- A "college gap" in family structure has emerged over the past four decades. Currently, 12% of children whose mothers have a four-year college degree live with an unpartnered mother. A whopping 29% of children whose mothers don't have a college degree and 30% of those whose mothers don't have a high school degree live without a second parent in their homes.
- This college gap exists among White families, Black families, and Hispanic families. Asian families are an exception, with uniformly high rates of two-parent families across all education groups.
- The rise in unpartnered-mother households has been driven by an increase in the share of mothers who are never married—not by a rise in divorce rates or in unmarried cohabiting couples.

- US children are more likely to live with only their mother than children around the world are.
- The widening college gap in family structure over recent decades has amplified widening earnings inequality, leading to an even greater degree of household income inequality than would have been experienced from labor-market changes alone.

**More than one in five American children
now live with an unpartnered mother.**

Figure 2.1 plots trends in the percentage of children living in various family arrangements between 1980 and 2019. The figure shows the steady, large decline in the share of children living with married

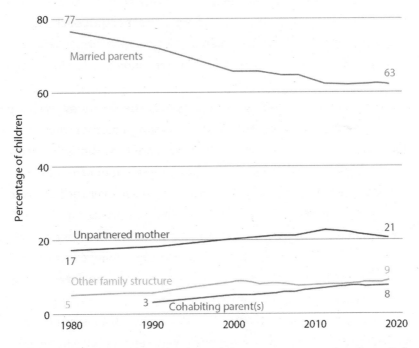

Figure 2.1 Share of children living with married parents, unpartnered mother, cohabiting parents, or in other arrangement
SOURCE: *Author's calculations using 1980 and 1990 US decennial census and 2000–2019 US Census American Community Survey.*
NOTES: *Observations weighted using child's survey weight. In the 1980 census, mothers who are cohabiting are recorded as unpartnered.*

parents. Only 63% of American children now live with married parents, down from 77% in 1980.

Where am I getting these statistics on children's living arrangements? The statistics are based on tabulations of public-use samples of the 1980 and 1990 US decennial censuses and the 2000–2019 American Community Survey, which is the largest household survey conducted by the US federal government. These samples include records on a combined 17.8 million children and 9.7 million mothers. The census also provides statistical weights for the observations in these public-use samples, which allow researchers to tabulate these statistics in a way that is accurate at a national level. The decennial census is conducted by the US Census Bureau every 10 years to determine the number of people living in the United States. It is required by the US Constitution. The American Community Survey, or ACS, was launched in 2000 and is conducted annually. Both the decennial census and the ACS are household-level surveys that collect data on basic demographic information about the people living in a household (including age, race, sex, marital status, and an individual's relationship to the head of household); economic data on the adults in the household (including work status, occupation, industry, and income); and other individual characteristics (including migration, disability, and veteran status). These are the most comprehensive data sources on where and with whom people in the US live.

What these data tell us is that most children who are not living with married parents are living in a household with only one parent, almost always their mother. Overall, 21% of American children live in a home with a mother who is neither married nor cohabiting. In comparison, only 8% of children live with either unmarried parents *or* a parent and an unmarried partner. Another 4.8% of children live with an unpartnered father. And 4.3% of children do not live in a home that includes a parent at all.[1]

To get a more precise sense of the relationship between children and the parental figures in the home, we have to go to another nationally representative survey conducted by the US Census Bureau: the 2018 Survey of Income and Program Participation, or SIPP. The

SIPP is a longitudinal survey (a study that follows participants over time—here, a span of several years) that collects comprehensive information on the dynamics of household composition, income, employment, and participation in government programs such as welfare. The 2018 SIPP compiled data on over 14,000 children. From these data we can see that among children living with married adults, nearly nine out of 10 live with two biological parents. Among children living with unmarried, cohabiting adults, the share living with two biological parents is between a half and three-quarters. In other words, the share of children living with two biological but unmarried parents is smaller than we might have thought.

When I tell friends about this book's central thesis—that marriage is in decline, and it's a driver of American inequality—they often counter with an argument that parents in the US are just adopting "a more European lifestyle": raising children in long-term committed cohabiting partnerships, free of labels but not different otherwise. As a matter of fact, this is simply not true. In addition to the fairly low rate of unmarried parental cohabitation in the US, it is also the case that cohabitation in the US is a rather fragile arrangement relative to cohabitation elsewhere.[2] Cohabitation among US adults tends to be less stable and of shorter duration than among cohabiting couples in Western Europe. US children are much more likely to experience two or three parental partnerships by age 15, as compared to children in other Western nations.[3]

None of these statistics should be misconstrued as suggesting that American parents don't want what is best for their children. I am inclined to believe that most every parent in every country, including the US, approaches having kids with the best of hopes and intentions. It is also true, however, that good intentions and best-laid plans have practical limits, especially when it comes to the challenges of parenting and domestic relationships. One thing these data tell us, then, is that marriage as an institution appears to offer institutional support for navigating those challenges.

In 1998 the renowned Princeton University sociologist Sara McLanahan and colleagues launched a study called the Fragile Families and Child Wellbeing Study, or FFCWS, arguably the most ambitious and influential study of unmarried parents ever conducted. (I took McLanahan's Sociology of Poverty class as an undergraduate student; her scholarship and objectivity on this topic has inspired and informed my research and thinking, as it has so many other scholars of the family.[4]) This innovative study gathered data on approximately 5,000 mothers and children in 20 large US cities across a series of parenthood milestones: just after they had given birth; while still in the hospital; and at regular intervals for more than two decades thereafter. Approximately three-quarters of the couples in the FFCWS sample were unmarried at the time of birth. The majority of the unmarried parents interviewed at the time of their child's birth expressed optimism about the future of their relationships: 74% of the unmarried mothers and 90% of the unmarried fathers said they believed that their chances of marrying the other parent were 50% or better.[5] But by the time of their child's fifth birthday, only a third of the unmarried parents were still together. Furthermore, new partners and new children were common, leading to high levels of instability and family complexity. A third of the fathers had virtually disappeared from their children's lives.[6]

Here it's important to note that while some mother-only households have another adult in the household, e.g., a child's grandparent or aunt, a majority of them do not: 67% of children living in an unpartnered-mother household have no adult living with them besides their mother. The remaining share of such households do include another adult—typically a member of their extended family. About one in five children of unpartnered mothers also live with their maternal grandparent in the house; about 3% have a maternal aunt or uncle in the house (this is without a maternal grandparent present); and 8% have some other adult in the home.[7] Of course, it should not be assumed that these households are arranged in a way that offers the equivalent of a second parent's resources to the mother and kids; in many cases the mother might be caring for the other adult (or adults) in the house, too. Again, families are complex, and these coarse descriptions are incomplete.

Family structure varies widely across mothers with different education levels.

Among children of college-educated mothers over the last 40 years, the share living with married parents hasn't changed much. In 1980, 90% of children of college graduates lived with married parents; in 2019 that number was holding strong at 84%. In contrast, among children of mothers with a high school degree or some college (but not a four-year college degree), only 60% lived with married parents in 2019—a huge drop from the 83% who did in 1980. This middle-education group accounts for the largest share of children today, which makes their situation very relevant to what is happening at a population level in the US today. Similar declines have occurred for children whose mothers have less than a high school degree, with less than 60% living with married parents, down from 80% in 1980.

In a country as large as the US, it is sometimes the case that population trends can skew differently by region or across urban and rural areas. That is not so in this case. This decline has remarkable symmetry across all swaths of the country. Among the children of mothers without a four-year college degree, the share living with married parents in 1980 was around 80% in all four major regions of the country (South, West, Northeast, and Midwest). Now that rate is at or just below 60% in three of these four; it is only slightly higher, at 65%, in the West. The shares in urban and rural areas are both at 60%.

Correspondingly, among children whose moms didn't go to college or didn't finish a four-year college degree, it has become more likely that they'll grow up in a single-parent home. Between 1990 and 2010, this proportion increased by nearly 50% (over 10 percentage points) after a period of relative stability during the 1980s. The share has generally remained flat since 2010, perhaps signaling that it has stabilized. An earlier jump could be observed among children whose mothers didn't finish high school: their share living with an unpartnered mother rose by 50%, from 20% to 30%, during the 1980s; the trend has been generally flat since. Meanwhile, there has not been a commensurate increase among the children of

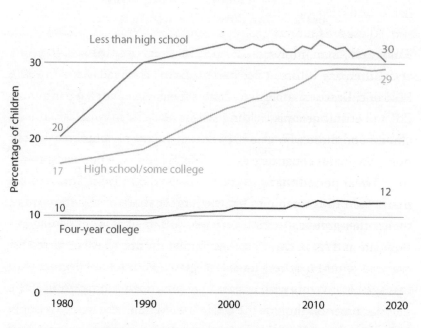

Figure 2.2 Share of children in unpartnered-mother households, by maternal education level

SOURCE: *Author's calculations using 1980 and 1990 US decennial census and 2000–2019 US Census American Community Survey.*

NOTES: *Observations are weighted using child's survey weight.*

college-educated mothers. The share of these children living with an unpartnered mother has hovered between 10% and 12% over the entire 40-year period. Figure 2.2 shows these trends.

Children's family structure varies across racial and ethnic groups and by mother's education level within racial and ethnic groups.

There have long been differences in children's family structures *across* racial and ethnic groups in the US. Those differences persist today. Meanwhile, a college gap in family structure has emerged *within* racial and ethnic groups. This book relies on economic data that can be tabulated for four major racial and ethnic groupings: White non-Hispanic, Black non-Hispanic, Asian non-Hispanic, and Hispanic.

For ease of exposition, I will refer to these groups as White, Black, Asian, and Hispanic. Unless otherwise noted, the reader should assume these are four mutually exclusive groups (meaning that White, Black, and Asian imply non-Hispanic). In the US today, about 55% of children are White, 13% are Black, 6% are Asian, and 23% are Hispanic. Unfortunately, what this schema leaves out are other racial and ethnic groups (including Native Americans and Pacific Islanders and those who identify as multiracial or multiethnic) whose numbers do not constitute a sufficient share of the population over the 40-year period that I study for there to be reliable statistics on them. I am thus unable to present national trends for children in these other groups.

White and Asian children are significantly more likely to live with married parents, as compared to Hispanic and Black children. In 2019, 77% of White children and 88% of Asian children lived with married parents. The share among Hispanic children was 62%. Only 38% of Black children lived with married parents—a historically low share that reflects a downward trend over four decades. In this book I am focused on the post-1980 change in children's family structures,[8] but it bears noting that a sizable racial gap in family structure existed before the late twentieth century, though it widened in the 1960s and 1970s.

Differences in parents' marriage rates across races and ethnic groups makes the almost uniform presence of a college gap all the more notable. Among children of White mothers, the share living with married parents is 88% for college-educated mothers; it's 69% and 60% among mothers with only high school degrees and without high school degrees, respectively. Among the children of Hispanic mothers, the share living with married parents is 76% for college-educated mothers, compared to 59% for each of the other two education groups. Children of Black mothers are twice as likely to live with married parents if their mom graduated from college than if their mom didn't: 60% versus 30%. Although there is a college gap in the married-parent share among Asian children, it is relatively small. The shares of Asian children living with married parents are 92% for those with college-educated mothers, versus 79% and 83% for the other two groups. For all four groups, the college gap was much more pronounced in 2019 than in 1980. This difference can be seen in the comparison of the upper and lower panels of figure 2.3.

These trends reflect a rise in nonmarital childbearing; divorce plays a smaller role.

The growing share of children living with unpartnered mothers over the past 40 years is an outgrowth of the dramatic increase in the prevalence of children born outside marriage during this period. Adults in the US today are much more likely to have—and subsequently raise—children outside the institution of marriage than they were in previous generations. In 2019, almost half of all babies in the US were born to unmarried mothers. This figure represents a dramatic increase since 1960, when only 5% of births were to unmarried mothers. The share increased to 18% by 1980, and it has continued to climb.[9] The dramatic increase in the share of children born outside a marital union has been the driving force behind the decline in the share of children living with married parents.

Today's unpartnered mothers are also more likely to have never been married than to have been married and then divorced. This finding also reflects a notable change from previous decades, when the reverse was true. In 1980, it was much more common for unpartnered mothers to have previously been married, typically to the father of their child: 64% of unpartnered mothers were divorced, leaving only 22% who had never been married. Things changed over the past 40 years, and today more unpartnered mothers have never married at all. In 2019, 52% of unpartnered mothers have never been married, compared to 39% who are divorced. (The remaining shares are married with an absent spouse [6%] or widowed [3%].)

A secondary college gap can also be seen in the differing circumstances of unpartnered mothers. Unpartnered mothers with a four-year college degree are more likely to be either divorced or have an absent spouse than to have never been married; this is not the case

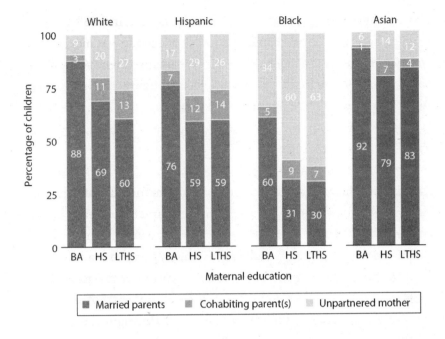

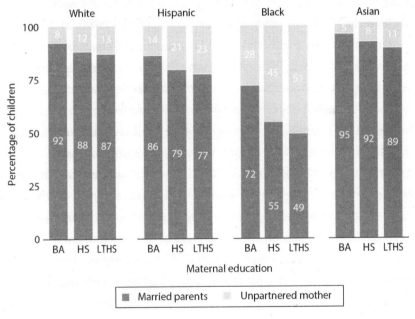

Figure 2.3 Children's family structure, by maternal race and education level: 2019 and 1980

SOURCE: *Author's calculations using 2019 US Census American Community Survey.*
NOTES: *Tabulations include all children ages 0 to 18 who live with their mother, weighted using children's weights. Cohabiting parents cannot be identified in the 1980 census. A, 2019; B, 1980.*

for mothers without a four-year college degree. In 2019, 32% of college-educated unpartnered mothers had never been married—a huge jump from 1980, when that number was 10%. As shown in figure 2.4, it is still a much lower share than among the other two education groups: 57% of unpartnered mothers with a high school degree and 59% of unpartnered mothers without a high school degree have never been married.

There are also sizable differences across racial and ethnic groups in the circumstances of unpartnered mothers. Black and Hispanic unpartnered mothers are much more likely to never have been married—70% and 54%, respectively—as compared to 38% of White mothers and 32% of Asian mothers. In addition, there is a college gap in the marital circumstances of unpartnered mothers within racial and ethnic groups. For all four racial and ethnic groups identified, unpartnered mothers with a college degree are substantially more likely to have been married at some point than their non-college-educated counterparts.

Does this gap matter? What's the difference between never-married and married-before in practical terms? The high prevalence of "never-married" among unpartnered mothers—especially those without a college degree—is not only illustrative of what is driving changes in children's living circumstances, it also matters for childhood resources. First, children whose parents were previously married are more likely to have had the benefit of two parents' time and resources in their home at some point during their childhood. Second, children whose parents were previously married are more likely to have current involvement with their father, as compared to children whose parents were unmarried at the time of their birth.[10] Third, children of divorced unpartnered mothers are more likely to live in households receiving child-support income. In the 2018 SIPP survey, these shares are 40% for the children of divorced mothers, as compared to 19% of never-married mothers. This finding holds true for mothers of all education levels.[11]

A side note here on child support: the shares of unmarried mothers receiving child support are far from 100%, for both divorced and

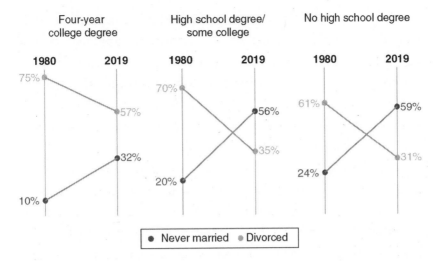

Figure 2.4 Change in marital circumstances of unpartnered mothers between 1980 and 2019, by maternal education level
SOURCE: *Author's calculations using 1980 US decennial census and 2019 US Census American Community Survey.*
NOTES: *Sample is limited to one observation per unpartnered mother, regardless of number of children. Observations are weighted using the mother's individual survey weight.*

never-married mothers. It is well known in the world of family policy that assignment of and compliance with child-support awards is far from complete. A special data-collection effort by the US Census Bureau in 2016 on this topic revealed that about 50% of all custodial parents had either legal or informal child-support agreements in the prior year. Among them, about 70% received some of their owed payment; only 44% received the full payment. The US Census Bureau reports that in 2015, $33.7 billion in child support was owed to custodial parents; 60% of that amount was received in total, averaging $3,447 per year received per custodial parent.[12]

What is going on in other countries?

Children in the United States are far more likely to live with only one parent than are children in other countries. The Pew Research Center published a study in 2019 reporting on the share of children living with one parent and no other adults in 130 countries and territories.

Utilizing a methodology that makes comparisons across countries possible, Pew estimated that 23% of US children under the age of 18 live with one parent and no other adults—more than three times the share of children around the world who live with just one parent (7%). In Canada, the rate is 15%; in Mexico, it is 7%. The share of children living in single-parent homes is especially low in Asian countries, which raises the possibility of a strong cultural-norm explanation for why the share of one-parent families is so low for ethnically Asian children in the United States.

Beyond a comparison across countries of the shares of children living in a one-parent home, it is interesting to consider whether there are similar patterns by education in countries outside the US, especially high-income countries with generally comparable levels of education. One source of data that allows us to investigate this question is a data set on the living arrangements of children in OECD countries. The OECD consists of 38 democratic countries with market-based economies, including the US, Canada, the United Kingdom, Australia, and a variety of countries in Europe and the Americas. Like children in the US, children in many of these countries are more likely to live with two parents if their mothers are highly educated. The OECD data categorizes mothers into three education groups: high, middle, and low. In the European Union countries, on average, 79% of children of the highest-educated mothers live in married-parent homes, as compared to 70% among the middle group and 62% among the lowest education group. The education gradient for cohabitation is reversed, with the highest-educated mothers having the lowest rates of cohabitation; the shares across education groups are 11%, 14%, and 18%, respectively. As is true for children in the US, European children with college-educated mothers are the least likely to be living with a single mother: 10%, as compared to 16% and 20% of the children of less educated mothers. Both the relatively higher rate of single-mother households in the US and the similar education gradient across high-income countries are noteworthy for what they do and do not suggest about potential drivers of US trends in family formation; I expand on this point below.

We can turn to the Luxembourg Income Study—a nationally representative data set of households in more than 50 countries—to learn more about the incidence of single motherhood globally and how it has changed since the 1980s.[13] The Luxembourg numbers show that in the late 1980s, the rates of single motherhood in the US were at 13%, 19%, and 30% among mothers categorized as being in the high, middle, and low education groups, respectively. The numbers both increased and fanned out by 2011–2015, to rates of 16%, 31%, and 32%, respectively, from the highest to lowest education group. Rates of single motherhood in the United Kingdom were lower for each group in the late 1980s: 10%, 16%, and 14% for the high, middle, and low education groups, respectively; between 2011 and 2015, those UK rates had increased and fanned out to 12%, 28%, and 34%. In other words: rates of single motherhood increased dramatically among all but the highest-educated women. Similar patterns can be observed for other countries, including Norway, Spain, and France.

These international comparisons are interesting in their own right, but they are also noteworthy for what they imply about likely causes of the decline in two-parent families in the US. Some observers are inclined to attribute the rise in single motherhood to US policy decisions—that safety-net programs like welfare promote single-parent household structures. Comparing the US data to equivalent data from other countries suggests this argument is wrong. The incidence of single-mother households is higher in the US than in many other countries that offer more generous safety-net programs, places like France and Sweden, for example. In addition, the striking education gradient relative to family structure—with the highest-educated mothers having by far the highest rates of marriage—has also emerged in countries other than the US. This suggests that the divergence in household structures between those with higher and lower levels of education likely reflects widespread economic and social changes that have also been experienced in other high-income countries, like the forces of the global labor market that have disadvantaged less educated workers and undermined the economic security of non-college-educated adults, men especially. I expand on this observation at length in chapter 4.

The growing class gap in family structure amplifies earnings inequality.

College-educated workers have seen their earnings rise unabated over the past 40 years, while they have continued getting married and raising families as married couples. At the same time, those in the middle of the education distribution have had their earnings stagnate or improve only slightly *and* they have become increasingly likely to set up a household without another adult. The combination of these labor-market trends (divergent earnings) and demographic trends (divergent household formation) means that inequality across households is even larger than it would have been from the rise in earnings inequality alone.

Figure 2.5 shows the change in median household earnings between 1980 and 2019 for households with children, by maternal education level and family structure. Panel A shows changes in median household earnings for two-parent families. Among college-educated mothers in such families, median household earnings increased 59% over this period. In comparison, median household earnings for a two-parent family with a high-school-educated mother increased only 8%; they declined by 14% for mothers with less than a high school degree. These differences, which hold constant family structure, reflect widening earning inequality, a topic which has received ample public-policy and media attention.

The middle panel reports on changes in median household earnings for unpartnered mothers. Among college-educated unpartnered mothers, household earnings increased by 60%, a similar increase to that among college-educated mothers in two-parent families. This finding reflects the fact that there was a large increase in earnings to all college-educated workers, women included. For unpartnered mothers with a high school degree, household earnings increased by a more modest 19%. For unpartnered mothers with less than a high

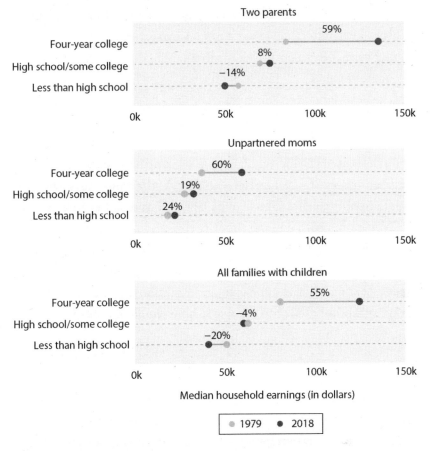

Figure 2.5 Change in median household earnings for families with children between 1980 and 2019, by maternal education level and family structure
SOURCE: *Author's calculations using 1980 census and 2019 US Census American Community Survey, reflecting prior-year earnings. All earnings reported in 2018 USD.*
NOTES: *The sample is limited to mothers with a child under age 18. There is one observation per mother, weighted by the mother's person weight.*

school degree, household earnings increased by 24%, rising from $17,797 to $22,000. This increase reflects the rise in employment rates among single mothers that accompanied welfare reform, expansions in the Earned Income Tax Credit, and a strong labor market in the 1990s. Still, the earnings levels among this cohort are so much lower than the earnings of college-educated mothers, even more so in the more recent years, reflecting, again, widening earning inequality between those with and without college degrees.

When we no longer condition on family structure, and look at all households combined, we see a net *decrease* in household earnings among non-college-educated mothers. This decline can be seen in the bottom panel of figure 2.5. Median household earnings among high-school-educated mothers *decreased* by 4%; among mothers without a high school degree, they *decreased* by 20%. Why? Because the earnings gains for mothers in these education groups were offset by an increased likelihood of not having a spouse or partner—and hence another potential earner—in their household. The decrease in the share of households headed by two parents—a fall from 81% to 67% for moms with a high school degree and from 79% to 66% for moms without a high school degree—led to a *decrease* in median household earnings for mothers without a college degree. These numbers show that the college gap in family structure has been a meaningful contributor to the rise in household earnings inequality.

Summary

The dramatic decline in the share of US children living with married parents over the past four decades has not been matched by a rise in the share of children living with two committed, unmarried parents. Rather, many more children today live with only their mother in their home. These changes have been especially pronounced for the children of mothers without a four-year college degree. Children with college-educated mothers are almost all still being raised in married-parent homes.

Furthermore, unpartnered mothers are not, in general, making up for the absence of a second parent in the home by having another adult in the household. Still, it is possible that mothers who raise children on their own are able to compensate for the lack of another adult in the home, perhaps with their own resources or the help of a network of family and friends. The facts and figures discussed in this chapter show clearly that there have been dramatic changes in the family structure of US children, and that these changes have not happened uniformly across groups with different education levels.

Remaining chapters of the book discuss why these changes matter, what factors have caused them, and what can be done to reverse them and/or ameliorate the negative consequences of them for affected children. The next chapter focuses on the link between family structure and childhood resources.

THREE

2 > 1

"It's just one of them, and they're doing everything on their own."

CARTIER CAREY, age 11, on why he's raising money to buy diapers and other supplies for single moms[1]

When it comes to the question of *why* marriage might matter for children's outcomes, there is a lot we could discuss. We could discuss what it might mean for children to see their parents love each other and work things out together when faced with challenges and disagreements. We could talk about what type of example that might set for children and their expectations for love and relationships in their own adult lives.

Of course we could also talk about what it might mean for children to live in a household that is filled with marital tension, where one or both parents are often unhappy or even mistreating the other. But I am not going to venture to say anything novel or new about any of those topics. It's simply not my expertise on marriage, coming at it as I do as an economist. I certainly recognize the importance of those issues, and in my personal life—like many women my age, I suspect—I have had many conversations about these kinds of questions with friends. But as an economist, I am focused on marriage as an institution that is defined by two people combining and sharing resources in a long-term contract. If you're looking for a book about marriage and love or about marriage and happiness, this is not that book. Marriage and resources? Let's talk about that!

In this simple economic approach, marriage is a long-term contract between two individuals to pool their resources and share household responsibilities, including (when it applies) raising children. Two is greater than one. And as we saw in chapter 2, a direct consequence of the decline in parental marriage is that fewer children are being raised in a two-parent home. This change is at the heart of the issue; it is key to why the decline in parental marriage matters for children. Pooling resources across two people means amassing more resources than one person has alone. And as any parent will readily attest, raising children takes a lot of resources—including money, time, emotional energy, and more. At the most basic level, a child raised by a married couple has steady and continued access to the resources of two adults. A child living with an unmarried parent, on average, has access to fewer resources during their childhood—a time in life when resources really matter.

When marriage is modeled in this way, it seems silly to deny that the institution would benefit children, at least on average. Conversely, it's easy to see why children growing up in a home with only one parent would be relatively disadvantaged on average. As 11-year-old Cartier Carey of Hampton, Virginia, told the *Washington Post* in a 2020 interview about his project to raise money for single moms, "It's just one of them, and they're doing everything on their own." President Barack Obama made a similar observation about the heroic efforts required of single mothers who take care of a family by themselves. "We need to help all the mothers out there who are raising these kids by themselves; the mothers who drop them off at school, go to work, pick up them up in the afternoon, work another shift, get dinner, make lunches, pay the bills, fix the house, and all the other things it takes both parents to do," said Obama in a 2008 speech. "So many of these women are doing a heroic job, but they need support. They need another parent. Their children need another parent. That's what keeps their foundation strong. It's what keeps the foundation of our country strong."[2]

Data backs up the common-sense view that families with two resident parents have a resource advantage. In one stark illustration, the official 2019 US Census statistics reveal that families headed by a single mother were five times more likely to live in poverty than families headed by a married couple; families headed by a single father were nearly twice as likely to live in poverty. For families headed by a woman without a spouse, the overall share living in poverty was 22.2%. For families headed by a man without a spouse, the share was 11.5%. These proportions compare to 4.0% among married-couple families.[3] Some of this discrepancy reflects the fact that poor adults are more likely to become single parents than are higher-income adults. But much of it is simple math: having two adults in the home who can bring in income lessens the chance that a family is poor.

The resource advantage of two-parent households extends beyond income. Consider the resource of parental time. Data show that nonresident fathers spend less time with their children, on average, than resident fathers do. Of course, many nonresident fathers still provide financial support to their children and spend time with them, just as many single mothers are economically secure and able to provide their children with materially enriched homes. But what we're talking about here is averages. And in general, we know from mounds of data, that children in two-parent homes tend to live in homes with a higher level of income and have more time with their parents than do children from single-parent homes. These resource advantages then set children up with more opportunities to get ahead in life.

In this chapter I review what the data show about outcome differences between children who grow up with a married versus unmarried mother or in a two- versus one-parent home, with an eye toward what the data imply about the *causal* effect of having two parents in the home instead of one. Though it is impossible to be absolutely precise about exactly how much of observed differences are due to the specific causal effect of this feature of a child's home versus other things that researchers can't see or observe about the home, study after study suggests that a married-parent family tends to confer benefits to children in the form of greater resources during childhood, and that these increased resources then translate into better opportunities and greater educational attainment, among other outcomes. I then move on to a discussion of how the benefits of parental marriage depend on context. Specifically, the potential gains to children from having a second parent figure in the house will depend on the mother's own level of resources, what the second parent figure would bring to the household, and what outcome we're interested in (say, a goal as basic as staying out of poverty or as advanced as graduating from college). Here I am sure plenty of readers are already asking, "but what about when the second parent is actually harmful to children? Or doesn't have any income to contribute?" These are important issues to consider, and they are part of the discussion, too.

Data show sizable gaps in the outcomes of children who grow up with married versus unmarried mothers, even when the married and unmarried mothers are the same age and have the same levels of education. The gaps may vary some depending on the mother's age and education or on what outcome for the child we're investigating. But by and large there is a consistent trend in which children growing up in mother-only households are at a relative disadvantage compared to children growing up in two-parent households, even despite all the parenting help that unpartnered mothers might get from nonresident fathers, other relatives, and government and community programs, among other sources. Some, but not all, of the gaps in children's outcomes are statistically attributable to the fact that married-parent households have higher income, which is important because it means policy makers can take steps to close these gaps by increasing the income of single-mother families. But it also means that even if policy makers were to *dramatically* scale up government support and shrink income gaps between one- and two-parent families, there would still be meaningful differences in children's experiences and outcomes.

Marriage allows for task specialization.

The economic approach to thinking about marriage emphasizes that when two people share the responsibilities of running a household and taking care of kids, the whole is greater than the sum of the parts. Basically, two people working together can do more for their household and their children than two people working apart can. As a concept, this principle mirrors the genius of the assembly line in production and manufacturing. Consider a manufacturing company making some product, a bicycle perhaps. If the process involved one worker per bicycle, it would be quite time consuming. Each worker would have to learn about each of the parts and how to put them together. But if instead, the workers work in assembly-line fashion, such that each worker specializes in one particular aspect of the bicycle-making process, each worker can become more proficient in their specific task or set of tasks and the process of making a bicycle becomes more efficient. More bicycles get produced in less time.

It's not hard to see how this concept applies to a household with two adults specializing in tasks such that the whole operation of running a home and raising a family is enhanced. Economists model marriage as allowing for specialization based on "comparative advantage." This notion of specialization in marriage was first proposed by the Nobel Prize–winning economist Gary Becker, who in the 1960s posited that marriage allows husbands to specialize in labor-market work while wives specialize in home production and child rearing.[4] Changing labor-market opportunities for women and evolving social norms mean that specialization today is not starkly divided between the genders in terms of market work, home production, and childcare as it once was. But the concept of specialization in a marriage still applies to many couples, allowing individual spouses to focus their efforts on the tasks they are relatively better at, thus using their time more efficiently.

As an example, in my own marriage, both my husband and I work outside the home, and we share household and child-rearing responsibilities. But within those buckets, we specialize. For example, I am a planner, and I thrive on organization. So, I generally manage the kids' schedules and activities and take care of meal planning and grocery shopping. Given how often my husband and kids ask me where something is, I sometimes think my greatest comparative advantage in the home is being able to find everything for them! Meanwhile, my husband deals with car and home maintenance and managing our health insurance and other bills. He also took the lead in teaching our kids how to read. Over the years, we have both become more efficient at the tasks we specialize in: it takes my husband far less time to navigate a health insurance issue than it would take me. Likewise, I can assemble our weekly grocery list and locate the items in their respective aisles in a quarter of the time it would take my husband. (Given how often I see men at the grocery store on the phone—confirming "which kind should I get?" or clarifying "they don't have that, what should I get instead?"—I am inclined to think this division of labor is common within couples.) If I were an unpartnered mother, or he were an unpartnered father, we would have to individually accomplish the tasks that two people complete in the time that just I alone (or he alone) would have. And neither one of us would be able to develop or focus our skills on a smaller set of tasks.

Economists write about such specialization and bargaining with elegant math equations, but I suspect this basic idea will feel intuitive and familiar to most readers. The key insight is that any specialization that happens among married parents further increases the relative resources of a two-parent household compared to a one-parent household.

The data say a lot about single motherhood and poverty in America.

The body of research on family structure and children's outcomes is vast, and it's typically centered around differences in maternal marital status—the experiences of the children of moms who are married compared to those of children of moms who aren't. This focus in part reflects the fact that large-scale data sets and surveys have tended to classify family structure into a very small set of (marriage-based) categories. Relevant to a book about the differences between one- and two-parent households, it is important to note that there is an *extremely* strong overlap between a mother's marital status and the number of parent figures in a home. As cohabitating has become more common, maternal marital status is less predictive of whether there is a father figure in the house than it used to be, but as we saw in chapter 2, there is still an extremely strong statistical link between a mother's marital status and the number of parental figures in the household. This background is all by way of explanation for why much of the research I describe is framed around single motherhood rather than one-parent households per se.

Scholars of US poverty have written extensively on the substantiated link between single motherhood (typically defined by marital status) and poverty in America. Foremost among them is the inimitable sociologist Sara McLanahan (whose work I mentioned in chapter 2, in reference to the Fragile Families and Child Wellbeing Study). McLanahan's 1986 book coauthored with economist and social-work scholar Irwin Garfinkel, *Single Mothers and Their Children: A New American Dilemma,*[5] marked an early milestone in the empirical study of vexing social problems, making a compelling descriptive case through data that the rise in single-mother households between 1960 and 1980 was a contributor to the concurrent rise in childhood poverty.

McLanahan and Garfinkel found that among White families, the share living in a household headed by a single mother increased from around 5% in 1960 to more than 10% in 1980; among Black families, the share increased from around 20% in 1960 to more than 45% in 1980. The conclusion from the 1986 book was uncomfortable— children from single-mother-headed households clearly seemed to be at a disadvantage. These disadvantages were apparent in the outcomes of both children raised by women who never married and by women who were divorced. As a descriptive matter, the authors showed that divorce tends to leave kids worse off, in large part because the income of the household falls precipitously after a divorce, and lower levels of family income translate into worse outcomes for children.

A follow-up book from McLanahan, published in 1994 with sociologist Gary Sandefur and titled *Growing Up with a Single Parent*, dug further into the link between family structure and children's outcomes, drawing again on data from multiple large-scale, nationally representative data sources.[6] The authors showed that White and Black children raised in a household headed by a single mother were more likely to become teen mothers, drop out of high school, and/or be both out of school and out of work during their early twenties, as compared to children raised in a married-parent family.

Is it family structure or some other, related factor that affects children's outcomes?

Other scholars have researched and written about the role of family structure in shaping children's outcomes since McLanahan's 1994 book. Much of this more recent research has focused on isolating the *causal* effects of family structure from correlations of children's outcomes with family structure. Researchers have worked to identify the extent to which the observed differences in outcomes by family structure are attributable—in a cause-and-effect sense—to the family structure or the marital status of the parents, rather than to some other associated factor or group of factors. For instance, it has been shown that unmarried mothers are statistically more likely than married mothers to have initiated childbearing as teenagers. But is it the fact that a mother started her family when she was very young or the fact that she doesn't have a partner in the family home that is the primary contributor—i.e., the causal factor—in the likely disadvantaged circumstances affecting her child's trajectory in life? Much of the work of scholars today centers on using statistical approaches to try to parse the respective roles of these types of confounding factors from the effect of family structure.

Social scientists' gold-standard research approach to identify the causal effect of a given factor is the *randomized controlled trial* (RCT). In an RCT, some people are randomly assigned to experience a policy reform or intervention, and others are not. This approach allows researchers to compare the outcomes of the two groups and confidently attribute differences to the policy or intervention. Obviously, that is not a feasible methodology for a study of how family structure affects children's outcomes—we could never randomly assign a child to live with two parents or one for the sake of a study. In practice, though, it is difficult to create situations that are "as good as random"—finding a set of families whose circumstances are impacted by only one factor being studied and not multiple factors at once. For instance, the death of a parent leaves a child with only one parent and might be viewed as random in some cases, but clearly the death of a parent does more than just strip the child of a second parent's resources. It is a traumatic event that is likely to affect a child (and the remaining parent) in many ways, including ways that are unknown or unobservable to researchers.

These methodological limitations make it very difficult for social scientists to determine conclusively that the presence of one parent versus two in a home is the thing that leads to different outcomes for children (as opposed to associated factors about the types of parents who are more or less likely to get or stay married—say, education level, attachment to employment, or personality traits). One promising approach that researchers have used to address these challenges is to use data from longitudinal data sets, which follow the same children and families over time and compare outcomes for a child before and after a change in family structure, thereby linking outcomes more directly to a change in family structure for an individual child. Another approach is to use longitudinal data for "sibling comparisons"—comparing the outcomes for siblings in the same family who experience more or fewer years of their childhood in a single- or married-parent home, or perhaps spend different segments of their childhoods in a single- or married-parent home. An advantage of sibling comparisons is that even though siblings might have a lot of unobserved underlying differences, they have the same mother and an overlapping gene pool, so a lot of important characteristics shaping outcomes are "held constant," as we say in the world of statistical analyses.

There is also a challenge of identifying the exact mechanisms that drive differences in outcomes by family structure—called "mediating factors," or the things that produce the difference in the outcomes being studied. If there are two parents in a family home, there are a bunch of things that will be different compared to a one-parent home. Having a second parent typically means a higher level of income, and all the associated advantages that higher income can buy for a family, such as a home in a safer neighborhood with better schools, healthier foods, enriching activities and trips, etc. A second parent also means another adult devoting time to the child, whether it be in the form of basic care (like feeding or dressing a young child), educational time (like reading to a child or helping them with their homework), travel time (like driving to sports practice or music lessons), or just time spent together in leisure and fun.

If we can identify the reasons why having two parents in the home leads to better outcomes for children—say, because two parents bring in more money than one parent or they collectively are able to spend more time teaching or supervising their children—that doesn't mean family structure doesn't matter. Rather, it means that the *reason* that children from married-parent or two-parent homes tend to have better educational, economic, and social outcomes in life is because of something that two-parent homes are more readily able to provide for their children.

Understanding what mechanisms drive the differences is crucially important, in part because it directs how we try to fix the problems or reduce the differences. For example, to the extent that gaps in outcomes by family structure are statistically explained by differences in income, then more income assistance to single-mother families would lessen the relative disadvantage of children in those families. To the extent that gaps are statistically explained by differences in fatherhood engagement or parental time, then increasing the likelihood that nonresident fathers are involved in their children's lives (in a positive way, obviously) or promoting the dedicated time from other positive adult role models or mentors might help lessen outcome gaps.

The most recent research, much of which incorporates advanced statistical techniques, continues to show that children who are raised in single-mother households tend to have lower levels of completed education and lower levels of income as adults, even after statistically accounting for observable demographic characteristics (for example, where the family lives or the mother's level of education). In attempting to identify the mechanisms for these disparities, the evidence suggests that household income during childhood is a key driver of outcome differences—but not the only driver. The sum of this research literature is vast, and too big to summarize here. What follows is a sort of best-of summary; I am not giving anything close to a comprehensive literature review here, which I suspect will disappoint research scholars reading this book but will be a relief to most readers.

Some social scientists have used longitudinal data, which follows research subjects for a long time, from the Panel Study of Income Dynamics (PSID) to trace children's outcomes during childhood and into adulthood. The PSID is the longest-running longitudinal household survey in the world: It began in 1968 with a nationally representative sample of over 18,000 individuals living in 5,000 families in the United States. Directed by researchers at the University of Michigan, survey conductors have been collecting detailed information on this initial sample and their children since then, gathering data on employment, income, wealth, expenditures, health, marriage, childbearing, child development, education, and numerous other topics.

A study published in 2014 using this data showed what is probably intuitive for most: that children who were raised in a household with a single mother grew up with a lower level of childhood household income over their childhood than children who grew with continuously married parents. This trend persisted even after the researchers statistically adjusted for the sex, race, and birth order of the child, the age of the mother at the time of her first birth, and the mother's level of education. The childhood income deficits were also larger for children whose mothers were never married, as compared to those whose mothers married after the child's birth or who were married at the time of birth but subsequently divorced.

Looking at the children's outcomes as they aged into adults, the same study showed that children of mothers who were never married have substantially lower income in adulthood than the children of continuously married parents (again after adjusting for demographic characteristics). The children of mothers who changed their marital status during kids' childhoods (either from unmarried to married or married to divorced) also had lower incomes during their adulthoods, with some modest differences based on demographics. The study indicates that having fewer economic resources during childhood statistically explains a lot of the gaps in adult educational and economic outcomes between the children of never-married mothers and continuously married parents. Differences in childhood income do not statistically explain as much of the gaps in outcomes between the children of divorced mothers and continuously married parents, however; presumably in these instances, the marital dissolution negatively impacts children in ways beyond the loss of household income.[7]

To this question of how divorce affects children's outcomes, scholars who have studied the impact of divorce on kids' well-being have generally found that children who experience a parental divorce exhibit more emotional and behavioral problems compared to kids whose parents stay together. A 2004 study by MIT economist Jonathan Gruber identified the causal effect by designing a study centered on unilateral divorce laws—state laws allowing one spouse to end a marriage without consent of the other, which became more common during the 1970s and led to a sizable increase in the number of divorces in the US.[8] Using data from the 1960, 1970, 1980, and 1990 US censuses (so, before and after the laws were implemented), Gruber found that this legal change led to more divorces and had the effect of worsening outcomes for children; namely, as a result of the increased incidence of parental divorce, children wound up having lower levels of education, lower levels of income, and more marital churn themselves (both more marriages and more separations), as compared to similarly situated children who did not live in places where unilateral divorce laws were in effect. The results of Gruber's analysis are consistent with a negative effect of divorce on children's long-term outcomes. (Although, to be clear, while the finding that the law-enabled increase in divorces produced negative effects for children, it does *not* necessarily mean that unilateral divorce laws aren't socially beneficial or desirable, all things considered. It is more likely the case that there were benefits to adults who were more readily able to end a harmful marriage.[9]) Other research shows that the divorce of parents has a causal effect on the likelihood that the children will subsequently live in poverty.[10] Lower household income after a divorce is clearly one way that divorce is, on average, disadvantageous for children.

Going back to longitudinal studies that look at family structure more generally, a 2022 study in a macroeconomics journal documents—again using data from the PSID—that family structure has become even more important over time in shaping a child's educational attainment.[11] The study shows that whether a child lives with one or two parents is an important predictor of college completion, even after statistically controlling for a host of other individual and family factors, including family income. The study further shows that the predictive power (in a statistical sense) of having two versus one parent in the home is *stronger* for individuals who turned 28 between 2006 and 2015, as compared to individuals who turned 28 between 1995 and 2005, holding other variables constant. The documented importance of early-childhood environments in determining college completion rates are so large that policy simulations the researchers ran implied that subsidizing pre-college investment for one-parent families has a larger impact on college completion and lifetime earnings than alternative interventions like tuition subsidies or cash transfers.

A 2009 study conducted by a team of economists used the 1997 National Longitudinal Survey of Youth (NLSY)—another highly detailed, nationally representative longitudinal survey of about 9,000 people ages 12–16 who were followed over time.[12] This study compared outcomes for a child before and after their family structure changed and compared outcomes across siblings who experienced different family structures at the same ages to isolate the relationship between family structure and children's young-adult outcomes. The NLSY study found that growing up without both biological parents in the home led to lower educational attainment and a higher incidence of unmarried parenthood or incarceration in young adulthood. The study authors reported that the employment and incarceration outcomes of young Black men were particularly strongly affected by growing up with a single mother. (I go into this thorny issue in more depth in chapter 6, where I discuss more recent evidence on the disparate impact of father absence from the home on boys' outcomes.) These statistical analyses show that the lower incomes of single-parent families—especially those headed by never-married mothers—account for some, but not all, of the observed relationship between family structure and young-adult outcomes. This finding about income being an important mediating factor, but not the only mediating factor, is consistent with what McLanahan and Sandefur found in their 1994 study and with what I found in my own research.

The absence of a father from a child's home appears to have direct effects on children's outcomes—and not only because of the loss of parental income. Nonfinancial engagement by a father has been found to have beneficial effects on children's outcomes. A 2006 study using data from an earlier NLSY (the 1979 cohort) found that children in single-mother families exhibited worse behavioral outcomes than children from two-parent families, even after accounting for individual characteristics such as the child's race and ethnicity and the mother's educational attainment and age at first birth. The study concluded that lower levels of father involvement can statistically explain some of that difference.[13] This same study also found that differences in the behavioral outcomes of children from single-mother families and children from otherwise similar situations are smaller when the nonresident father is more engaged. A 2013 comprehensive review of the academic research on the causal effect of not having a father in one's home concluded that a father's absence has a negative causal effect on children's social-emotional development, in particular by increasing externalizing behaviors, which are defined as disruptive, harmful, or problem behaviors directed outward—things like getting into fights or bullying.[14] (Again, the importance of fathers to children's outcomes, boys in particular, is a topic I return to in later chapters.)

Despite the statistical adjustments made in many studies to isolate causal effects at play in their research, we still need to be cautious about assigning a causal interpretation to the full range of differences observed across children in different family structures. As I noted before, family structure and parental relationship status are not *randomly assigned*—that is, they aren't designed for easy study. Even if researchers take steps to statistically account for all the things that can be observed in the data that might be confounding factors, there is still the possibility that there is something unobserved about single parents, something that researchers can't see in the data, that would make them less well-equipped to parent even if they were married, such that their children's outcomes would still be inferior to those of the children of married parents. But at some point—a point I think we are well past, given the body of research—the weight of the evidence is so strong that the most reasonable conclusion is that even if there were some unobservable differences between single and married parents, the thing staring at us from the data is overwhelming: having a second parent in the home, with the added resources (money, time, etc.) that second parent brings, is, on average, beneficial for children's outcomes.

The gaps in outcomes between children of married and unmarried mothers depend on the resource context.

At the conference I described at the opening of the book, I brought up the topic of class gaps in family structure to a room full of economists and policy scholars during a conversation about income inequality and social mobility. It was followed by the one-on-one conversation with the probing economist in the hotel lobby after the group meeting ended. I reflected on that conversation later that night and in the days that followed, and I soon realized that I had dismissed his questioning too quickly when I said I wasn't concerned about the kids of higher-income parents whose parents might be divorced or not married—that I was worried about all the kids growing up in lower-income single-parent homes. It's true that this is the issue that worries me the most. But I also wondered, how does family structure matter—or does it even matter—for people with higher levels of resources? If an unpartnered mother is well-educated and highly resourced, do her kids tend to do just as well as the kids of her married peers? I had read countless studies about the link between single motherhood and poverty, some of which I have described here. But I realized after that conversation with the other economist that I didn't really know what the data said about nonmarital childbearing or raising a child as an unpartnered mother for people who have greater resources and aren't in danger of slipping into poverty. Surely, having a child outside of marriage has different implications for a 19-year-old woman without a high school degree than for a 25-year-old with some college, or a 35-year-old college graduate. Wouldn't the advantages of a marriage—or more to the point, the advantages of having a second parent in the home—be different for children based on their mothers' circumstances?

I called my frequent collaborator, Phil Levine, an economics professor at Wellesley College, and I asked him if he knew of any research on the "heterogeneous"—economist speak for "different" or "varied"—benefits of marriage for different types of mothers. We started talking about what we'd expect the effects to be and looking for existing studies on the subject and we didn't find studies that directly answered the question we were mulling over. So we did what economist friends do when they get together: we wrote down a model (meaning, we wrote down mathematical equations to reflect hypothesized relationships) and then we sketched out an approach for estimating those relationships and investigating the question with data we knew to be available.

We started with a simple theory: that the gains to marriage (for a child) will depend on a mother's individual resources, the additional resources that her partner/the dad would bring to the household, and the returns to those additional partner resources. We used the term "resources" to refer broadly to resources relevant to raising children, including parental income, wealth, time, and emotional energy, among other things. The third part of our theory—the returns to resources—is akin to a "production function" that turns inputs into outputs. For those who aren't accustomed to thinking about raising children in the same terms that are used to describe a car factory, this might feel like a strange concept. But think of it this way: You spend time with your kid, you read to them, you buy them books and pay for educational experiences and enriching activities. Those things—the time and money and energy you pour into them—are the resource inputs. Your child's outcomes—including the level of education they attain and their ultimate earnings—are outputs, or outcomes. The "production function" in this relationship—here, a process of child development—takes all those inputs and ultimately generates outcomes. The different inputs, along with the way they interact, will generate "heterogeneous marriage premiums"— different levels of benefit for having married parents. We used the term "marriage premium for children" as a shorthand measure for the difference in outcomes between children who are born to married parents as compared to a single mother.[15]

For example, for some women, a partner's additional contributions won't be sufficient to alter certain outcomes, because those contributions would be too low. Even if a teen mother married the father of her child, their combined low resources might not be sufficient to keep their child out of poverty or ensure that she completes high school. In contrast, a professional woman is likely able to keep her child out of poverty and ensure that the child graduates high school with her resources alone. For both these women—one with limited income and one with high income—the addition of a spouse to the home would likely not affect the probability that the child lives in poverty or graduates from high school. For them, the marriage premium for children would be low. By contrast, a marriage between a mother with modest resources and a man with modest (but positive) earnings might produce enough of a boost in resources to really make a difference in their child's life. Their children would have a high marriage premium.

To test our idea, Levine and I used data on children and families from the PSID (the nationally representative longitudinal data set described earlier). We classified children based on their mother's marital status at birth, which it turns out is highly predictive of the family structure a child will experience during his/her childhood: 75% of children observed in the data as being born to married parents were still living with married parents at the age of 14. Of children born to a single mother, 65% were still living with only their mother at age 14. The data revealed that unmarried mothers were younger, less educated, and had lower household income when they had their first birth compared to married mothers when they had their first. Unmarried mothers also had their first child at age 23.7, on average, as compared to age 29.8 among married mothers. They had completed 12.8 years of education, on average, versus 14.6 for married mothers. Median household income at the time a mother had her first child was twice as high among married mothers compared to unmarried mothers: $73,255 versus $31,329 (in 2013 dollars).

The data also showed dramatic gaps in household income during childhood. Childhood family income averaged $35,430 for children born to unmarried mothers, as compared to $82,454 for children born to married mothers (again, in 2013 dollars). Children born to single mothers also spent a much larger share of their lives in poverty: 36.4% of their childhood, as compared to 8.6% for the children of married mothers.[16]

We then looked directly at four outcomes for the children of married vs. unmarried mothers: being out of poverty at age 25; completing high school by age 20; having household income over 400%

of the poverty line at age 25 (to indicate high income); and completing college by age 25. We called avoiding poverty and graduating from high school "primary outcomes"—basic things that most people, on average, will achieve. In contrast, we referred to having a high income and graduating from college as "advanced outcomes"—harder-to-accomplish outcomes that fewer children will grow up to achieve. These labels gave us a shorthand way to refer to outcomes that are easier or harder to achieve. (In retrospect, I suppose we could have just referred to them as easier outcomes or harder outcomes.)

We expected different patterns in the marriage premium for primary and advanced outcomes. Recall that we proposed that the "marriage premium" would depend on three factors in particular: a mother's own level of resources, the resources the dad would bring to the household if they were married, and the returns to those resources (i.e., the way the resources in a household translate into children's outcomes). This logic implies that for primary outcomes, the benefit of marriage will be greatest for moderately resourced mothers: they don't need much to get them over the threshold of core milestones like having a child stay out of poverty and graduate high school. A young single mother with a high school degree might not have sufficient resources to clear that bar on her own, but having a similarly situated spouse in the home might be enough to ensure that their child will graduate high school and earn a high enough wage to avoid poverty as a young adult. Meanwhile, an older, college-educated single mother will likely be able to raise her child with sufficient resources on her own to help them complete high school and avoid poverty. There won't be a sizable marriage premium for the most highly resourced mothers when it comes to primary outcomes.

For advanced outcomes, the returns to marriage are likely greatest for relatively more resourced mothers. Consider the advanced outcome of college completion. College completion rates are quite low among children from low-income households, but they go up with family income.[17] A young, less educated mother and her partner might not have sufficient resources, even when combined, to achieve a high likelihood of their child completing college. In general, it will require the resources of two well-resourced parents combined to create the kind of environment and set of opportunities that yield a high likelihood of an advanced outcome, namely, a child completing college and earning a very high income as a young adult. That implies that the difference in college completion outcomes will be largest among children of highly resourced moms, since the majority of children born to young, less educated mothers will not complete college, regardless of whether their parents are married.

The patterns in the data fit these predictions. For the primary outcomes of graduating high school and being out of poverty at age 25, the marriage premium (the gap in outcomes between children born to married and unmarried mothers) is smallest for the youngest, least educated mothers and the oldest, most highly educated mothers. In other words, the potential resource gain from marriage is not sufficient at the low end, and is unnecessary at the high end, to increase substantially a child's probability of graduating high school or avoiding poverty or completing high school. The greatest marriage premium occurs in the middle of the maternal age and education distribution: for mothers in their early to mid-20s and those with a high school degree, marriage is associated with the largest differences in these two outcomes.

For the advanced outcomes of graduating from college and having a high level of income at age 25, the marriage premium increases steadily with maternal age and education. This finding is also consistent with the predictions of our model. When it comes to reaching harder-to-obtain outcomes, marriage is increasingly associated with them as maternal age and education increase. Married parents are the through-line for many of society's most consequential milestones.

These patterns can be seen in table 3.1, which reports children's educational attainment by maternal marital status and level of education at the time of the child's birth.[18] (These are raw numbers, with no other adjustments made to the data.) The marriage premium— the difference in the percentage of children who have a high school

Table 3.1 Children's educational outcomes by maternal marital status and maternal education level

Maternal education level	Married mother	Unmarried mother	Difference ("marriage premium")
	Percentage of children with a high school degree by age 20		
Less than high school degree	73.6	67.9	5.6
High school degree	87.7	78.5	9.3
Some college	90.7	82.9	7.7
Four-year college degree	93.0	88.8	4.2
	Percentage of children with a four-year college degree by age 25		
Less than high school degree	7.4	4.9	2.5
High school degree	18.0	4.8	13.2
Some college	31.1	13.8	17.3
Four-year college degree	57.0	28.6	28.4

NOTES: *An observation is a child born between 1960 and 1989 in the PSID. Each observation is weighted by the child's individual-level PSID sampling weight in the year the outcome is observed.*

degree by age 20 based on mothers' marriage status—is greatest among children of mothers with a high school degree and some college: 9.3 and 7.7 percentage points, respectively. The gap is lowest for the children of mothers without a high school degree and for the children of mothers with a college degree. On one end, the smallness of the gap is because there is a high rate of high school noncompletion among the children of high school dropouts, even among those who are married; at the other end, there is a very low rate of high school noncompletion among the children of college-educated mothers, even unmarried ones. For instance, 88.8% of children of unmarried college-educated mothers have a high school degree by age 20. This is higher than the 73.6% of children of married mothers without a high school degree who earn a high school degree by age 20. This comparison highlights how important the mother's own level of education is in predicting her child's educational attainment, regardless of marital status.

The differences in college completion rates between the children of unmarried and married mothers by maternal education level

show a very different pattern than is seen for high school completion. Among children of mothers without a high school degree, very
few graduate from college, regardless of their mom's marital status:
only 7.4% of children born to married mothers and only 4.9% of
children born to unmarried mothers have a college degree by age 25.
Both rates are very low, which means the marriage premium is very
low. However, among the children of mothers with a college degree,
57.0% of children born to married mothers and 28.6% of children
born to unmarried mothers have a college degree by age 25. This is
a sizable difference of 28.4 percentage points.

The numbers reported in table 3.1 report unconditional differences, meaning that these are differences tabulated by only the two
variables reported: mother's marital status at the time of birth and
mother's education level. They don't account for other, correlated
factors. In our academic study, we reported differences in outcomes
by maternal marriage status for the two primary and two advanced
outcomes, after adjusting for the child's age, race, ethnicity, and year
of birth. The patterns described above based on the unconditional
differences are also seen in the more detailed results for *adjusted* differences. The analysis further reveals that household income at birth
is only *partly* responsible for the differences in outcomes. Even when
we statistically adjust for household income (in addition to the demographic factors), sizable differences in outcomes remain. Put another way, a child born in a two-parent household with a family income of $50,000 has, on average, better outcomes than a child born
in a single-parent household earning the same income.

The finding that household income is an important factor, but
not the only factor, that contributes to differences in outcomes between children from single- and married-parent families is consistent with the findings of other studies, including those cited above.
There are a variety of mechanisms beyond income through which
children might benefit from living in a married-parent home. For
instance, parents in two-parent households might have more time
and energy to devote to parenting. Furthermore, low levels of income and single parenthood are often associated with other stress

factors that are directly harmful to children's development, such as residential instability, maternal stress, and less positive parenting practices. Chapters 5 and 6 delve deeper into these issues.

The key takeaway from this discussion is that the so-called marriage premium for children depends crucially on resource context. It is noteworthy that the largest "gains to marriage" from a child's perspective exist for mothers in the middle or upper part of the maternal age and education distribution, depending on outcome. As we saw in chapter 2, the largest increase in single-mother childbearing and child rearing in recent decades has occurred for this demographic group—women with a high school degree or some college.

Related to the point of varied effects depending on context, a 2020 study by sociologist Christina Cross uses PSID data to examine the differential relationship between family structure and educational attainment for Black, White, and Hispanic children.[19] Cross documents that the negative association between spending a higher share of one's childhood without two biological parents in the home and the likelihood of graduating high school is stronger for White and Hispanic children than it is for Black children. She shows that part of this difference appears to be statistically explained by differences in maternal education and age of single mothers across racial and ethnic groups. This interpretation would be consistent with the model and results I described above, showing that the size of the "marriage premium" depends on maternal characteristics and on the level of resources that a second parent would bring into the home.

These observations bring us to a key point: A naïve conclusion to the challenges described above would be that more parents should simply get married. Perhaps. Or perhaps not. It depends crucially on why so many parents have been choosing not to get married in recent decades. Insofar as the reduction in marriage and the rise in nonmarital childbearing reflects an erosion of men's (and father's) economic standing, then dads in more recent decades would bring lower resources into the home than they would have in previous decades. As a preview to the discussion in chapter 4, this does seem to be at least part of the problem—to put it in stark (coldhearted) terms: the economic attractiveness of non-college-educated men has been diminished. This diminishment is part of the underlying problem. It means that even if there were a magic wand that one could wave to increase rates of marriage, class gaps in household resources would remain. Of course, most of us would never want to wave such a magic wand anyway. The ideal would be to address the underlying causes of the marriage decline, so that more parents *choose* to marry, and their marriages (i.e., their long-term contracts to pool resources and share the responsibilities of running a household and raising children) would then confer benefits to their children.

What about resource sharing and co-parenting among parents who aren't married or a child's biological parents?

Given the emphasis on resources, a few obvious questions emerge:

- First, does a couple need to be formally married to confer the relevant benefits of the institution on their children?
- Second, what about remarriage or stepfamilies?
- Third, do the benefits of marriage depend on the sex of the partners, or are opposite-sex and same-sex marriages equivalent from the perspective of resources?
- Fourth, what if the decline in marriage among parents is a result of a decline in fathers' resources?

To the first question, if two adults maintain a long-term partnership and a shared commitment to raising and caring for their children, then presumably there would be no resource gap between this arrangement and an arrangement wherein the adults were legally or religiously wed. To the extent that the beneficial effects of marriage for children are derived from the resource advantage of that arrangement, the actual marriage is irrelevant. However, the practical truth is that, to date, there has been no alternative institution to marriage that is characterized by the same long-term partnership and commitment in the United States. Cohabitation partnerships in the US are simply not as stable as marriages. This comparative instability helps explain *why* observed gaps in household resources, childhood experiences, and children's outcomes exist between married-parent and unmarried households.

Put another way: if all unmarried mothers were in committed long-term relationships with their children's father, and those unmarried parents pooled household resources and shared parenting responsibilities as married couples do, then we wouldn't see such large gaps in household resources and children's outcomes between married and unmarried households. We might still see some gaps in children's outcomes, if there are underlying differences between the kinds of people who marry and those who don't (i.e., if marrying types are somehow better parents, for reasons we can't observe in the data). But, given how large the observed differences are in the outcomes between children from single-parent and married-parent homes, even after adjusting (statistically) for the large array of characteristics and factors that are observable, it is a stretch to think these differences are all because marrying parents are somehow better parents. It is far more likely that these differences are due to the additional resources (monetary and otherwise) available to the children of married parents.

The issue of remarriage and stepfamilies moves the discussion away from a focus on *resources* to a focus on *relationships*. The main social issue that motivates me to write this book is the dramatic increase in mother-only households among a large segment of the US population since 1980, given the widely documented gap in household resources and children's outcomes that exists between children from mother-only and two-parent married homes. Questions about how children fare across different parental relationships are a bit tangential to the main challenges highlighted in this book. That said, there is some social science evidence suggesting that children tend to have better outcomes when they live with two biological parents. For example, there is a study using large-scale, nationally representative data showing that stepmothers generally do not invest as much in their stepchildren's health as do biological mothers, even after adjusting for household income and other relevant characteristics.[20] Another large-scale study finds that adolescents who experienced their mother marrying a stepfather after parental divorce had worse behavioral outcomes and more negative feelings than adolescents whose biological parents remained continuously married.[21] That situation additionally brings up issues of transitions and instability, which are generally understood to be difficult for children. In a 2005 article published in the *Future of Children*, sociologist Paul Amato concluded that studies consistently indicate that children in step-families tend to exhibit social and behavioral problems on a similar scale to children in single-parent homes, and more so than children living with continuously married biological parents.[22]

On the topic of same-sex parenting partnerships, to the extent that the beneficial effects of marriage for children are derived solely from the resource advantage of that arrangement, the genders of the parents are irrelevant. Some have argued that children do best when they are raised by a man and a woman, as compared to two adults of the same gender. But to the best of my knowledge, there is no empirical evidence showing that children raised by married same-sex parents have different outcomes than children raised by similarly situated married opposite-sex parents. A research brief on the topic prepared by a team of sociologists for the American Sociological Association's 2013 amicus curiae brief to the Supreme Court concluded that the social science literature indicates that American children living within same-sex parent households fare just as well as those children residing within different-sex parent households over a wide array of well-being measures, once socioeconomic status and family stability measures are accounted for.[23]

In some cases, wouldn't children be better off without one of their parents in the home?

The discussion in this chapter frames marriage as an institution that brings the resources of a second parent, typically a father, into the home. The model I described above emphasizes that the potential benefit of marriage for children—the "marriage premium for children," as Levine and I labeled it—will depend on context. Specifically, it will depend on a mother's own resources and the resource the child's father would bring to the family. If a father doesn't have any positive resources (financial or otherwise) to bring into the household, then there would be no household gain to marriage. Conversely, if that father would bring violence or chaos or stress into the household, the gains to marriage could be, and probably would be, negative.

Consider the case of a criminal parent who is incarcerated. Incarceration is obviously an extreme form of parental or father absence, but one that is relevant to the question of whether having a second parent in the home would, in some instances, be worse than the alternative. Two recent studies by economists document the causal effect of parental incarceration on children's outcomes.[24] These papers speak to the question of what happens to children's outcomes when a parent who is convicted of a crime is sentenced to prison, as compared to not being sent to prison. Both papers identify the causal effect of incarceration, conditional on criminal conviction, by statistically taking advantage of the fact that criminal defendants are randomly assigned to judges who have different propensities for sending criminals to jail.

One of these studies (published in 2021 in the most prestigious academic journal in the field of economics) uses 30 years of administrative data from the state of Ohio. The other study (also published in 2021 in a very prestigious economics journal) uses data from the country of Colombia. Both papers find that the incarceration of a parent charged with a crime is on net beneficial for children's outcomes. The evidence from Ohio shows no causal effect (positive or negative) of parental incarceration on children's educational performance nor on teen childbearing. But, it does reveal that children whose parents are incarcerated—due to a randomly assigned judge's propensity to incarcerate convicted criminals—are substantially less likely to engage in criminal activity themselves before the age of 25. They consider multiple potential mechanisms for this finding; the evidence points to a deterrent effect. The study that uses data from Colombia finds that having a criminal father who is sent to prison (again, due to random assignment to a particular judge) leads to an increase in children's educational attainment. The researcher observes that these findings are consistent with previous research that finds that removing a violent parent or negative role model from the household can create a safer environment for a child. She also notes that parental incarceration may result in the child being placed with an alternative caregiver who has better resources to care for the child, such as a grandparent.

Though important, these studies about parental incarceration reveal the causal effect of father absence in the very specific case of a father convicted of a crime. They should not be used to draw general conclusions about how father absence affects children more generally. They do, however, underscore the importance of thinking about parental circumstances and parenting resources when speculating about the benefits of marriage, a two-parent household, or committed co-parenting. In later chapters, I discuss ongoing fatherhood initiatives that are aimed at helping dads be better parents to their children. Some of these initiatives specifically address the barriers that men who have been in prison face.

Summary

The data and evidence highlighted in this chapter show clearly that there are gaps in outcomes between children of married and unmarried mothers, including among more-educated mothers. But what can be done to close these gaps? Increased rates of marriage among unmarried parents might be beneficial to children in some instances, but likely not all. If the mothers who are not married are not married precisely because the men with whom they have fathered children would not meaningfully contribute positive resources to the raising of their children, then the observed marriage gap in children's outcomes is not a good approximation for what their children would gain from parental marriage.

This raises the question—is it really the case that close to 40% of births in the US are to men who would not bring any positive resources (on net) into the home? Is it likely to be true that roughly 70% of births to non-college-educated mothers are fathered by men with no positive resources to contribute to a family environment? If the answer to these questions is even close to yes, then that does not suggest single parenthood is not a social problem. Rather, it implies that the social problem extends far beyond the issue of how children are being raised, to the issue of why so many men are not fit to be marriage partners or engaged fathers. The next chapter delves into the question of why rates of marriage have fallen so much among non-college-educated adults.

FOUR

Marriageable Men (or Not)

"I'm telling you, as soon as I start getting more hours, the first thing I do is get my own place."

NICK SOBOTKA to his girlfriend Aimee, explaining that he needs more hours at his union job so that he can afford a place where they can live together with their daughter (he currently lives in his parents' basement), "Hot Shots," *The Wire*, season 2, episode 3

To understand the decline in the fraction of children in the US being raised in two-parent homes, we need to first understand why fewer adults are getting married. And to understand why fewer adults are getting married, it is instructive to begin with a discussion of *who* exactly is statistically less likely to get married today. The statistical answer to that question is stark: marriage rates among non-college-educated adults have plummeted, especially in comparison to marriage rates among college-educated adults, both men and women. Economic factors have played a role in driving these social and demographic changes. The same forces that have eroded economic security for a large swath of Americans have also contributed to social malaise, including a reduction in marriage; a rise in nonmarital childbearing; and a rise in the share of children being raised without two parents in their home. These types of economic and social factors reinforce each other: they both reflect inequality and are a driving force behind the growth of inequality.

In some ways it is surprising that marriage rates are down given how easy it is now to meet someone. The proliferation of dating apps has not only expanded individuals' pool of potential partners (a pool that was formerly composed only of people they encountered in the physical world, whether at school, work, church, or a bar); it has also produced an environment in which people are more declarative and transparent about their interests for partnerships. The adorable audacity of Tom Hanks and Meg Ryan accidentally falling in love over email in the sappy 1998 movie *You've Got Mail* has evolved over two decades into an environment of greater intentionality: users sort prospective partners by their shared interests in long-term partnerships, including marriage or not-marriage. We might have expected that as it has become easier to meet people over recent decades, marriage rates would have increased. As it turns out, other forces have prevailed.

The share of American adults who are married is at a historic low. Among adults ages 30 to 50, in 2020, 60% of men and 63% of women were married. In 1980, the corresponding shares were 79% and 76%. That's a 24% decrease among men and a 17% decrease among women. Going back another decade, the decline is even more dramatic—the shares married in 1970 were 87% of men and 83% of women. This reduction in the share of adults married reflects two trends: fewer adults are getting married now; and among those who do, they are marrying later in life than they used to. (Notably, the reduction is not driven by a rise in divorce. In fact, married couples today are less likely to get divorced than they were in the 1980s.)

When I talk with people about my work and my research, they are often quick to offer theories for what's driving these demographic trends. Young adults, they often say, are choosing to invest in their education and careers instead of getting married. The idea is that these "go-getters" are choosing to remain single, so that they have more flexibility to move around for job opportunities and put in long hours at work. (Here, I admit, sometimes I can't help but fact check these types of claims when they are casually thrown around at cocktail parties and backyard gatherings. In these moments I often catch my husband watching me, waiting to see how long I'm going to let a conversation about social and economic trends continue before I do the professor thing and interject "well, actually, what the data show . . .") Granted, some of this narrative-fitting does reflect actual trends—college-educated adults *do* move around more for economic opportunity, and they *do* put in longer hours at work. But they are actually *less* likely to remain single than those with less education. For women, this reflects a reversal from trends in earlier decades. Overall, both men and women with college degrees are now more likely to be married than others.

The changes in marriage patterns that I describe have all taken place *after* the cultural revolution of the 1960s and 1970s. The watershed social movements of those earlier decades liberated women from traditional gender roles, catapulted their educational and occupational ambitions into a new tier, and had profound effects on marriage, childbearing, and family life. The preeminent Harvard economic historian Claudia Goldin refers to these earlier decades as a period when women, in particular college-educated women, started to perceive their lifetime labor-force involvement as more long-term than intermittent and their work life as part of a professional identity, rather than just a method of supplementing a husband's income.[1] During these decades, married women's labor-force participation increased dramatically, and college-educated women delayed marriage and childbearing to pursue educational degrees.

This period of revolution in women's roles in society opened up opportunities for so many women, myself included. In my family, I was the first to grow up in the era during which women might expect to both build a career and a family at the same time. I grew up as a girl who loved school and confidently aimed to go to college and have a career. I met my would-be husband in college in the mid-1990s, and then we lived in separate cities while we pursued graduate degrees, finally getting married and starting our family after I completed my PhD. My nonny, meanwhile, was mystified by my choice to pursue so much education. Hers was a different era and a different socioeconomic reality. She grew up in New York City, the daughter of Italian immigrants. She completed her schooling at the eighth grade, and at age 20 she married my grandfather. She raised her children in an apartment building with her siblings and their children, working as a seamstress to supplement the money her husband brought home. (Their way of life, typical of many Italian immigrants in NYC at that time, is now chronicled in the fabulous Tenement Museum in the Lower East Side of NYC.[2])

Between my and my grandmother's generations, my mother's generation was raised with a set of social norms and expectations that fell somewhere between. She completed high school and began working as a secretary at the age of 18. She married her high school sweetheart at the age of 21 and had her first child (me) at age 25. She spent the next 20 years raising her four daughters alongside her husband, being a homemaker, volunteering with the PTA, and working as a part-time secretary. At the age of 43—when her daughters were ages 16, 14, 12, and 8—she enrolled in a local public college and began the journey toward becoming a teacher. First she had her family and her part-time job, and only when she deemed her daughters old enough, did she go to college and pursue a teaching career. In contrast, my sisters and I fit the mold of college-educated women graduating in the 1990s and after, among the generation of women whom Claudia Goldin labels as "career and family": we went to college, we embarked on careers, and then we began our families in our 30s at the same time as we invested in our careers. These generational social changes continue to evolve; I often wonder what choices my own children will make when it comes to marriage and having children. The world they inhabit is different from the one I experienced growing up, just as it was different for my parents and their parents before them. And it will continue to change in ways that will matter for people's choices about how to live their lives. We are products of our times and the economic and social environments we grow up in.

After the changes of the 1960s and 1970s, economic and societal forces emerged in the 1980s and 1990s that affected different groups differently. Income inequality grew. Americans with four-year college degrees did extremely well. Others, not as much. Marriage rates fell further, but mostly for those without college degrees.[3] These are the forces and changes that this book is focused on.

Marriage shares have been falling, with the largest declines occurring among those with a high school degree or some college.

Amid the cultural changes of the 1960s and 1970s, marriage rates fell among men, with relatively equal rates of decline across men with different levels of education. In the early 1960s, 85% to 90% of men between the ages of 30 and 50 were married. By 1980, these shares had fallen to the range of 75% to 80%. Then, during the eighties, the pace of decline in men getting married continued among high-school-educated men, accelerated among men with less than a high school degree, and leveled off among college-educated men; marriage became relatively more common among elites. Figure 4.1 plots the share of men ages 30 to 50 married, by the three levels of education. The share of high-school-educated men (including those who've completed some college) who are married is now on par with the low rate of marriage among high school dropouts.

Figure 4.2 shows the analogous numbers for women. It illustrates how, from the 1960s to 1990, women with college degrees were less likely to be married than women with high school degrees. By the mid-1990s, these women became the *most* likely to be married. Here again, the 1980s were an inflection point. While all demographic groups are less likely to marry, the women who are marrying least are those with less education.

A clear education gradient in marriage has emerged in the past 40 years for most major racial and ethnic groups.

The predictive relationship between education and marriage is complicated by the fact that, in America and most places, educational

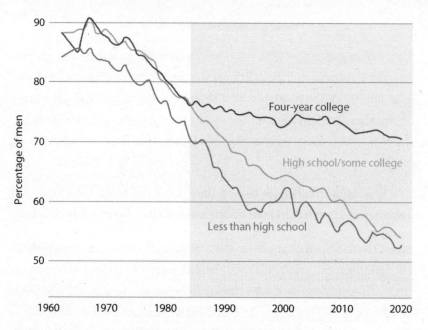

Figure 4.1 Share of men ages 30–50 married, by education level
SOURCE: *March Current Population Survey, 1962–2020.*
NOTES: *Sample includes noninstitutionalized men between the ages of 30 and 50, weighted using CPS person weights. In 2020, the shares of men in the three education-level groups (those with less than a high school degree, those with a high school degree and some college, and those with a four-year college degree) were 9%, 52%, and 39%, respectively.*

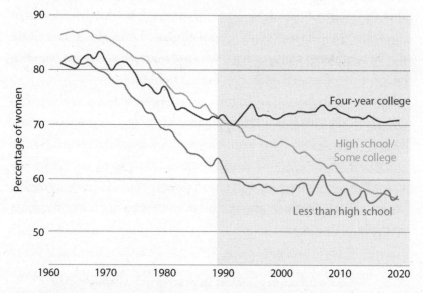

Figure 4.2 Share of women ages 30–50 married, by education level
SOURCE: *March Current Population Survey, 1962–2020.*
NOTES: *Sample includes noninstitutionalized women between the ages of 30 and 50, weighted using CPS person weights. In 2020, the shares of women in each of the three education-level groups (those with less than a high school degree, those with a high school degree or some college, and those with a four-year college degree) were 7%, 47%, and 45%, respectively.*

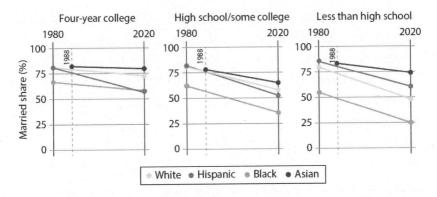

Figure 4.3 Men's marriage rates ages 30–50, by race and education level: 1980 and 2020
SOURCE: *March Current Population Survey, 1980, 1988, and 2020.*
NOTES: *Data is tabulated from the 1980 and 2020 CPS for all racial and ethnic groups except Asians; marriage rates among Asians are tabulated from the 1988 instead of the 1980 CPS, which is the first year that racial category was separately recorded. Sample includes noninstitutionalized men between the ages of 30 and 50, weighted using person weights.*

attainment is less available to some groups than others. (The marriage rates among women, based on these same values and date ranges, are detailed in chapter 2.) Between 1980 and 2020, the married share of men ages 30–50 fell from 81% to 65% among White men (a decline of 20%), from 60% to 41% among Black men (a decline of 32%), and from 84% to 55% among Hispanic men (a decline of 35%). The share of Asian men who are married did not fall much: 81% to 75%.

The decline in marriage has been driven by a decline in marriage among those without a college degree. But the specific pattern in marriage across education levels differs a bit across the four major racial and ethnic groups tracked. Figure 4.3 shows how the proportion of men married changed between 1980 and 2020, separated by education *and* race/ethnicity. In 1980, among both Black and White men, the shares of men married were similar across education groups. This is no longer the case. Now, for both Black and White men, married shares are much higher among men with college degrees than among those without.

For Hispanic and Asian men, the relationship between married shares and education level takes on a U-shape. Hispanic men without a high school degree and men with a four-year college degree had similar married shares in 2020 (60% and 57%); those with a high school degree had a lower married share (52%). Among Asian men, the 2020 married share was also highest among those with a four-year college degree (79%) and those without a high school degree (73%), and lowest for those with a high school degree (65%). This U-shape pattern is largely driven by relatively high rates of marriage among immigrants with a low level of education. In fact, among native-born Hispanic and Asian men, there is a positive education gradient, not a U-shaped relationship.

Harvard sociologist William Julius Wilson wrote about the correlation between the "marriageability" of men and rates of marriages more than 30 years ago, focusing on Black/White differences.

In 1987, the sociologist William Julius Wilson wrote a seminal book, *The Truly Disadvantaged: The Inner City, the Underclass, and Public Policy*, that called attention to the rising share of families headed by single mothers among Black families living in US cities in the 1960s and 1970s.[4] Wilson posited that high rates of nonmarriage among certain groups in society might reflect the low economic "marriageability" of men. The basic premise of this hypothesis was that a man who does not reliably hold down a job and bring in a steady, decent income might be considered less "marriageable." Wilson suggested that this phenomenon might be part of the explanation for the rise of single-mother families among Black families in US cities at the time.

Wilson introduced a concept that he called the "marriageable men pool index": the number of employed men in a given race and age group compared to the number of women. Wilson calculated that in the 1950s and 1960s, that index was comparable for Black and White adults. But the index began to diverge between Blacks and Whites in the 1960s. By the late 1970s, the ratio of employed young men to young women was only 40 for Black young adults, as compared to 63 for White young adults. This simple metric reflects a host of economic and social challenges that disproportionately affected Black men, contributing to their low rates of employment, including discrimination, incarceration, and mortality, among other factors. Wilson described his scholarly findings to a *Washington Post* reporter as follows: a "shrinking of the pool of marriageable black men seems a likely explanation for at least some of the increase in out-of-wedlock births and single-parent households among blacks."[5]

Echoes of this theory about the "marriageability" of men are evident in the more recent work of sociologists Kathrin Edin and Maria Kafalas, whose ethnographic accounts of single mothers were the center of their 2005 book *Promises I Can Keep: Why Poor Women Put Motherhood before Marriage*.[6] Based on interviews with 162 single mothers about their lives and views on marriage and children, Edin and Kafalas's book suggests that many women don't marry the father of their child because they do not see him as a reliable source of economic security or stability. Based on their conversations with the women in their study, the researchers conclude that these women do not generally avoid marriage because they reject the institution or concept of marriage. Rather, many appear to have a higher bar for a potential spouse than their partners—and the fathers of their children—have met.

More than 30 years after Wilson's book, his observation of a link between the economic struggles of men and the breakdown of the two-parent family extends far beyond Black families living in urban neighborhoods. In his 2016 memoir *Hillbilly Elegy: A Memoir of a Family and Culture in Crisis*, venture capitalist J. D. Vance wrote that Wilson's observations about urban Black families in the 1960s and 1970s seemed to describe his upbringing as a White boy in rural Ohio. Vance writes about the poverty, social isolation, family instability, and violence that characterized his childhood and the lives of his poor White neighbors in the Appalachian region of the US. Vance himself makes the connection between his childhood and Wilson's observations. "Wilson's book spoke to me," he writes. "I wanted to write him a letter and tell him that he had described my home perfectly. That it resonated so personally is odd, however, because he wasn't writing about the hillbilly transplants from Appalachia—he was writing about black people in the inner cities."[7]

Where men's earnings have fallen, so too have marriage rates.

Since the 1980s, economic trends have favored workers with college degrees, making it harder for those without a college degree to obtain a secure footing in the workforce with a steady, well-paying job. Men without college degrees have seen their earnings stagnate and employment rates fall. Women, meanwhile, have experienced increases in average earnings regardless of their education level. This change has stripped many men of their traditional role as breadwinner for the family and, in simple terms, made them less desirable marriage partners.

Figure 4.4 plots the median earnings of men ages 30 to 50 who are employed full-time, all year round. As can be seen clearly in the figure, median earnings among working men with college degrees (measured in constant 2018 dollars, which eliminates the effects of inflation in this comparison) have, like the wages of women, been on a general upward trend since 1980. They increased over these 40 years from about $60,300 per year to about $83,800 per year, in real terms. The same cannot be said of the earnings of working men without a college degree. Among working men with a high school degree, median real earnings hardly changed; they were just below $49,000 in both 1980 and 2020. Among working men without a high school degree, median real earnings fell slightly from $35,400 to $34,000 a year. Making the relative economic standing of men without college degrees even worse than what is captured in declining earnings among workers is the fact that they are now less likely to be employed than they were 20 and 40 years ago. There has not been a meaningful decline in employment rates among college-educated men.

The corresponding patterns in economic outcomes and marriage for men is striking. The largest decline in marriage rates between 1980 and 2020 occurred among non-college-educated men— the same group that experienced stagnant earnings and falling

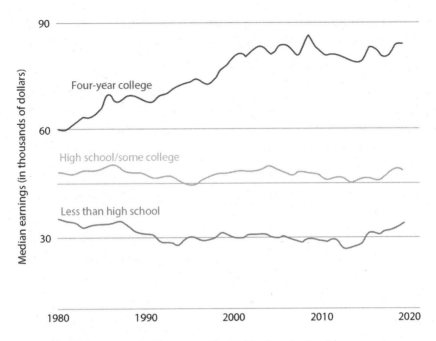

Figure 4.4 Median earnings of men ages 30–50, by education level
SOURCE: *March Current Population Survey, 1962–2020.*
NOTES: *Sample includes noninstitutionalized men between the ages of 30 and 50 who reported that they usually worked at least 35 hours and had worked for at least 40 weeks in the previous year, weighted using person weights. Earnings reported in 2018 USD.*

employment. Meanwhile, there was very little decline in marriage rates among college-educated men—the group whose employment rates remained high and whose earnings increased.

If we dig further into the data parsed by both education level and race/ethnicity, the correspondence between education and marriage persists within the smaller groups. For instance, Asian college-educated men, White college-educated men, and Black college-educated men experienced the largest increases in median earnings over the 40-year period (in that order); these same groups had low relative declines in their married shares. At the other end of the distribution, Hispanic men with and without a high school degree, White men with and without a high school degree, and Black men with a high school degree experienced very small increases in median earnings over this period; these are the groups with the largest reductions in married shares.

The earnings/marriage patterns of non-college-educated Asian men do not follow the trend. Asian men with and without high school degrees experienced very small increases in median earnings over this 40-year period; yet they experienced relatively small declines in marriage. Why have less educated Asian adults in the US not retreated from marriage, while their White, Black, and Hispanic counterparts have? It's a really interesting question, and unfortunately, I don't have an answer for it. I suspect the answer has a cultural or social explanation, but that is purely a speculative direction of inquiry.

Parsing and analyzing men's earnings between 1980 and 2020 is one part of understanding the value proposition of marriage—the resources a man would bring to a marriage or a household. But to fully understand the economic-value proposition of marriage, we also have to consider what a woman can earn on her own. After all, if the primary value of marriage for a child is the increase in overall parental resources, then who's to say a child needs two parents if one, likely the mom, is making enough to get by? This observation is related to the resource-based model of the "marriage premium for children" that I described in the previous chapter: the benefit of parental marriage for a child depends on how much a mother could materially provide for her child as a single mother, how much a second partner (typically the child's dad) would bring into the home, and how those combined resources would translate into experiences and outcomes for the child. When we think about the value proposition of marriage more generally, we also have to think about how much a spouse would bring into the marriage *and* how much a woman could make on her own in the absence of that spouse.

So, from the perspective of a woman considering whether to marry a man, the "gains to marriage" will depend not just on how much he would bring, but on how much she could make on her own, if she chose to work. This is a standard economics approach to modeling marriage. (Again, I realize the economic approach sounds cold-hearted and heteronormative—there is truth to these criticisms. But these are the broad strokes in which we tend to operate in order to understand overarching trends and patterns at a population level.) Of course, the marriage proposition is also—perhaps even *mostly*—about love and companionship. But that does not negate the reality that marriage is, as a practical and child-raising matter, also an economic institution. Remember the economic framework introduced earlier for thinking about marriage: it is a long-term contract between two individuals to pool and contribute resources.

Within that economics framework, it is instructive to consider how women's own economic prospects, as captured by earnings, changed relative to men's earnings during the period from 1980 to 2020. Among college-educated workers, women made about 70% of what men made (using median earnings) throughout the 1990s and 2000s.[8] (Prior to that, the ratio was closer to 65% in the 1980s.) Between 2013 and 2020, it inched up to 76%. This is to say, the gender gap between highly educated men and highly educated women has been mostly as advertised, with women making somewhere around three-quarters of their male counterparts.

Meanwhile, among non-college-educated adults, the earnings gap between men and women has shrunk dramatically. Among workers with only a high school degree, the ratio of women's median wages to men's median wages increased from 54% in 1980 to 74% in 2020. While women with less education saw pay that was approximately half that of similarly educated men in 1980, the ratio of women's median wages to men's median wages increased from 57% in 1980 to 71% in 2020—a more substantial shift than the one measured among women with more education. In other words, among workers without a four-year college degree, the gap between men's earnings and women's earnings shrank considerably (on account of both increasing earnings among women and stagnant earnings among men), which lessened the economic incentive (and imperative) for some women to marry.

These economic accounts presume that people tend to marry within their same education class (generally the case) and that men are generally expected to be breadwinners, or at least financial contributors, to a marriage. Of course, there is an alternative option

here: men could up their game on the home front. Instead of pull-
ing away from marriage when men's traditional role of breadwinner is undermined, it is possible (and anecdotally, it is happening
in some households) that couples agree for the husband to cede the
role of primary earner to the wife, and for him to take up the role
of primary homemaker and childcare provider (at least within the
context of a heterosexual marriage). Though I don't deny the possibility of this role shift happening more in the future, we don't seem
to be there yet in American culture. Existing evidence shows that
when men's primary economic position has weakened, marriage
rates have fallen—that men have retreated from marriage structures. Relatedly, an economics paper published in 2015 provides
evidence that traditional gender norms continue to govern many
marriages, such that the following patterns are seen in nationally
representative data: the earnings of wives tend not to exceed that
of their husbands, and when they do, there is an increased incidence
of divorce. That study also provides evidence that the expectation
that men outearn their wives affects marriage formation, not just
existing marriages—in geographic areas where women tend to earn
more than men, marriage rates are lower.[9]

**Research has established a causal link from men's
declining economic status to a decline in marriage shares.**

The statistical correspondence between the declining economic position of non-college-educated men and the decline in marriage
among non-college-educated adults is clear. However, it takes a lot
more work (in a statistical sense) to establish that there is a *causal*
link—actual cause and effect—between the weakened economic
position of these men and their lower rates of marriage. It would
be misleading to simply compare marriage rates among high- and
low- earning men and conclude that high earnings are the *reason*
why higher-income men are more likely to be married. It could be,
for example, that high-earning men get married more because they
have some other personality trait that makes them successful both

in the workplace and marriage market. Such a trait would be what economists call a "confounding unobserved factor": a factor that is highly relevant to observing cause and effect but isn't necessarily visible or observed. A man who is super responsible in general is probably more likely to both hold down a steady, high-paying job *and* commit to being a husband. Thus, we can't simply compare the marriage rates of high-earning men to the marriage rates of low-earning men and attribute the difference in marriage rates to the difference in earnings.

The same is true when it comes to the geography of a given dynamic. Say we observe in the data that one place, call it Town A, has a lot of high-earning men and a high rate of marriage, while another place, call it Town B, has a lot of low-earning men and a low rate of marriage. It is not necessarily true that the good job opportunities for men in place A lead to the higher rate of marriage in the town. It could be the case that Town A just raises or attracts responsible men, and Town B raises or attracts less responsible men. Maybe Town B has more of the type of amenities that less responsible men like— say, bars or gambling establishments—and Town A has a specific culture that fosters marriage in certain ways. Determining whether the better economic outcomes experienced by men in Town A are partially responsible for the higher rate of marriage in Town A requires researchers to identify causality.

Causality is a fixation of economists. It is also exceedingly difficult to study and to prove, especially in a space as complex and nuanced as human relationships and marriage. But through a remarkably clever paper, a 2018 study by a team of US economists overcame this "identification challenge" (as empirical economists call it) to document a *causal* link between the eroding economic position of men and lower marriage rates. The authors do so by studying the specific case of non-college-educated men in US manufacturing towns in the aftermath of increased import competition from China in recent decades. In 2000, China joined the World Trade Organization, and the US rather rapidly began importing a range of products that had previously been manufactured domestically (at a higher cost). This development meaningfully changed the economic prospects of men living in some parts of the country, especially those where a large share of the workforce had been previously involved in manufacturing the types of goods that were now being imported more cheaply from China, leading to a decline in men's earnings and employment rates. This external change—not to the types of men who live in a place, but to the economic reality of the place—allowed the economists to investigate statistically whether a change in men's economic prospects can cause a change in marriage rates. The answer was yes.

The economists published their findings in a 2019 paper titled "When Work Disappears: Manufacturing Decline and the Falling Marriage Market Value of Young Men," which was an explicit reference to a 1996 book by William Julius Wilson titled *When Work Disappears: The World of the New Urban Poor*.[10] Their study showed that the trade-induced reduction in men's relative earnings led to lower levels of marriage and a higher share of unmarried mothers. It also led to an increase in the share of children living in single-mother households with below-poverty levels of income.

Additional evidence of a causal link between men's declining economic position and marriage rates came from a 2021 study on the increased use of industrial robots in workplaces during the first decade of the 2000s, which in turn led to decreased earnings and employment among non-college-educated men.[11] Factories in many US manufacturing towns—though not necessarily the same manufacturing towns that were economically harmed by imports from China—increased their use of industrial robots in their production plants, driving down the earnings and employment of men without college degrees who worked in affected industries. This study documented how the adoption of industrial robots had a negative impact on the employment and wages of workers in affected industries and regions, with worse effects for men than for women. The study also demonstrated that US regions affected by more use of robots to do work subsequently experienced a decrease in new marriages and an increase in the share of births to unmarried women. Both these recent studies make a very compelling case that declines in male economic status have led to reductions in marriage rates and a rise in the share of children living without a father in the home.

The story of how economic forces have eroded the standing of men without college degrees—and in turn, reduced rates of marriage and increased rates of single mother families—can be told through any number of these academic studies, which use cutting-edge statistical techniques to establish causal statistical linkages. But the story will also feel familiar to anyone who grew up in a manufacturing town in America that was hit by these global forces. Orion Martin is a former college and professional football player who coached high school football in Martinsville, Virginia, shortly after his playing career ended in 2009. Martinsville, located 15 miles from the North Carolina border to the south, was a twentieth-century hotbed of manufacturing activity, specializing in the production of furniture and textiles. The hugely successful Bassett furniture company was founded in the Martinsville area in the early 1900s, and in the 1940s the DuPont company built a large nylon-manufacturing plant elsewhere in town. Martin recalls how "back in the day," men graduating high school would go work for the Bassett plant or the DuPont plant or other smaller plants in town. These jobs offered good pay and the possibility to provide for a middle-class family.

But that all changed in the 1990s. Martin, whose father grew up in Martinsville, recalls how the city once boasted that it was home to more millionaires per capita than any other city in America—a bastion of economic growth and upward mobility. (Note: I have not fact checked that claim, but nobody would even attempt such a boast today.) The changing global economic landscape of the 1990s rendered much of the manufacturing in Martinsville unsustainable. Many of the plants in town closed, workers were laid off, and a promising economic pipeline that moved so many young men from the local high school to a secure middle-class job vanished. By the 2010s, poverty and joblessness were widespread. On the high school football team Martin coached in his hometown, he estimates that perhaps five of the 60 or so boys on the team had a father in their home.

The link Martin observed—a decline in manufacturing jobs in

his hometown and a rise in the share of families headed by a single mother—has been established in large-scale data sets. In addition to the studies about manufacturing imports and the rise of industrial robots, a 2016 study looking at the adults in the National Longitudinal Survey of Youth between 1997 to 2011 documented a greater likelihood that people get married before having a child when they live in a place where there are more jobs paying high school graduates above-poverty wages.[12] Another 2022 study investigated the impact of the decline in US manufacturing jobs from 1960 to 2010 on a range of economic and social outcomes, including their impacts on White and Black Americans.[13] The study analyzed how national trends in manufacturing employment differentially affected areas with higher initial levels of baseline employment in the manufacturing sector. To see how this empirical approach works, consider two towns again, Town A and Town B, where Town A had only a small share of adults working in manufacturing at the beginning of the period being studied and Town B had a large share in that same year. Over the ensuing decades, as the country experienced an overall loss in manufacturing jobs, how did the outcomes of adults in Town B change as compared to the changes in outcomes of adults in Town A? Using data from the 1960, 1970, 1980, 1990, and 2000 US censuses, along with data from the 2009, 2010, and 2011 American Community Surveys, the study statistically detailed the relationship between the loss of manufacturing jobs in a particular geographic area—as driven by national trends, not by things happening specifically in that area—and changes in outcomes like marriage and single motherhood.

The study found that the decline in US manufacturing jobs led to a decrease in wages, a decrease in employment, a decrease in marriage rates, and an increase in wage inequality—along with other adverse impacts—for both Black and White men. But the study also found that for Black women, the loss of manufacturing jobs in an area led to decreased rates of marriage and increased rates of single motherhood, teen motherhood, and poverty, among other adverse outcomes. For White women, there was an increase in single motherhood and poverty. The study goes on to document the downstream effects on children: for both Black and White children, the decline in manufacturing jobs in an area led to an increase in the share of children living in a single-parent household and an increase in poverty. The study also found larger adverse effects for Black individuals than for Whites, suggesting that the decline in manufacturing jobs has exacerbated racial gaps in these outcomes. This study demonstrated that the decline in manufacturing jobs in areas around the country has increased inequality on multiple dimensions—widening gaps in socioeconomic outcomes within and across White adults and Black adults.

Martin told me that the single mothers in his hometown worked hard but often struggled to keep the boys off the streets. His players were often unsupervised in the evenings and would "do dumb things"—sometimes landing themselves in jail, or worse. The story Martin told overall—of economic forces leading to a loss of jobs leading to an increasing number of children being raised by single moms leading to struggles for children (boys in particular) in the manufacturing town he grew up in—was the real-life version of what academic studies have documented from nationally representative data sets.

We are living in a vicious cycle: the forces that have eroded the economic position of non-college-educated men are now having widespread, multifaceted effects on families and how children are raised. These affected children are straddled with disadvantages that make it harder for them to flourish. The changes in family structure lead to further inequality and cement class gaps across generations. This theme is central to today's trends in household economics, and a key thread throughout the chapters of this book.

There is also corroborating evidence from earlier studies showing that a decline in "marriageable men" causally leads to lower rates of marriage. A 2010 paper found that increased rates of male incarceration due to policy shifts led to decreased rates of marriage in affected marriage markets.[14] Simply put, having more men in jail made for fewer men to marry. The researchers confirmed that a reduction in marriage among young Black women was a secondary consequence of harsher sentencing guidelines that put more young Black men in prison over the 1980s and 1990s. The tragically high rate of incarceration among non-college-educated Black men in America is a different, albeit related, challenge from the more widespread economic changes that have disadvantaged non-college-educated men over the past 40 years. But this incarceration rate is an important societal factor that has amplified the challenges facing Black families beyond more general economic forces.

The decrease in men's earnings *relative* to women's earnings has also led to a reduction in marriage. The standard model of marriage in the economics literature posits that as female wages rise relative to male wages, there will be a reduction in marriage because the returns to marriage are lower.[15] This means that women have less to gain by entering into a marriage contract. It follows, then, that an increase in women's relative wages will lead to a reduction in marriage and an increase in divorce because the female "outside option" has improved.[16] Women, economic theory holds, will be more likely to forgo marriage when the amount of money they can make on their own is higher.

A 2021 study by the economist Na'ama Shenhav provides empirical support for this prediction.[17] Focusing on the time period from 1980 to 2010, when women's wages increased by 20% relative to men's, Shenhav zeroed in on the fact that men and women faced different shifts in wages based on their representation in different industries and occupations: occupations that men were more likely to work in saw wage declines, while female-dominated industries saw wage increases. Her careful empirical work determined that an increase in women's relative wages reduced marriage, both through a meaningful decline in first marriages and through an increase in divorce. A 10% increase in women's relative wages produced a 3.1% increase in the share of never-married women and a 1.7% increase in the share of divorced women. Shenhav also found that the first-marriage decisions of less educated and younger women were particularly responsive to the relative wage, with the overall relative wage effect accounting for 20% of the overall decline in marriage between 1980 and 2010. Critically, Shenhav's paper also considered whether the relative-wage-induced reduction in marriage was offset by an increase in cohabitation; she found that it was not. Her analysis showed that 65% of women who did not marry in the presence of a higher relative wage instead opted to live with a female roommate or live alone.

Would solving the marriageability problem solve the marriage problem?

For years, whenever I was part of academic or policy conversations about the decline in two-parent families, I would speculate that reversing the trend would likely require an improvement in the economic circumstances of less educated men. My thinking on this issue was greatly influenced by the work and studies I've described in this chapter, which together suggest that the declining economic position of men—in both absolute and relative terms—has been a key driver of the decline in marriage among affected groups. If the eroding economic position of non-college-educated men is driving these trends, then one could reasonably conclude that an improvement in the economic position of less educated men might help reverse these trends.

That's what I thought, anyway, until I studied how recent increases in male employment and earnings prospects influenced family formation. The results of that research cast doubt on the notion that an improvement in men's economic position will necessarily increase marriage rates. The fracking boom of the first decade of the 2000s, which gave rise to economic booms in US towns and cities where they wouldn't have occurred otherwise, provided a rare opportunity to investigate whether an improvement in the economic prospects of men without a four-year college degree would lead to a reduction in the nonmarital birth share. In a 2018 study that I wrote with my coauthor Riley Wilson, we used the fracking boom to test a "reverse marriageable men" hypothesis.[18] I say "reverse" because this research was centered on the possibility that an improvement in men's economic position would lead to an increase in marriage rates and a reduction in nonmarital childbearing—effectively the converse of William Julius Wilson's marriageable men hypothesis. The research represented a rare opportunity because in recent decades, most secular changes—including increased imports from China, the adoption of robots in workplaces, and the decline in union representation—have weakened the economic position of men without four-year college degrees in the United States, without any predictable vector for reversal. The fracking boom, and its impacts on men's wages and economic position, was a notable exception.

The practice of fracking in rural communities—extracting oil and gas from underground rock formations—has been associated with more jobs and enhanced income in those communities. The ability of communities to engage in such activity is almost entirely driven by geographic factors buried deep in the earth. This limitation creates an ideal experiment from the point of view of econometric research: there is no other reason why the geological conditions of a place would predict a sudden change in family formation and fertility outcomes around 2005. Any changes we see in these outcomes are likely attributable to the economic changes associated with the fracking of those geological shale plays.

The study found that local fracking activity between 1997 and 2012 (the incidence of which was arbitrary, or at least determined in part by geology) led to an increase in employment and earnings among non-college-educated men—not just in oil and gas extraction jobs, but in other industries as well, consistent with the existence of broader job-creation effects from local fracking activity. Although there was no discernible increase in employment among non-college-educated women, the data suggest that *earnings* went up for these women, albeit only by half as much (on average) as for non-college-educated men.

Wilson and I investigated whether this improvement in non-college-educated men's employment and earnings prospects—both in absolute terms and relative to women—had also led to an increase in marriage among young adults (ages 18 to 34) or a decrease in the share of births to unmarried women.[19] Our first finding was that these local fracking booms led to overall increases in total births, an increase of roughly 3 births per 1,000 women. This result was consistent with the known effects of income on birth rates established by earlier research across many contexts: when people experience an increase in income or wealth, they tend to have more children.[20] Why does more income lead people to have more children? It's impossible to generalize this in universal terms, but research supports a conclusion that, in a nutshell, most people generally want to have kids, but kids are expensive. So when people get more income, they are more likely to have a child or more children than they otherwise would. This finding was an important takeaway from our study, but it wasn't really the point of it. We wanted to know how the share of births to unmarried mothers changed when there were more jobs and higher wages available for men.

To our surprise, the increase in births associated with fracking booms occurred as much with unmarried parents as with married ones. The "reverse marriageable men" hypothesis, which predicted that improvements in the economic circumstance of men would lead to an increase in marriage and a reduction in the share of births outside marriage, was not what the data showed. More babies were being born, but they were being born to an approximately unchanged share of unwed parents. Though fracking activity led to an increase in employment and earnings for men, which in turn led to an increase in births, it did not have any effect on the percent of adults ages 18 to 34 who were newly married, never married, or currently married.[21] Nor was there any change in divorce or cohabitation rates.

We wondered: *Why not?* If the trend toward unwed births had correlated so closely to diminished economic standing among men, wouldn't the reinstatement of their earlier stature have produced at least *some* return to the earlier mode of marriage and children? One possibility was (and is) that the social norms surrounding childbearing and marriage have changed enough that men and women didn't feel the need to get married, or the desire to get married, even if the man had a well-paying job and the couple had a baby together.

In speaking about social norms, I mean simply that the way someone thinks about marriage and having kids is influenced by the way people around them live. This idea that people approach family and marriage in a way that reflects the prevailing social norms of where they grow up is hard for social scientists to prove, but it will likely strike most readers as intuitive. The research assistant who helped me to write this book—currently a PhD student in economics at the University of Maryland—grew up in a small rural town in Pennsylvania, where most of her high school friends still live and are now married with kids. As she was helping me with this chapter, she told me that she and her boyfriend had been having conversations about marriage and kids and had come to realize that they have divergent views about the appropriate time (and age) to get married—a reflection of the fact that they grew up in very different communities. "I can't help but feel old when I'm home [where I grew up] and see my friends' kids in elementary school," she said. "But then I remind myself: I'm only 26." In her hometown, the poverty rate is 23%. The share of adults ages 25 and older with a college degree is 35%. In contrast, her boyfriend grew up in a high-income town in New Jersey, one that has only a 5% poverty rate and boasts a 62% college graduation rate. None of his friends or acquaintances from high school has kids yet, and he can't remember anyone having kids in high school or dropping out due to pregnancy. Their childhood environments and the lives of their friends have shaped their own thoughts about marriage and childbearing. For most of us, the experience is much the same: either we fall in with the prevailing social norms of our friends or families or, very deliberately and unusually, we buck the trends.

To investigate whether social norms might help explain the family-formation response in the context of the local fracking booms, Wilson and I proceeded to examine whether the response to the sudden economic shock was different in places where nonmarital childbearing was more and less common. It was. In places where very few births occurred outside marriage before the start of fracking, the local fracking boom led to a sizable increase in births only to married women, not to unmarried women. In places where a sizable share of births occurred to unmarried women before the fracking boom, the economic boom led to relatively equal increases in births to unmarried and married women.

To further investigate this theory that social context matters to how births proceed, Wilson and I revisited the economic and demographic data surrounding the Appalachian coal boom and bust of the 1970s and 1980s. The economic shock brought about by the coal boom was very similar to that of fracking, but it occurred during a period when it was much less common—and much less socially acceptable—to have a child outside of a marital union. An earlier economics study, published in 2013, had shown how the coal boom and bust of the 1970s and 1980s led to an increase, then decrease, in men's incomes in the Appalachian coal-mining region of the United States, which in turn produced a similar pattern of increase and decrease in births to married couples.[22] This prior finding led the researchers to frame their study in interesting terms: are kids "normal goods," i.e., things people have more of when they have more money? For married couples in these coal towns, the answer appeared to be yes. Wilson and I revisited their work and historical context to investigate whether unmarried couples *also* had more kids when their income went up on account of the coal boom. Unlike what we found during the fracking boom, the answer was no. But the increase in male earnings associated with the coal boom of those earlier decades *did* lead to an increase in marriage.

The contrast in how people responded to having more money from the coal boom of the 1970s and the fracking boom of the first decade of the 2000s is consistent with the notion that social context matters. In the earlier period, when nonmarital births were still far from the norm, couples responded to an increase in earnings by getting married and, if married, having more kids. But there was no increase in births among unmarried women; social norms were such that women didn't do that. In the later period, both marital and nonmarital births increased in response to the economic shock. And unlike during the Appalachian coal boom, there was no discernible increase in marriage in response to the economic benefit associated with fracking.

Though not definitive, this evidence is consistent with the idea that social norms play an important role in shaping how people respond to economic conditions. Our study suggested that, in a time when an increasing share of kids are born to unmarried parents, there may be no going back—at least not through economic changes alone. Improvements in the economic prospects of less educated men have not been shown, by Riley Wilson and me or by others, to usher in an increase in marriage and married-parent families. Crucially, however, this fact does not mean that certain men's declining economic position over the past four decades has not been a primary driver of the increase in both nonmarital birth rates and overall marriage rates. Evidence remains that the stalled or reduced earnings of non-college-educated men during earlier decades—alongside the increased earnings among women—was a driving force that led to a decline in marriage and a corresponding rise in nonmarital childbearing among this population. The remaining question is whether things these things can be reversed, and our study suggests the answer is no, at least not solely by reversing the economic trends that brought us here. Now that nonmarital childbearing has become fairly common, we are likely in a new social paradigm. Reversing recent trends in family structure will likely require both economic *and* social changes.

A note: The reduction in marriage is not about welfare.

One frequently suggested explanation for the reduction in marriage and the rise in single-mother families in the US is so persistent that I want to explicitly raise and dispense with it. The reduction in marriage, and with it the coterminous rise in one-parent families, *cannot* be explained by citing the public provision of increasingly generous welfare payments.

A bit of welfare history is necessary here. For decades, the main cash welfare program in the US was the Aid to Families with Dependent Children (AFDC) program, established by the Social Security Act of 1935 as a federal program administered by states. AFDC provided cash welfare payments for "needy" children who had been deprived of parental support or care because their father or mother was absent from the home, incapacitated, deceased, or unemployed. States had significant leeway over setting benefit levels and determining income and resource limits to establish who qualified as "needy."

In general, by the 1980s, the AFDC program, which had been established in the 1930s mainly as a way of helping mothers whose husbands were deceased or out of work, served primarily never-married mothers. This shift led to a lot of policy concern and political backlash, driven by worries that the program was encouraging the establishment of single-mother households and causing welfare dependency. As a result, many states started experimenting with new program rules in the 1980s and 1990s.

This experimentation culminated with the Personal Responsibility and Work Opportunity Reconciliation Act of 1996 (PRWORA)—passed by a bipartisan Congress and signed into law by President Bill Clinton—which replaced AFDC with a cash welfare block grant called the Temporary Assistance for Needy Families (TANF) program. Key elements of TANF include a lifetime limit of five years (60 months) on the amount of time a family with an adult can receive assistance funded with federal funds, higher work-participation-rate requirements that states are required to meet, and broad state flexibility on program design. Spending through the TANF block grant is capped and funded at $16.5 billion per year, only slightly above fiscal year 1995 federal expenditures for AFDC and related expenditures replaced by TANF.

In the context of these evolving policies, there are four main reasons why we can be confident that cash welfare has not been a driver of the changes of family structure we have witnessed over the past 40 years. First, cash welfare benefits to low-income families are quite meager and have declined since 1980. Cash benefit amounts under

TANF vary at the state level, as they did under AFDC. The most common way to measure the generosity of these cash benefits is in terms of the maximum benefit available to a family consisting of a single mother and two children. The median benefit value (in constant 2012 dollars) across states was $321 per month in 1980, $539 in 1990, $645 in 1995, and down to $427 in 2012.[23]

Second, it is well documented across dozens, if not hundreds, of academic studies that any link between welfare generosity and the incidence of single-mother households in the US is, at most, small. As succinctly summarized by preeminent Johns Hopkins economist Robert Moffitt in a 1998 book titled *Welfare, the Family, and Reproductive Behavior*, a large body of studies on the topic produces estimates that are consistent with a small real effect on marriage and family formation outcomes, but one that is sensitive to methodology.[24] If there were a sizable effect, it would be more readily and consistently replicable across studies and statistical approaches.

Third, the landmark PRWORA federal welfare-reform legislation of 1996 really did make it much harder for families to access welfare benefits. The act was designed to "end welfare as we know it," in the words of President Clinton, who signed the bipartisan bill. The legislation was passed with four explicit goals: (1) provide assistance to needy families so that children may be cared for in their own homes or in the homes of relatives; (2) end the dependence of needy parents on government benefits; (3) prevent and reduce the incidence of out-of-wedlock pregnancies; and (4) encourage the formation and maintenance of two-parent families. The legislation included a number of provisions designed explicitly to reduce welfare dependence and stem the rise in single-mother households. These included time limits on benefit receipt, work requirements for beneficiaries, a "family cap" that eliminated the practice of increasing a family's benefit amount when a new child was born into the family unit, and requirements that teen mothers live with their parents in order to qualify for TANF benefits, among other provisions.

In fact, the PRWORA legislation is quite remarkable in how

explicitly it favors marriage. The following excerpt is taken directly from the legislation:[25]

> The Congress makes the following findings: (1) Marriage is the foundation of a successful society. (2) Marriage is an essential institution of a successful society which promotes the interests of children. (3) Promotion of responsible fatherhood and motherhood is integral to successful child rearing and the well-being of children. (4) In 1992, only 54 percent of single-parent families with children had a child support order established and, of that 54 percent, only about one-half received the full amount due. Of the cases enforced through the public child support enforcement system, only 18 percent of the caseload has a collection. (5) The number of individuals receiving aid to families with dependent children (in this section referred to as "AFDC") has more than tripled since 1965.

Welfare reform did, unambiguously, lead to a reduction in welfare caseloads. Caseloads plummeted in the 1990s, falling from around 14 million in the early 1990s to around six million by the year 2000.[26] However, it did not appreciably affect marriage and birth rates, and the prevalence of mother-only families has continued its steady upward climb, despite the legislation's wide-reaching changes.[27]

Fourth, government transfer payments account for only a small fraction of income among mother-only households. We can see this in data from the US Census SIPP data set, a nationally representative data set that is the most comprehensive source of information on household income and program participation. In the 2018 SIPP, annualized family income among unpartnered-mother households averaged $50,403. The lion's share of this amount came from personal earnings: 82%, or $41,365. On average, benefits from means-tested government transfer programs (including, but not limited to TANF and SSI) accounted for only 2% of family income, or $1,055, and benefits from social insurance programs (including, but not limited to, social security and unemployment insurance) accounted for 6%, or $3,236. Another 3% came from child-support payments and the remainder came from other sources, including investment income. It is clearly not the case that unpartnered mothers are, in general, providing for their families primarily via government benefits, though these families surely benefit from the additional income such programs provide. To argue, however, that the rising incidence of one-parent households in the US has been driven by the availability of generous welfare benefits is simply untrue and unfounded.

Summary

Since the 1980s, the share of American adults getting married has fallen considerably, driven by a reduction in marriage among adults without a four-year college degree. There is now a sizable college gap in marriage rates—both overall and among White adults, Black adults, and Hispanic adults. (Asian Americans are an exception to this trend, with relatively high rates of marriage even among those with lower levels of education.) The decline in marriage among non-college-educated adults appears to reflect both economic forces and changing social norms. In the past 40 years, the economic position of men without a four-year college degree has eroded, both in absolute terms and relative to women, making them less reliable breadwinners and less suitable marriage partners.

While economic forces have been a key driver of the decline in marriage—and the corresponding increase in single-mother homes—it seems that we are now in a new social paradigm, where nonmarriage is common outside the college-educated class, including among adults with children. This development has not been good for children. It has meant that an increasing share of American children are growing up without the benefits of two parents in their home, and specifically, without their dad present. Reversing these trends—if at all possible—would likely require both economic and social changes on a grand scale.

FIVE

Parenting Is Hard

"Making a child is the easy part. The hard part is everything else."

GLORIA DELGADO-PRITCHETT, "Arrested," *Modern Family*, season 4, episode 7

Bringing an infant home for the first time is a uniquely terrifying experience. When I was a new mom, I often found myself staring in desperation at my crying newborn, wondering what to do, desperately wanting to just walk away and go to sleep. It didn't get easier, either: years later, another of my babies was colicky. She cried, all the time. Nonstop. For months. She wouldn't let me put her down. In the stroller, she screamed. In the car seat, she screamed. She scratched her own face. She would only nap if she was lying on me. One night when my husband wasn't home and the baby was at this for hours, I went outside and walked her up and down the street, feeling dazed and somewhat desperate. A neighbor came out of her house, took her out of my arms, and said, "Let me take her for a few minutes." That mother of four knew I needed a break at that moment.

Not long ago, I was speaking with a graduate student whose wife had given birth to their first child a month earlier. He said all the things one expects a new parent to say, about how in love they were with the baby, and how grateful they were, and so on. I finally said, "But it's hard, right?" And he answered quickly and emphatically, sounding almost relieved that I had brought it up first. "Oh my G-d, yes! She cries all the time. I take the graveyard shift so my wife can sleep at night. When I'm up with her in the middle of the night and she's crying and I'm exhausted, I keep thinking 'I can't believe how many people I know who have done this.'" Another, quieter version of this conversation is an accounting for the personal fortune of having someone else to parent with: "I don't know how single parents do it." I have thought that so many times over the years.

Now that my children are older, the specific worries and challenges of parenting are different but no less acute. Parenting is still hard. It is expensive and exhausting. It is also wonderful and exhilarating and the greatest responsibility and joy I will ever know in my life. I am grateful every day for my three children and the amazing privilege of raising them. (Yes, even as I write this during the COVID pandemic, when we are all working and doing Zoom school from home.) I am also very grateful for the many people who help me raise my kids, especially my husband, my parents, his parents, our siblings, our babysitter, our kids' friends' parents, our family friends, the kids' teachers, and the many generous adults in our community who volunteer their time to coach and run activities. It is trite to say, but it *does* take a village to raise children. It also takes lots of resources.

Parenting means more than just having given birth to and loving a child. In a discussion of differences in parenting practices, one can reasonably take it as a given that all parents *love* their children and that no group of parents loves their children more or less than any other group of parents; if you've had a child, you love that child pretty immediately. If loving our children were enough to ensure they would be okay, then all children would be okay. When my firstborn was about five hours old, I called my sister and said through tears, "Oh my goodness, now I know why Mom is crazy! I would die if anything ever happened to this little boy!" What I didn't know then, and what no new parent can, was the breadth of challenges that awaited. Being a parent means worrying because so much is out of our control. It means trying to protect, love, and guide our children with the full force of whatever resources we have. Parenting means, in addition to loving one's child, devoting time, money, and energy to the raising of one's child or children. Aside from love, there are limits to how much parents can provide.

The pouring of time, money, and energy into children can be described in economic terms: We invest resources and parenting inputs into our children in the hopes of producing healthy, happy, well-adjusted, successful adults. Success means different things to different people, but for most, it likely includes some level of educational attainment and economic security in adulthood. This isn't to say that people only raise children to be adults. We also want to give them happy childhoods and enjoy time with them, and I don't mean to discount any of that. So much of what I do with my own children is because I simply love being with them. I love seeing them laugh, hearing their stories, and feeling their hugs. This has nothing at all to do with goals or visions of the future. *But* this book is motivated by issues of inequality and social mobility, and so this chapter is necessarily focused on the process by which parents shape their children's experiences and impact their educational and economic outcomes.

This chapter details what is known about how key parenting inputs—financial expenditures, time use, and emotional and mental energy—vary, on average, across more and less resourced parents. Much of the research reviewed in this chapter refers to differences produced by socioeconomic status. Socioeconomic status—commonly referred to as SES—is a catchall measure of social and economic standing that typically encompasses family income, parental education, family structure, or some combination of those factors. It is common in social science and psychology research to refer to parents as being high- or low-SES, but different sources of data measure SES differently. Given that families headed by a single mother generally have lower levels of resources, they are more likely to be categorized as low-SES households. Since much of the existing research in this space uses these socioeconomic measures (as opposed to terms of family structure), I will lean on the SES classification a bit when describing the evidence below.

Data confirm that having access to more resources enables parents to invest more in their children. More highly resourced parents tend to spend more money and time investing in their children. Why? The evidence suggests that it's not because more and less resourced parents have different views about what their children need or different preferences about what they want to do for or with their children. Rather, a highly resourced couple has way more resources to draw on when it comes to raising children. A lack of resources, meanwhile, makes it harder for low-income, single parents to do all they would like to do for their children. Some of this difficulty is about money (since one working adult tends to bring in less income than two working adults, especially if they have the same level of education), but some of it is about having another committed adult to split the workload with, to watch the kids while you're working or doing something else, or to pick up the emotional load when you're just too drained.

In the same way that a child who lives in a one-parent home tends to have access to fewer parental resources, the inherent challenges of parenting make it such that children who grow up in single-mother households tend to experience lower levels of parental investments. This is not because single parents don't *want* to provide their kids with the same types of advantages as kids from two-parent homes are often getting. Rather, it is because they are resource constrained: one parent tends to have fewer resources (of all kinds) to devote to parenting than two.

Kids are expensive.

According to US government statistics from 2015, a middle-income married couple with two children spends more than $230,000, on average, to raise a child from birth to age 17.[1] (So that doesn't even count college!) That amounts to an average of more than $13,500 per year in each child's life. Not surprisingly, this observed spending on kids is higher among higher-income households and lower among lower-income households. Among families in the lower third of the household income distribution—households with annual income below $59,200—annual expenditures were around $9,700 per year.[2] Among married-couple families in the upper third—defined as those with annual income above $107,400—annual expenditures were around $21,000. Housing, food, and childcare or education accounted for the largest budgetary shares.[3]

These average expenses mask a great deal of variation across families, not only by income, but also their children's ages, geography, and other factors that drive differences in spending. In general, families with older children tend to spend more on their children than families with younger children. Families in urban areas spend more than families in rural areas, and families in the urban Northeast region of the US spend more than families in urban areas in the West, South, and Midwest (ordered from highest to lowest). Most relevant to the themes of this book, higher-income families report much higher child-directed expenditures, especially enrichment-oriented expenditures, than do lower-income families, a gap that has increased over the past half-century. Because children in single-parent homes are more likely to be growing up with lower levels of income, they are less likely to be getting the benefits of high levels of investment expenditures.

There is a large class gap in parental spending on investment in children.

While it sounds materialistic, spending money on children and their enrichment is one of the main forms parental investment takes. Not all spending on kids is investment, but much of it is, and the fact that higher-income households can and do spend much more on their children—for higher-quality childcare, for private school, for tutors, for enriching activities and books and games, among other expenditures—is one mechanism through which more highly re-sourced parents transfer advantages to their children.

Much of what we know about spending on kids, including the government statistics reported above, is based on the Consumer Ex-penditure Survey, a national household survey collected by the US Bureau of Labor Statistics to determine how Americans are spend-ing their money every year. The data come from a quarterly survey that collects data on large and recurring expenditures that respon-dents can recall over the prior three-month period, things like rent and utilities, as well as from a "diary survey" that collects data on small, frequently purchased items, including most food and cloth-ing. Scholars interested in family economics and child well-being have routinely used these data to document patterns and trends in spending on children.

A pair of sociologists used this data in a 2013 study on invest-ment spending across demographic groups. The researchers defined investment spending as expenditures on education, childcare, les-sons, and certain goods like toys and games—spending that is likely to contribute to children's educational and economic success in life. They found striking differences in this discretionary spending be-tween higher- and lower-income households.[4] Their analysis of the data found not only that parents at the top of the income distribu-tion spent much more on child investment than do lower-income parents, but also that the gap in spending (as measured in real dol-lars, meaning inflation-adjusted) has widened substantially since the 1970s.[5] Figure 5.1 plots data from their analysis. Parents in the highest income decile increased their investment spending per child from $2,832 in the early 1970s to $5,551 in the early 1990s and to $6,573 per year in 2006–2007 (all in inflation-adjusted 2008 dol-lars). These calculations don't even fully capture inequality in invest-ment spending because these amounts don't include housing costs, and spending more for a home in a more highly rated school district is one of the most common ways that parents with higher income invest in their children.

Some of the widening of this income gap in spending on kids

reflects the widening of income inequality in recent decades, with the income of those at and near the top of the distribution taking off. But that's not the full story. Between the 1970s and 1990s, high-income parents increased the share of their total household income that they devoted to child investment goods. This corresponds to a period when parenting, in general, became a more intensive activity.

The spending by high-income households on kids' education and enrichment has pulled further and further away from what families in the middle and bottom of the distribution are spending—and likely what they're able to spend. Among families in the middle of the distribution, per-child investment spending increased (in 2008 dollars) from $1,143 in the early 1970s to $1,548 in the early 1990s, to $1,421 in 2006–2007. The authors estimate that these amounts reflect spending shares of 4.2%, 6.5%, and 5.2% of (equivalized) income, respectively. The real dollar amount that families in the lowest income decile spend on per-child investment has also been mostly steady across the three highlighted decades, at amounts of $607, $779, and $750, respectively.

This kind of investment spending is yet another way that the children of higher-income parents are having an abundance of resources thrown at them and their development, making it increasingly difficult for kids from less advantaged home circumstances to keep up or compete.

Another way to look at the gaps in the experiences that more and less resourced parents can offer their children is to look at engagement in enrichment activities. Not surprisingly, children from more highly resourced homes are more likely to participate in a variety of extracurricular enrichment activities. A 2015 survey of parents conducted by the Pew Research Center revealed large income gaps in the rate at which kids experience enrichment activities.[6] Among parents with family income of more than $75,000, 84% report having a child who participated in sports or athletic activities in the past year, as compared to 69% of parents with family income between $30,000 and $74,999 and 59% of parents with family income below $30,000.

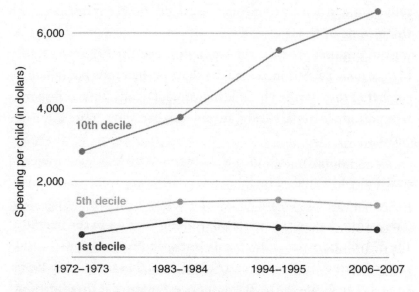

Figure 5.1 Parental spending per child, by household income decile
SOURCE: *Kornrich and Furstenberg, "Investing in Children," table 3.*

Across these three income groups, the shares reporting that their child took lessons in music, dance, or art were 62%, 53%, and 41%, from highest to lowest income group—that's a 21-percentage-point gap in the likelihood that a child takes music lessons between families with at least $75,000 and families with less than $30,000 in annual income.

How does this finding relate to family structure? Recall that family structure is highly determinant of household income: Two-parent households are much more likely to have a higher level of household income and thus to be able to afford—or even spend lavishly—on children's activities. Activities like being on a sports team or playing an instrument help children develop their talents, their mind, their passions, their focus and dedication—and simply experience joy. They give them meaningful things to do with their time, outside of school and off their phones and devices. It is quite sad, really, that whether a child participates in such activities is so dependent on their family's level of resources. It is yet another way that the experiences of children from different family home environments diverge. (Ideally, community and philanthropic groups could help close these gaps, making sure children from less resourced families - whatever their family structure– have ample access to sports, music, art, and camp. There are many such amazing programs around the country, and from an economic, policy, and indeed *human* perspective, it would be beneficial to see them scale up and grow. But I digress.)

I think of these trends of divergency when I see how much money kids' activities cost, and accordingly the exorbitant amount of both money and time some families spend on things like youth sports or dance or niche hobbies. My mom comments on it, too, seeing the activities her various grandchildren are involved with. She often makes remarks along the lines of, "Goodness, we never would have been able to afford any of that when you guys were kids." A 2019 study by the RAND Corporation confirms the impression that kids from below-median-income homes are deterred by the costs of youth sports today.[7] Researchers conducting the study surveyed approximately 2,800 parents, public school administrators, and community sports program leaders. They found that the financial costs and required family time commitments—through volunteering and providing transportation, for instance—were barriers to sports participation for middle and high school youth from lower-income homes.

None of my sisters played lacrosse until encountering it in our public high school in New Jersey. And yet, all three of my sisters were recruited to play lacrosse at an elite East Coast college. (Fortunately, I, as the oldest child, didn't have to feel too badly about not following in their superstar athletic footsteps). There aren't data available to check this claim, but anecdotally, my sisters' experiences would be extraordinarily unlikely to occur today. Today, families whose kids are aiming to play a sport at the college level are likely to have spent extreme amounts of money and time on sports teams and training activities before a child is even in high school. Whatever one might think of the trend toward intense child enrichment, be it in sports or the arts or wherever, one thing is quite certain: Kids from highly resourced homes are at a tremendous advantage when it comes to parental spending on child investment.

Also, it's not just parental spending on kids when they're little.

Prior to the 1990s, parents spent the most money on child investment during their kids' teenage years. After the 1990s, parental investment spending became greatest when children were under age
six—*and then again in their midtwenties!* A high level of spending
on children under the age of six reflects an increased awareness of
the importance of early-childhood experiences to child development
outcomes. The increase in parental spending on children during their
young-adult years—again, something that more highly resourced
parents are much more readily able to afford—is yet another way
that better-resourced kids are getting a leg up in the climb to economic security and success in today's sometimes punishing economy
and housing market. This new norm of sustained parental spending
into young adulthood amplifies the relative importance of a child's
family structure and parental resources to a child's adult outcomes.

Time is another parental resource.

Kids aren't just expensive, they are also exhausting—um, I mean,
time consuming. Any parent will tell you, sometimes even without
you asking, that raising children takes a lot of time. When children
are little, they need their parents to spend time feeding them and
bathing them and dressing them. As they grow, they need—or at
least desire and benefit from—parents reading to them, playing with
them, and driving them to their activities. The time they require of
their parents when they are teenagers is different, but given their
emotional, educational, and mental health needs, the teen years can
nevertheless be a very time-intensive (and emotionally draining) period of parenting. So how does parental time vary across different
types of families? I suspect most of you have picked up on the pattern by now: there is a gap in parental time devoted to children, in
favor of children from higher-income, married-parent homes.

The rise in income gaps in child investment since the 1970s and
1980s is mirrored by a rise in income gaps in parental time use. Parents today spend *way* more time engaged in enriching activities with

their children as compared to parents in previous generations. I am sure many of you have heard it said or remarked yourself—"Back in the day, our parents just sent us off to play in the street!" The rise of intensive parenting is a real thing. We know this from the American Time Use Survey data, a nationally representative data set collected by the US Census Bureau. The data was collected in over 210,000 interviews conducted from 2003 to 2019, with surveyors asking subjects for a 24-hour recall of the previous day's activities to elicit time-diary information. Each day of the week, including weekends, is equally represented within the survey.

This shift in how parents spend their time reflects changing attitudes about parenting and the ways in which children's experiences and environment shape their well-being and later life outcomes. But this increase in parental time investment has not occurred evenly across the population—predictably, the shift toward more time spent with one's children has been especially pronounced among more-educated, highly resourced parents.

More-educated parents spend more time with their children than less-educated parents.

Economists think extensively about the ways in which people use their time, including how different uses of it produce different benefits and costs. When it comes to childcare, economists have frequently categorized it as a "household production" activity—a sort of feeding-and-watering activity that amounts to basic maintenance of a household, in this case a household with children. But in a 2008 paper that I coauthored with the economists Jonathan Guryan and Erik Hurst, we found that patterns of childcare by parental education level look very different from patterns of either household production or leisure by education level.[8] Taking care of one's children seems to deserve its own category of time use. Using data from the 2004–2006 American Time Use Survey, we found that more highly educated mothers and fathers spend less time doing household production activities like cleaning and vacuuming; they also spend less time in leisure activities like sleeping, watching TV, and hanging out with friends. What did they do with this time? They were spending more of it directly engaged with their children in so-called childcare activities.

As a working mom myself, I find that the notion that I spend the bulk of my time either working at my job or with my kids rings pretty close to accurate. I readily admit that I can do that in part because I am able to pay for things that buy me time with my children, like paying someone to help with cleaning and laundry. I say that as both part confession and part illustration: parents with more resources are more able to spend time doing things like reading to their young children and driving their older kids to activities because they can afford to spend less time doing household chores. However, the educational differences in childcare time—time spent with children— are not explained by differences in rates of paid work: Moms with college degrees are spending more time both in childcare *and* in paid market work, at the expense of things like sleep and watching TV, as compared to moms without high school degrees. The fact that more highly educated parents spend more time engaged with their kids, but less time in household chores or leisure activities, suggests that these parents view parenting activities as different, and indeed separate, from both household chores and leisure. Parents likely think of time spent with their kids at least in part as an *investment* in their children's development. I return to this idea below.

Not only is there a gap in the amount of parental childcare time by parental education, there is a gap in the developmentally appropriate structure of parental childcare time.[9] More-educated mothers spend more time with their children in precisely the ways that development psychology suggests are most beneficial to kids at various ages. Gaps in childcare time between mothers with a college degree and those with only a high school degree are largest in basic care and play time when children are infants and toddlers. As children's needs change, so too do these gaps. When children are preschool age, more highly educated moms spend more time teaching their children; when children are between the ages of 6 and 13, more highly educated moms spend more time managing their children's activities.

Married parents spend more time with their children than unmarried parents.

Like the discernible difference in childcare time between more- and less-educated parents, there is a gap in childcare time by marital status. On average, married mothers spend more time per week engaged with their children than do unmarried mothers.[10] Married mothers with at least one child under age 18 spend an average of 15.1 hours per week in dedicated childcare, meaning that their primary activity is related to the child—dressing them, reading to them, driving them to an activity, and the like. They also spend, on average, 45.4 hours with their child(ren), meaning that their child or at least one of their children is with them, even if their primary activity isn't centered on the child. Unmarried mothers spend an average of 12.7 hours per week in dedicated childcare and 37.8 hours with their child or at least one of their children. If there is at least one child under the age of five in the home, both married and unmarried mothers spend more time in childcare activities or with their child, still with married mothers spending more time: 23.4 hours in childcare activities and 59.4 hours with a child among married mothers, compared to 21.2 hours and 53 hours for unmarried mothers. Some of this difference is attributable to the fact that unmarried mothers are more likely to work outside the home, leaving them with less time than married mothers to actively engage with their children. In the 2019 American Time Use Survey, 78% of unmarried mothers report working outside the home, as compared to 71% of married mothers. They also work more hours in paid labor, on average: 28.2 versus 23.5 hours per week. In general, married mothers are not likely to be the sole or even primary breadwinners in their families (recall the discussion from chapter 4 about the ongoing prevalence of traditional gender roles in many marriages), which

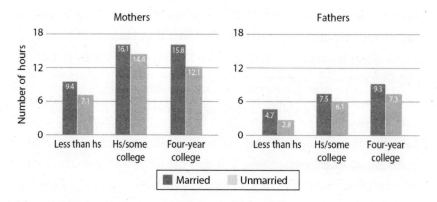

Figure 5.2 Hours per week parents spend on childcare activities, by parental education level and marital status
SOURCE: *Author's tabulations of 2019 American Time Use Survey.*

presumably gives them more flexibility to work fewer hours for pay. The luxury of being able to spend less time working and more time engaged with one's child can be thought of in just that way—as a luxury that married mothers, on average, more often have because there is another adult in the household.

The gap in childcare hours between married and unmarried mothers is observed across all mothers, regardless of education level. More-educated mothers spend more time actively engaged in childcare activities than less educated mothers (despite also working more hours outside the home), but within education groups, married mothers spend more time in childcare activities and more time with their children, as compared to unmarried mothers with the same level of education. These differences can be seen in figure 5.2. It is also the case that for all three levels of education, married mothers spend fewer hours in market work. The same pattern holds within racial and ethnic groups as well. For White, Black, Hispanic, and Asian mothers, married mothers spend more time in childcare and with their children than do unmarried mothers.

What about dads? Both married and unmarried dads spend less time than mothers either actively engaged in childcare activities or passively being with their own children. But married dads tend to spend more time with their children than unmarried dads. In the 2019 American Time Use survey, married dads reported an average of 8.0 hours in dedicated childcare activities and 30 hours with their children per week. Unmarried dads reported 5.9 and 23.8 hours per week, respectively. As with moms, this marriage gap in time spent with children is observed for dads of all three education levels. Dads with four-year college degrees spend the most amount of time in childcare, even though they also spend the most hours in paid work: 9.3 hours per week among married dads and 7.3 hours per week among unmarried dads. Dads without a high school degree spend the least amount of time in childcare, even though they also work the fewest hours: 4.7 hours a week in childcare activities among married dads and only 2.8 hours per week among unmarried dads.

The data I have presented above from the 2019 American Time Use Survey show how much time mothers and fathers spend with their children, based on parents' marital status and education. But a limitation of this survey is that it does not collect data at the family level, only from one individual per household. Therefore, we cannot use that data to investigate the total time a child receives from their two parents. However, we can observe variations in the total time children receive across caregivers based on a child's family structure thanks to a 2014 study that examined time-use data from the care of more than 2,700 children in the 1997 Panel Study of Income Dynamics (PSID) Child Development Supplement.[11] The data showed that children living with two biological married parents received more total caregiving time than those living with an unpartnered mother or with a mother and her cohabiting boyfriend. Notably, children living with two cohabitating biological parents, a mother and a stepfather, or in a multigenerational family received comparable time as children living with married biological parents. The children in multigenerational households benefited from substantial time investments from their grandparents, and those living with a mother and stepfather received substantial time investments from their nonresident biological father (note: not their resident stepfather).

Does all that extra time and money produce better child outcomes?

The rise in income gaps in parental investments—both in terms of expenditures and time—corresponds to a rise in income gaps in childhood achievement. Stanford University education researcher Sean Reardon studied kindergarten test scores and found that the gap in test scores between children of parents at the 90th percentile of the income distribution and those at the 10th percentile grew over time, with larger differences observed for children born in the 1990s as compared to those born in the 1980s and 1970s.[12] His analysis shows that racial and ethnic achievement gaps declined during the same period.

Some good news on this front is that in newer work, Reardon and a coauthor analyzed data on a more recent kindergarten cohort and found that income gaps in math and reading test scores narrowed modestly from 1998 to 2010.[13] (Data on kindergarteners from 2010 is the most recent available.) Still, while a narrowing of gaps is encouraging, the gaps themselves are large, and would take decades to close at current rates of convergence. (And regrettably, the 2020–2021 US COVID pandemic and associated widespread school closures undid a lot of this progress and exacerbated gaps in learning outcomes.) Although these achievement gaps cannot be definitively linked to differences in parental investments, the fact that they are observed in kindergarten suggests that they are driven by factors that predate (in the children's lives) anything that could be attributed to the school environment. That shines a spotlight on home environment, early-childhood experience, and even in-utero experiences. In fact, the recent experience of the COVID pandemic underscores this point. When schools were closed and children were sent home, learning outcomes widened between those from higher- and lower-resourced households. Home environment matters.

Research findings are consistent with the notion that the more time parents spend with their children, especially in developmentally appropriate activities, the better the child does academically and emotionally, though it is hard to quantify the precise return on specific or individual parental investments. There are many studies, however, that find a positive connection between the amount of time parents spend with their children and children's subsequent academic and behavioral outcomes. Two are especially compelling from a research methodology perspective.

A 2019 study looked at differences between siblings in the same households based on the amount of time they spent reading with their mothers and their subsequent reading test scores on standardized tests.[14] A comparison of siblings is useful because siblings share parents, a home environment, and many other characteristics that would make comparisons across children in different families hard to interpret. Differences between siblings' outcomes are much more likely to reflect a causal difference that can be attributed to the difference in parental activity. But still, a mom might spend more time reading to one of her young children than another one of her children at the same age—either because the first was more reading inclined or because the arrival of the second gave the mom less time to devote to reading to her kids. The authors of the study cleverly took advantage of this latter tendency in designing their study, noting also that extra reading time is even greater for first-born children who are further apart in age from their younger sibling. Exploiting such differences, the researchers provided evidence that extra reading time with one's mother leads to a sizable improvement in standardized reading test scores.

More evidence on the positive effects of parental time with children on children's outcomes came from a 2014 study that examined data on more than 4,900 children from the Longitudinal Study of Australian Children, which began collecting data in 2004.[15] The researchers linked children's time spent in various activities to subsequent measures of cognitive skills, as captured by test scores, as well as parents' reports of children's behavioral, social, and emotional traits and outcomes. Their analysis found that after statistically controlling for a slew of personal characteristics, time spent in educational activities, especially with parents, is the input that yields the highest improvements in cognitive skills as measured by test scores.

In contrast, they found that behavioral, social, and emotional out-comes were most affected by parenting style—with a style that com-bines effective but not harsh discipline and parental warmth pro-ducing the best outcomes along these lines—as opposed to time. (The researchers only consider maternal parenting measures, which allowed them to include children from mother-only families in the analyses.)

Why do more highly resourced parents spend more time investing in their children?

There are a variety of possible explanations for why more highly re-sourced parents spend more time engaged in activities with their children, despite *also* spending more time working outside the home. One explanation is that perhaps more highly educated or higher-income parents place more weight on the educational and labor-market outcomes of their children and are thus more likely to make investments to advance those outcomes. University of Pennsylva-nia sociologist Annette Lareau put this thesis forward in her 2003 book, *Unequal Childhoods*.[16] Based on the in-depth observation of 12 families that were part of a sample of 88 families Lareau and her team of graduate students studied in the 1990s, Lareau examined how middle-class families raise their children in a way deliberately designed to preserve their middle-class status. She calls the middle-class parenting style of talking to kids, driving them to activities, and structuring their time "concerted cultivation."

In contrast, Lareau described the parenting approach of the poor and working-class families whom she observed as "natural growth parenting"—an approach with an emphasis on unstructured time and less interference. She speculated that these differences would manifest in unequal outcomes for the children in later life, a conjec-ture that was confirmed in her follow-up with the families ten years later (though these observations are simply correlational and can-not be interpreted as necessarily causal). Lareau's core argument and finding was that children who had experienced middle-class "concerted cultivation" parenting were more successful in their careers and in their relationships. While Lareau's observations are intriguing, no large-scale survey or data have substantiated the notion that middle- and low- income parents have systematically different preferences or beliefs about how they should or want to parent. I thus offer this idea as a *possible* explanation, while also expressing some skepticism for the claim that parents of different social classes have expressly different ideas about parenting, as opposed to different advantages and constraints.

A second, related explanation for the education gradient in parental childcare is that perhaps the return on investment in children of more highly educated parents is higher. If the children of more highly educated parents have greater potential or greater opportunities, the return on time invested in such children could be higher. Consider that the children of more highly educated parents are more likely to go to college, not because they are necessarily more capable but because college is more in reach for them given how hard it is to navigate the enrollment process and finance a college education. If that's the case, then perhaps the incremental time that more highly educated parents devote to their children will make a difference "on the margin" (as we economists like to say) in whether they get into college and what kind of college they attend. In contrast, perhaps less educated parents think that spending more time reading to their child or driving them to enrichment activities won't make a difference in the types of opportunities their children have access to or whether or not they will be able to go to college.

In other words, maybe it's the case that the more children stand to gain from a so-called leg up, the more parents are likely to invest in them. This is the idea behind a 2010 paper by two economists on the "Rug Rat Race"—the tendency for college-educated parents to spend a ton of time in educational activities with their kids and driving them to various activities, much more so than in previous decades.[17] The authors document that since the mid-1990s, college-educated mothers have increased the amount of time they spent in childcare by 9 hours per week, as compared to 4 hours per week among less

educated mothers. This "reallocation" of time away from other activities to childcare activities occurred at the same time as competition to get into college increased. Since college-going is much more
common among the children of college-educated parents, it makes
sense, in these researchers' view, that the increase in rug-rat-race
behavior has been concentrated among college-educated parents.
Furthermore, they note that parental time with children has not
changed much, even among college-educated parents in neighbor-
ing Canada, where college competition is much lower. To lend further credence to their hypothesis that increased time investment in
children among more highly educated parents is driven by the desire
to help one's child earn admission to a competitive college, the authors document that parental time investment in children is higher
in parts of the country where college competition is more severe.
Economists Matthias Doepke and Fabrizio Zilibotti drew on data
from around the world and over time to show how economic incentives can explain differences in parenting approaches. In their 2019
book, *Love, Parenting, and Money*, Doepke and Zilibotti connect differences in income inequality across countries to differences in parenting approaches.[18] They argue that in nations with less economic
inequality, such as Sweden, the stakes of parenting are less high, and
social mobility is not under threat. Parents in Sweden are therefore
less likely than parents in the United States to obsess about their
kids' time and activities. In other words, the more children stand to
gain from parental investments, the more likely parents are to make
those investments. Though it's hard to definitively confirm or reject
this particular explanation, the patterns in the data are consistent
with it, and the logic is compelling.

A third possible explanation for why more highly resourced parents devote more time to active childcare activities is because they
have more emotional bandwidth to do so. Note that having more
emotional bandwidth is different from having more time, per se;
we've already seen that more highly educated parents spend more
time with their kids even though they also spend more time in
paid work, regardless of work status or education level. Emotional

bandwidth is different from time. Having emotional bandwidth means not being so weighed down by stress that you can't sit and read to your child, or help them with homework, or volunteer to drive them to an activity or event. Parents with fewer resources—money, time, emotional support from a committed spouse and co-parent—live with a higher level of daily stress, which likely impinges on their ability to do the kinds of activities they might otherwise want to do with their children. I expand on the role of stress in shaping parenting below.

Financial strain leads to toxic stress, which in turn makes parenting harder.

I'm reminded of a line in one of my favorite songs from the movie *Frozen*, which my daughters had me watch with them more times than I can count when they were younger. The hilarious trolls sing a song about Kristoff when they first meet Anna. In the song, a troll makes the observation that when people are mad or scared or stressed, they make bad choices. Isn't that the truth? And it applies to parenting decisions as well.

I will be the first to admit that when I am stressed or tired or running late, I am much more likely to be impatient with my kids or to try to grab a moment of alone time than to sit and play a board game or even have a meaningful conversation about what happened to them at school that day. One evening I was being cranky and short with my kids, and presumably with my husband, too. It didn't take long for one of my kids to call me out on it. She said, "Hey, Mom, clearly you had a stressful day at work, but don't take it out on us." I knew she was right; I *was* taking my stress out on them. Of course, her pointing it out just made me more agitated. I don't remember exactly how I responded, but I definitely felt chastened by the fact that even my 10-year-old kid realized I just didn't have the mental energy to engage with her and her siblings as I should, or as I wanted to.

Perhaps it's the case that more highly resourced parents spend more time with their children and more time in developmentally appropriate and enriching activities not because they have different information or values or preferences but because they have more mental energy for it. And perhaps it is also the case that more highly resourced parents are less likely to live with what development psychologists call "toxic stress." Low-income families face significant economic pressure as they struggle to pay bills and purchase important goods and services, and these economic pressures can create high levels of psychological distress that affect marital and family relationships.

Plenty of descriptive evidence shows that lower-income parents experience greater family and environmental stress, which in turn predicts worse mental health, higher levels of family conflict, and harsher, more detached parent-child interactions. Given the link between single motherhood and lower income, much of this descriptive evidence also comes from single mothers.

Recent studies move beyond showing such correlations and demonstrate a plausibly causal link between income loss and worsened family outcomes. For instance, one study examined children's behavior over time and found that children exhibit fewer externalizing problems—things like getting into fights or lashing out—when their families' incomes were relatively high, as compared to times when their families' incomes were relatively low. This same study found that the estimated benefits of increased income were greatest for children whose families were chronically poor.[19] A separate study found that when fathers lost their jobs because of economic shocks affecting male-dominated industries, rates of child maltreatment increased. But when mothers lost their jobs because of similar shocks, rates of child maltreatment decreased.[20] This pattern could be explained by mothers being more protective of their children when they are home, but fathers, on net, being harsher with their children when they are home and out of work.

Research conducted in recent years by behavioral economists supports the notion that financial stress impedes people's ability to focus and make good decisions. Research by Eldar Shafir, Sendhil Mullainathan, and collaborators suggests that poverty imposes a mental cost on individuals that impedes cognitive functioning.[21] For instance, in an experiment conducted in a shopping mall in New Jersey, the researchers presented 101 people with hypothetical financial challenges, like needing to pay a certain amount to get their car repaired. The researchers found that describing a financially costly hypothetical situation to low-income individuals led them to subsequently perform poorly on a test of unrelated spatial and reasoning tasks; test performance was not negatively affected if the hypothetical situation was not costly. The performance of higher-income individuals on the test was not affected by having to think about financial challenges, either large or small, presumably because it wasn't as hard for these participants to think of a way to deal with the situation. In another experiment with 464 sugarcane farmers in India, the researchers tested the cognitive performance of farmers over the planting cycle. They found that individual farmers show diminished cognitive performance before harvest, when their income is low, as compared to after harvest when their income is relatively higher. Their analysis suggests that although farmers do exhibit more stress before harvest, it is not the stress that accounts for diminished cognitive performance, but rather the poverty itself, which consumes mental resources and leaves less cognitive bandwidth for other tasks.

These behavioral economists interpret the pattern of results between these two experiments as being consistent with the hypothesis that financial strain imposes a mental burden that impedes cognitive functioning. Though their research doesn't look specifically at cognitive functioning around parental decision-making, the logic could be readily extended to that context (and especially considering the always-on nature and challenge of parenting). If I am constantly worried about how I am going to pay my bills, then making decisions about my child's education or helping them with their homework might demand cognitive bandwidth that I simply don't have. As a friend remarked to me: "Now that I am no longer the child of poor or financially struggling parents, and I am no longer a single parent who is also struggling financially, I have so much more compassion for what my parents went through and understand why they often seemed so disengaged."

All parents deal with this kind of stress to some extent, but, given that a single parent is more likely to face these daily challenges alone and with a lower level of resources, it is reasonable, even logical, to think that toxic stress is particularly acute and persistent for less resourced lone parents.

Well-designed parenting programs—and additional income—can potentially close parenting gaps.

A variety of government parenting programs have been implemented and studied over the years aimed at improving parenting practices among low-income (and often single) mothers. The United States Department of Health and Human Services runs the Maternal, Infant, and Early Childhood Home Visiting (MIECHV) program, which facilitates collaboration and partnership across programs at the federal, state, and community levels. The stated goal of this program is "to improve the health of at-risk children through evidence-based home visiting programs. The home visiting programs reach pregnant women, expectant fathers, and parents and caregivers of children under the age of 5."[22] In operation since 2010, MIECHV remains relatively new, but its work and data have potential to offer unique insights about the drivers of parenting behaviors and ways to close the gaps in positive parenting practice between more and less resourced parents.

Three other federally supported programs that have been widely adopted and rigorously evaluated are the Nurse-Family Partnership, the Early Head Start Home Visiting program, and Healthy Families America. Like MIECHV, each of these programs is centered on home visits. The Nurse-Family Partnership is a nonprofit that focuses on first-time mothers living in poverty: during pregnancy and until a child is two, program nurses visit moms at home to educate them on parenting, share resources, and perform health checks. Early Head Start (EHS) is a federal government initiative that provides child development and parent-support services to low-income pregnant women and families with children from zero to three years old. EHS includes home visits and group socialization activities for parents and their young children. Healthy Families America is a home-visiting program that works with families who tend to have histories of trauma, intimate partner violence, mental health issues, and/or substance abuse issues. Expectant or new parents are screened and assessed based on the risk for child maltreatment or poor early-childhood outcomes. Families are offered weekly home visits, and parents are linked to other services in the community as needed.

Developmental psychologists Ariel Kalil and Rebecca Ryan reviewed the large body of evidence about the effectiveness of these three home-visiting programs in 2020, finding that the programs' efficacies varied by program models and implementation approaches.[23] The two experts were cautious in characterizing the capacity of these programs to meaningfully alter parenting behaviors and child outcomes, noting that even with the programs that have been found to generate positive effects, the effects were modest and diminished within a few years. Kalil and Ryan further emphasize that the effects are largest and most consistent with respect to reducing harsh parenting practices and/or child maltreatment, not increasing maternal sensitivity or stimulation. That suggests that even within the highly targeted population served by these programs—mostly families living in poverty—home-visiting programs are most effective at preventing acutely poor parenting, as opposed to encouraging particularly good practices.

The Parents and Children Together (PACT) program is a promising intervention aimed at getting low-income parents to read more to their preschool-age children. This experimental program was implemented with a sample of parents whose children were attending a federal Head Start preschool and evaluated by the Behavioral Insights and Parenting Lab at the University of Chicago.[24] For six weeks, the PACT program lent 169 parents an electronic tablet with a preloaded app that included children's books in English and Spanish. Half the parents in the PACT program were randomly assigned to a treatment group that received an intensive version of the program. This version of the program included three behavioral elements designed to encourage parents to read more to their children: goal-setting exercises, regular text reminders, and recognition of high levels of reading. The other half of parents did not receive intensive encouragement to read, so they served as the comparison group. To measure the impact of the PACT program on parents' reading efforts, researchers used data collected by the app on the time spent reading and the number of books completed.

The behavioral encouragement tools of the intensive program were effective at increasing parental reading time. Over the six weeks in the PACT program, parents in the treatment group spent significantly more time reading with their children than the comparison group, as measured by the app on the provided devices. Furthermore, the behavioral encouragements had a greater effect on parents who exhibited lower levels of patience on a survey that was designed to measure parents' level of "present bias." Present bias refers to the tendency to put more weight on current circumstances than on future outcomes. Spending a lot of money on some enticing item now, even though you might be trying to save money, is an example of succumbing to present bias. The PACT study was deliberately designed to test the hypothesis that present bias may be a key reason why some parents don't read more to their children; the behavioral tools of goal setting, frequent reminders, and social rewards were designed to "bring the future to the present." It appears to have been an effective approach.

This study is important because it shows that behavioral motivators could succeed at getting low-income parents to read more to their young children. It also contradicted—through extensive survey work conducted as part of the study—two potential explanations for why low-income parents might not spend more time reading to their children the way higher-income parents do. First, on baseline surveys, parents in both groups reported that they thought reading to their children was important, that they believed their child would be better prepared for kindergarten if they spent more time reading to them, and that they viewed it as their responsibility to read to and teach their children. This finding suggests that the relatively limited time that lower-income parents spend reading to their children is *not* reflective of dismissive attitudes. Second, parents reported that access to reading materials was not a barrier. The fact that neither attitudes nor access seem to be general explanations for limited reading time is consistent with behavioral explanations being more important.

Beyond specific parenting programs, alleviating the income pressures on low-income families leads to documented improvements in maternal health and parenting practices. For example, research has found that an increase in income transfers to low-income single mothers due to an expansion of the Earned Income Tax Credit has produced improvements in the mental health of qualifying single mothers.[25] More generally, there is now substantial evidence that an increase in household income leads to an improvement in outcomes for children from low-income families.

The final chapter of this book will get to the core discussion of how the US as a country might thoughtfully address these challenges. But I can't help saying it here: In order to address the relative disadvantages of children growing up in single-mother families (and low-income families more generally) and to shrink class gaps in children's outcomes, the US is going to have to do much more than we currently do to alleviate the material burdens of low-income families. By making families more economically secure, parents (whether single or married or unpartnered or cohabitating) will be better able to provide for their children, better equipped to give their children safe, enriching childhood experiences, and more likely to send their children out into the world prepared to thrive and reach their human potential.

Summary

The children of more-educated, higher-income, and married parents get more of all kinds of resources—more spending on educational and enrichment goods and activities, more parental time, and more attentive parenting. The additional parental investments that these children receive from both their mothers and their fathers on a regular basis contribute to the relative advantages they enjoy in life and perpetuate class gaps in opportunities and outcomes.

Well-designed parenting interventions can potentially improve parenting practices in low-income and single-mother families. This evidence provides justification for philanthropic and public funding to scale up parenting programs with evidence of success. However, we should be clear in our expectations. Such programs can make a positive difference, and they should be supported on those grounds, but we cannot expect parenting interventions alone to close class gaps in children's outcomes.

Even with community and government support, how can a parent who is raising her child or children without another parent figure in the home lavish the kind of spending, time, and emotional bandwidth on her children that children growing up in a highly resourced two-parent home are frequently being showered with?

To make progress closing class gaps in parenting resources—and childhood environments—will require strengthening families and bringing more fathers into the family fold. Doing so will require addressing the many economic challenges facing men today, as described in the previous chapter, so that more men are "marriageable"—meaning, stably employed, reliable, and dependable. It will also require addressing the social changes that have fostered the normalization of the widespread separation of marriage from the act of raising children. We must recognize that the rise in one-parent households has not been good for children, boys especially. That is the topic of the next chapter.

SIX

Boys and Dads

"Of all the rocks upon which we build our lives, we are reminded today that family is the most important. And we are called to recognize and honor how critical every father is to that foundation. They are teachers and coaches. They are mentors and role models. They are examples of success and the men who constantly push us toward it. But if we are honest with ourselves, we'll admit that what too many fathers also are is missing—missing from too many lives and too many homes."

BARACK OBAMA, in his 2008 Father's Day Speech at the Apostolic Church of God in Chicago[1]

Boys today are substantially more likely than girls to get in trouble at school. They are more likely to get in trouble with the criminal justice system. They are less likely to go to college or obtain an advanced degree. Boys are struggling and falling behind. There is not one simple explanation for why boys are having more trouble in school and completing college at lower rates than girls and women. When it comes to getting in trouble at school and with the law, there are any number of reasons why boys might be more susceptible to the kind of "externalizing," or risky behavior, that attracts negative attention. Some of this gender gap could be due to boys' temperaments and brain wiring. Some of it could be due to unfair or discriminatory attitudes on the part of teachers and other adults, especially with respect to Black boys. Some of it might be due to current social norms, in schools and society more broadly, that are less tolerant or indulgent of energetic, rambunctious boys, who in general take longer to mature than girls. But something else is also happening with boys, and more often than it used to: many more of them are growing up without dads in their homes. Insofar as dads are teachers and coaches and role models and even disciplinarians, the absence of dads from so many homes is—not surprisingly—having an adverse effect on children, boys especially. Parents are critical role models for their children. Dads are important role models for their sons. Boys are at an acute disadvantage by not having a loving dad in their home.

The struggles of boys today are a downstream consequence of the struggles of men that have been discussed in previous chapters. The challenges facing boys and men are mutually reinforcing. As too many men (particularly those without a four-year college degree) struggle, they become less likely to be suitable or desirable husbands and live-in dads, which means more boys are growing up without the positive influence of a father in their home, which makes it harder for boys, who then grow up to be less reliable workers, partners, and fathers. And this cycle, tragically, repeats—with increasingly widespread and negative consequences for society.

The current trends affecting men and boys cross racial and ethnic groups, but they are of greatest impact on Black boys in the US. An influential 2019 study (described in more detail below) showed that a high incidence of Black dads in neighborhood homes is one of the strongest positive predictors of upward mobility rates for Black boys in the same neighborhood. The problem, though, is that many Black boys do not have the benefit of growing up in a neighborhood with the beneficial attributes of a low rate of poverty and a high share of Black father presence. The question of why so many Black dads are missing from their children's homes and neighborhoods is another complex issue without a simple explanation. Some of it reflects structural discrimination in the labor market and the criminal justice system. The loss of middle-wage jobs for so many men over the past 40 years—Black men included—has worsened the situation. The persistent challenges of being a Black man in America have been compounded by the fact that men without a college degree have faced economic headwinds more generally.

Boys are struggling.

Boys' struggles are apparent in a variety of ways. Two critical outcomes can be traced to illustrate this point, one from childhood—behavior and punishment at school—and one from young adulthood—college degree attainment. Boys are much more likely than girls to get suspended from school. In-school and out-of-school suspension rates for boys are 7.2% and 7.3%, respectively, as compared to 3.6% and 3.2% among girls. This difference matters because a higher incidence of suspension is associated with a lower likelihood of completing high school.

The rates of in- and out-of-school suspension are especially high among Black boys and girls. Among Black boys, the in-school suspension rate is 14%, and the out-of-school suspension rate is 17.6%. Among Black girls, the comparable rates are 8.5% and 9.6%. Among Hispanic students, the two suspension rates are 6.7% and 6.4% for boys, as compared to 3.4% and 2.6% for girls. Among White students, the rates are 5.9% and 5.0% among boys, versus 2.4% and 1.7% among girls. Both the overall levels and the gender gaps are much smaller among Asian students, with rates below 2% for boys and below 1% for girls.[2] The suspension rates among Black youth are shockingly high, raising a host of questions about the fairness and effectiveness of suspension as a disciplinary procedure for students, as well as the role of discriminatory attitudes in schools. Though such questions about school disciplinary procedures are outside the scope of this book, the statistics themselves highlight a key fact: boys are much more likely than girls to get in trouble at school for externalizing behaviors—meaning, problem behaviors that are directed outward, like fighting, cursing, disobeying rules, or vandalizing property.

A second key outcome for which there is a gender gap favoring girls is college degree attainment among young adults. For men and women over the age of 25, the aggregate four-year college degree (BA) attainment rates are relatively close: 32% for men and 34% for women. The gender gap emerges, however, in looking at the educational attainment of young adults ages 24 to 35, who were born between 1984 and 1995. Young men in this age group are 8 percentage points less likely to have a BA than are young women: 33% versus 41%. The gender gap in BA attainment is widest among White, non-Hispanic young adults: 38.3% of White men have a BA or higher, as compared to 47.7% of White women. Among Black young adults, 20.1% of Black men have a BA or higher, as compared to 27.2% of Black women. Only 17.3% of Hispanic men ages 24 to 35 have a BA or higher, as compared to 24% of Hispanic women. The gender gap is very small among Asians: 65.3% of Asian men have a BA or higher, as compared to 68.5% of Asian women.[3]

Boys do relatively worse when they grow up in a home without a dad.

What does this finding have to do with family and home environment? Well, as it turns out, boys' development and behavior—including their educational outcomes—appear especially responsive to family environment, both over time and across demographic groups. As the share of children growing up in single-mother homes has increased, so has the relative disadvantage of boys (as captured by things like their level of completed education). Is there something causal at play within these dynamics? Is the absence of a father figure from the home especially disadvantageous for boys? The evidence suggests yes.

To be sure, many factors other than family structure likely contribute to these associations between the presence of dads and boys' thriving or struggling. For instance, over the same decades that single-mother families became more prevalent, it's possible that schools became less tolerant of rambunctious behavior (more often associated with boys than girls). When one observes that single-mother families are more common among Black households than among other racial and ethnic groups, one must also account for the fact that racial animus and discrimination against Black men and boys is rampant, which surely contributes to the harsh treatment of Black male students in school and by the criminal justice system. To point out a potential role of family structure in the production of the gender gap is not to discount or diminish the importance of other contributing factors, such as racial prejudice. The point is to highlight evidence showing that the absence of a father from the home has been shown to correlate to behavioral problems for boys, which in turn can lead to longer-term challenges with school and work.

One especially striking and important study on this relationship was published in 2013 by economists Marianne Bertrand and Jessica Pan.[4] Their study was motivated by an observation that boys appear to have more problems with "noncognitive skills" than girls do. What are noncognitive skills? Social scientists outside of economics tend to refer to these skills as "socioemotional skills." Others might call them "life skills," specifically as a thing separate from, say, "book smarts." Ample research has shown that noncognitive skills, not just the more cognitive book smarts, play a role in determining one's success in school and the labor market. These same noncognitive skills—traits like self-control, grit, patience, and conscientiousness—can also predict whether someone will get in trouble in school, complete high school, enroll in and persist in college, and ultimately earn high wages.

Theories of the brain suggest that boys' brains develop differently than girls' brains do during adolescence, creating a gender gap in noncognitive skills that favors girls. But the big open question that remained, and which the economists Bertrand and Pan sought to answer, was what role, if any, does environment play in noncognitive skill development? Beyond nature, what about nurture? Bertrand and Pan specifically investigated the role that family and school environments play in the development of noncognitive skills for boys and girls. The researchers' main data source for the study was the

Early Childhood Longitudinal Study: Kindergarten Cohort (ECLS-K), a longitudinal study conducted by the National Center for Education Statistics. The data come from a nationally representative sample of over 20,000 children in about 1,000 schools who entered kindergarten in 1998. Bertrand and Pan's study used information from children, parents, teachers, and schools about the children's cognitive, social, emotional, and physical development—as well as about the children's home and school environments.

The researchers found that family structure was a key determinant of the gender gap in behavioral outcomes, more so than early school environment. Boys misbehaved more than girls, and that gap was greater among the children of single mothers than among children in two-parent homes. Bertrand and Pan found that the gender gap in externalizing problems among fifth graders was nearly twice as large for children raised by single mothers compared to children raised in a family with their two biological parents. By eighth grade, the gender gap in school suspension was close to 25 percentage points among children raised by single mothers, versus 10 percentage points among children from two-biological-parent families.

The researchers also investigated whether these observed gender differences by home environment were in part reflections of the types of school or classroom environments that children from single-parent homes are likely to encounter, including ones with more female teachers or disruptive students. If so, that would suggest that it's not family environment per se that is leading boys to act out more often, but rather the correlated factor of school environment. The data showed this was not the case. Even within the confines of similar school environments, there is a larger gender gap in behavioral outcomes for the children of single mothers than for those raised in a two-parent home. In particular, the researchers did not find systematic differences in the gender gap based on age of kindergarten entry, being assigned to a female teacher in earlier years of school, or having more disruptive peers.

A related study published in 2019 by a different team of economists similarly found that family disadvantage disproportionately

damages the early life development of boys.[5] These researchers examined the records of over a million elementary-school-age children in Florida born between 1992 and 2002. Like Bertrand and
Pan, the researchers found that boys growing up in families with
lower socioeconomic status—which in their study was defined by
a combination of having an unmarried mother, a younger mother,
a less educated mother, or a mother whose pregnancy was covered
by Medicaid—have more disciplinary and school problems than do
girls. This finding held true even when they looked specifically at siblings, using a sample of more than 280,000 sibling pairs, and thereby
comparing boys and girls from the same home environment. The
relatively higher incidence of behavioral problems for brothers, as
compared to their sisters, was larger for children from disadvantaged
home settings. The analysis further found that home environment,
above and beyond characteristics of the neighborhood a child lives
in or the school they attend, substantially and differentially shapes
the trajectory of boys' outcomes as compared to girls'. Though their
study is not as squarely focused on family structure as the study by
Bertrand and Pan is, their results reinforce the finding that home
environment impacts the gender gap in outcomes.

Returning to the study by Marianne Bertrand and Jessica Pan,
why were the boys who grew up in single-mother families so much
more likely than girls to exhibit externalizing behaviors? The researchers investigated that question as part of their study. They first
considered whether sons systematically received less parental time
and nurturing than daughters did within single-mother homes, as
compared to boys and girls in two-parent homes. There is some evidence of small differences in this regard. In the ECLS-K data, single
mothers reported being relatively more emotionally distant from
their sons (exhibiting less "parental warmth") and also more likely
to report having spanked their sons (exhibiting "harsher discipline").
In addition, data from the American Time Use Survey revealed that
single mothers spend relatively less time engaging in childcare-
related activities with their sons as compared to their daughters.
However, such gender differences observed for the children of single

mothers are only slightly larger than those observed in two-parent families.

The researchers' analysis finds that boys' outcomes are more affected by parental time and nurturing than are girls, so small differences in parenting led to a large gender gap in outcomes. Boys' noncognitive development appears extremely responsive to parental nurturing and time, much more so than girls. For example, they found that for boys, the likelihood of externalizing behavior in fifth grade is greatly reduced when they receive a higher measure of parental warmth at home; for girls, there is virtually no association. Similarly, for boys, the likelihood of conduct problems in kindergarten is higher if spanking is used as a disciplinary method at home; for girls, there is virtually no association. The authors report that families with two biological parents tend to have higher measures of parental warmth and a lower reliance on spanking. Given how responsive boys appear to be to these types of parental inputs, that difference between two-parent and single-mother home environments matters more for the outcomes of boys than for girls, even though both boys and girls experience similar home environments within family type.

This explanation aligns with the resource-based framework of family structure: the idea that parents contribute resources to a child's home environment and childhood experiences—including outlays of spending on children, parental time, and emotional engagement, among other resources. These parental resources then shape the opportunities and outcomes of children, such that higher resources generally produce better outcomes for children. The novel finding of the Bertrand and Pan study is that the behavioral outcomes of boys are especially responsive to the parental inputs of time and nurturing behavior. Consequently, the lower levels of parental time and parental warmth available in single-mother homes, on average, puts boys who are growing up in such families at a particularly large disadvantage, more so than girls.

These studies present an unforgiving reality: children are not only sensitive to their household environments; they are in many ways shaped by them. So when the challenges of everyday life leave a single mom unable to give her child as much time as she would like, and when the stakes and scale of that time-loss are better understood thanks to studies like the one from Bertrand and Pan, we have a window into how inequality gets made, propagated, and compounded. The results are as unfair as they are distressing—and not just for the kids. For every child not getting as much attention, there's a mom working to pay the bills and take care of and supervise a child (or children) to the extent that her time and energy allows, often on her own. We should feel also for the dads, many of whom have their own very real struggles and are unable to be the type of dads they would like to be.

It bears repeating: Parenting is hard. It is stressful. Single mothers are generally under more stress than those who parent with a committed spouse and partner. And anyone who's ever cared for a child is probably not surprised that single mothers are more likely to resort to harsh discipline or show less warmth to their children, because the more constructive approaches to parenting require reserves of patience and time that are difficult to muster in times of stress. The acute effects of this dynamic on young boys, documented by Bertrand and Pan, give it a new and pernicious dimension: growing up in environments with less attention produces some of the male behaviors that are today posing challenges among not just kids, but adults. Bertrand and Pan document how many male children respond to this type of parenting by acting out, starting around kindergarten but even more so when they get into middle school. This behavior sets them on a path toward even more trouble, in the form of involvement with the criminal justice system and lower levels of educational attainment. This unfortunate trajectory is part of the reason that so many boys are falling short of their human potential.

In the 2019 study based on administrative data from Florida, the researchers found that the gender gap in outcomes between boys and girls was most pronounced among Black children: Black boys were more affected than other groups of boys by the absence of one parent and the tendency toward behavior problems in school. And we saw above, the gender gap in suspension rates (with boys having higher rates) and college degree attainment (with young men having lower rates) is widest among Black Americans. The analysis by the authors of that 2019 study suggests that the greater share of Black children being raised in single-mother families explains *part* of this large divergence in boys' and girls' outcomes for Black children. I would also speculate (with a fair degree of confidence) that part of the gender gap is also due to the pernicious forces of discrimination and racial animus against Black boys and men in the United States. The disadvantages Black boys face are mutually reinforcing, with tragic effects.

Another component of this conversation is the role of so-called missing dads, which has long been studied as an important social issue with greatest impact on Black families. The topic was explored most extensively in the landmark scholarship of Harvard sociologist William Julius Wilson, who wrote about the relatively low rates of marriage among Black men and related it to lower rates of employment among Black men. As structural discrimination has played a persistent role in exacerbating the limited economic opportunities available to Black men, it has also led to lower rates of marriage among Black adults. Relatedly, the mass incarceration of Black men in the US contributes to the removal of Black men from families and communities. Research has documented a causal channel from mandatory drug sentencing policies implemented in the 1980s to increased male incarceration rates to lower marriage rates.[6]

Though a major theme of this book is the importance of *class* gaps in children's living arrangements today, it is impossible to ignore the fact that Black children are substantially more likely than White, Hispanic, and Asian children to be raised without a father in the home. As reported in chapter 2, 54% of Black children live with an unpartnered mother, as compared to 15% of White children, 27% of Hispanic children, and 9% of Asian children, with an even higher rate for the children of Black mothers without a four-year college degree.

Having Black dads in the neighborhood is good for the upward mobility prospects of Black boys.

The absence of dads from many Black families disadvantages not only the children in those families but also the other boys growing up in the neighborhood. A 2019 study from the Opportunity Insights research lab at Harvard University, coauthored by economists Raj Chetty, Nathan Hendren, Maggie Jones, and Sonya Porter, showed that the presence of Black fathers in a neighborhood is one of the strongest predictors of positive upward mobility rates for Black boys.[7] It was, and remains, a milestone piece of evidence: this research showed that the presence of more dads in a neighborhood benefits not just the children of those dads but other boys in the neighborhood as well.

The benefits that come from having a father or father figure present in the midst of challenging circumstances will seem obvious to those of us who have loving fathers in our own lives or who know someone who is good at being a dad. The presence of a dad can provide a sense of warmth and security. In 2021 a news story from Shreveport, Louisiana went viral for its illustration of these truths, as a group of fathers volunteered at their kids' high school in the wake of surging violence among students that had resulted in nearly two dozen arrests, suspensions, and other disciplinary actions within a 72-hour span.[8] In a *Good Morning America* feature, the five fathers told the story of starting "Dads on Duty USA"—a practice of showing up at school every day, and eventually at sporting events and school dances, to do nothing other than be dads. The five men were not security officers, and they didn't police anything. Their presence was centered on acting like friendly and even corny dads: wearing "Dads on Duty" branded T-shirts, welcoming the students to school in the mornings, telling dad jokes, and walking and talking with students in between and after classes. As one of the dads explained:

"Although we're titled 'dads on duty,' we also serve as uncles on duty, we serve as men of the community on duty," he said. "Because there are some folks who don't have a father or don't have such a great relationship with their father, and it's our goal to let them see what the right relationship with a male figure is supposed to look like."[9]

The principal of the Louisiana high school reported that the dads' efforts produced hugely positive results. The school faced serious gang violence at the beginning of the school year, a problem that tapered off once the dads came around. In effect, the five Louisiana dads illustrated anecdotally what the Opportunity Insights team did statistically (and using data on millions of people!): how helpful the presence of Black dads is to the life outcomes of Black children, especially Black boys.

The study by the Harvard/Opportunity Insights researchers was extensive, measuring not just the impacts of Black fathers on boys' outcomes, but presenting a detailed picture of economic mobility for a generation of Americans. "Intergenerational mobility" is a concept that measures a person's childhood household income (or its position in the income distribution), then compares it to that person's corresponding income or position in the income distribution as an adult. For their study, Chetty and his colleagues followed the income progressions of some 20 million children (not a typo—it was *twenty million*) born in the US between 1978 and 1983—basically, every person born in the US within those five years. Using redacted tax records, the researchers calculated multiple measures of intergenerational mobility, including the likelihood that a child from a low-income family earns a high income in adulthood. They then further analyzed the data to quantify gender and racial gaps—in effect, to determine who experienced greater and lower levels of economic mobility.

The study produced several revelatory findings. In tracing the Black-White gap in intergenerational mobility rates for girls, the researchers found that it was generally nonexistent: Black and White girls who grew up with the same levels of parental income experienced similar levels of earnings as adults. In fact, conditional on parental income, Black women ended up about one percentile higher in the income distribution than White women and worked a similar number of hours. In a similar comparison of Black and White men raised in households with similar incomes, the researchers found that Black men had substantially lower wages (and employment rates) than White men as they aged into adulthood.

More broadly, Black boys who were born to families at the bottom of the income distribution had the lowest chance of moving up the income distribution as adults—not only when compared to White, Hispanic, and Asian boys born to low-income families, but compared to Black girls from low-income families, too. The study also documented sizable Black-White gaps among men, based on parental income, in high school dropout rates, college attendance rates, occupation, and incarceration rates. In all cases, the Black-White gaps were larger for men than women.

The researchers also examined what types of neighborhood features were associated with higher rates of upward mobility for Black boys and smaller Black-White gaps in intergenerational mobility measures. The data revealed that, on average, Black boys had lower changes of moving up in the income distribution than White boys even when they grow up in the same census tracts, i.e., neighborhoods. That means that Black-White differences in intergenerational mobility rates for boys could not be fully explained by the fact that Black boys were more likely to grow up in low-income neighborhoods with inferior schools and more limited economic opportunities. The researchers found that both Black and White boys enjoyed significantly higher incomes as adults if they grew up in neighborhoods with low poverty rates, high test scores, or a large fraction of college graduates. However, the Black-White gaps are *larger*, on average, for boys who grow up in such neighborhoods because White boys do especially well when they grow up in places with these advantages.

Two neighborhood characteristics stood out as especially beneficial to Black boys from low-income backgrounds in the pursuit of higher income as adults: lower rates of racial animosity where they live and a higher share of Black dads living with their children. Black men who grew up in low-poverty neighborhoods with lower rates of measured racial bias among Whites (as captured by the prevalence of racially biased Google searches) make more money and are less likely to be incarcerated as adults. Second, a higher share of fathers present in low-income Black households in a neighborhood is associated with better outcomes for Black boys. It is *not* predictive of adult outcomes for Black girls, nor for White boys. In other words, Black father presence at the neighborhood level strongly predicts better adult outcomes for Black boys and smaller Black-White gaps in measures of upward mobility.

To put these findings in specific terms, Black boys appeared to have high rates of upward mobility if they grew up in places like Silver Spring, Maryland (with a poverty rate of 4.7% and 63% of low-income Black boys being raised in a home with a father present), or Alexandria, Virginia (poverty rate of 7.3%; 53% of low-income Black boys being raised in a home with a father present), or Queens Village, New York (poverty rate of 8.1%; 56% of low-income Black boys being raised in a home with a father present). Black boys fared less well if they grew up in places like Cook County, Chicago, or Southern Los Angeles—areas where poverty rates exceeded 40% and only about 25% of low-income Black boys had a father in the home.

But these geographic trends produce limited opportunities in terms of the total population: fewer than 5% of Black children currently reside in census tracts with a low poverty rate (below 10%) *and* fathers present in more than half of homes. In contrast, 62.5% of White children live in low-poverty areas with fathers living in more than half of children's homes. Here we can see the contemporary legacy of racial neighborhood segregation in the US, which was cemented by decades of the discriminatory and harmful practice of "redlining" in US mortgage and housing markets.[10]

Can responsible-fatherhood programs fix America's dad problem?

The body of research on the economic benefits of having fathers around—not just one's own father, but other fathers in the neighborhood—raises an obvious question: What would it take to get more fathers engaged in family and neighborhood life? It's a big and sensitive question, one that innovative fatherhood programs around the country are currently working to answer. Many of these programs espouse a mission of meeting fathers where they are currently—i.e., taking an approach that acknowledges the myriad economic, relationship, and personal obstacles that may keep them from greater engagement with their children—while also recognizing the benefits of having a father in a child's life.

The US Department of Health and Human Services Office of Family Assistance currently funds dozens of grants to fatherhood and family programs through state and local governments and community-based organizations.[11] This federal office also maintains the National Responsible Fatherhood Clearinghouse (available on the internet at www.fatherhood.gov) as a federally funded national resource for fathers, practitioners, programs, state governments, and others "interested in supporting strong fathers and families." Efforts such as these reflect an important shift in social policy—away from the almost complete focus in the past on financially helping single moms while essentially writing off dads outside of child-support enforcement efforts. These programs have also evolved over time, from a focus on strengthening marriages (as was the explicit focus of the Healthy Marriage initiative launched by the Bush administration in 2001) to strengthening all kinds of families, regardless of parental marriage status.

In 2011, the US Department of Health and Human Services contracted with Mathematica, Inc., a private research firm, to conduct a large-scale randomized controlled trial (RCT) study of various initiatives intended to strengthen families. Between 2012 and 2015, four responsible-fatherhood programs serving a combined 5,500 fathers were studied using the random assignment design, meaning that some fathers were randomly assigned to receive program services and others were not, allowing researchers to attribute any differences in subsequent outcomes to the causal effect of the program.[12] (Conversely, a study that wasn't random, specifically one that was composed of only fathers who self-selected into fatherhood programs, would have produced far less reliable results.) Most of the fathers served by these programs did not live with their children and were not romantically involved with the children's mothers.

The results of the trial showed, encouragingly, that fathers who participated in one of these programs showed improved parenting engagement one year after participation, as measured by their self-reported nurturing behavior and engagement in age-appropriate activities with children. Nurturing behaviors included showing patience when the child was upset or encouraging the child to talk about his or her feelings. Depending on the age of the child, age-appropriate activities included reading books or telling stories to the child, feeding the child or having a meal together, playing with the child, or working on homework together.

However, there were also some disappointing results. Participation did not lead to more in-person contact between fathers and their children, nor more financial support. Neither did participation in these programs lead to meaningful improvements in measures of co-parenting or measures of the fathers' social-emotional and mental well-being.

In their final report about the program, the researchers shared some observations that help explain why these types of interventions weren't more successful at changing outcomes. They observed that some of the fathers in the programs had highly conflicted or disengaged relationships with their children's mothers, and in some cases that mothers would serve as "gatekeepers," restricting a father's access to his child. The researchers suggested that programs may need to focus on helping parents improve their relationships with one another, whether amorous or not, in order to be able to help dads have more positive engagement with their children. Another qualitative finding was that many of the fathers faced significant barriers to being involved, supportive fathers—such as economic instability, criminal justice involvement, or substance abuse—but still wanted to be. This theme also comes up in Kathryn Edin and Timothy Nelson's 2014 ethnographic account of low-income fathers, *Doing the Best I Can: Fatherhood in the Inner City*: the desire, but not the practical means, to be a better father.

The economic instability in many men's lives suggests that helping them be more supportive fathers will require more intensive or comprehensive services to address the multitude of barriers some fathers face. The reason that so many children are now being raised by only one parent—or at least only living with one parent—is not necessarily because adults have simply decided they're less interested in marriage or cohabitation as parents in previous generations. Nor is it because dads have decided they don't want to be steady presences in their children's lives. The current, highly inequitable state of children's home environments is a reflection of widespread economic and social challenges—in many cases likely reflecting challenges from the adults' own disadvantaged family backgrounds.

In other words, these trends are compounding. As increasing numbers of men are out of work or in and out of jail, it follows that an increasing number of them are not actively providing for their children or engaged in family life; economic challenges notwithstanding, it is also extraordinarily difficult to restart a personal relationship after a period of estrangement. So it shouldn't surprise us that fatherhood programs aimed at bolstering fatherhood engagement are limited in their potential success by the weight of other forces gripping so many American men—joblessness, alcohol and drug addiction, criminal activity, and general idleness.[13] Addressing the decline of the two-parent family will require efforts on multiple fronts.

To the credit of government agencies, they are trying different approaches. Another element of the government's push to encourage healthy families is the "Take Time to Be a Dad Today" media campaign, which primarily takes the form of advertisements at bus stops and on TV or social media. These fatherhood.gov ads were launched in 2008, and they feature heart-tugging images of dads doing things like making their young daughter laugh or cooking while wearing their baby son in a carrier. They are, by design, very adorable. Do they work? I'm not sure, and to the best of my knowledge, we don't have good evidence on the effectiveness of this media campaign or others like it. But the campaign itself reflects a recognition that children benefit from positive attention and engagement from their dads, and that society has an interest in promoting fathers' involvement in their children's lives. While the important work of engaging fathers is ongoing, other new and long-running initiatives aim to positively augment children's lives from other sides.

Community mentors and positive role models can help fill some gaps.

Parents play a primary, critical role in their children's lives, but children interact with, engage with, and learn from other adults, too. Teachers, neighbors, coaches, and after-school caregivers, to name but a few, can all shape the way children see themselves and their world. All of these adults have the potential to alter a child's life trajectory, either by amplifying the advantages given to a child by their parents, or in some cases helping to compensate for a lack of positive attention, supervision, inspiration, or support in a child's home. Looking at who lives in a child's neighborhood offers a glimpse into the types of adult role models that children are likely to know. Here, again, children from low-income families are at a disadvantage: they are less likely to have economically successful role models and mentors in their own families and neighborhoods.

A typical low-income child lives in a neighborhood where 18.5% of adults dropped out of high school, compared to 11.7% nationally and 5.6% for the typical high-income neighborhood. In the same low-income neighborhood, 15.5% of working-age men are out of the labor force, nearly twice the 8.1% in the typical high-income child's neighborhood. The typical low-income child's neighborhood has twice as many households headed by an unmarried parent as compared to a typical high-income child's neighborhood: 38% versus 19%.[14] As inequality has widened, neighborhoods have become more economically segregated.[15]

If children are shaping their aspirations and perceptions of themselves based on how they see the adults around them living, then these differences in the kinds of adults in the neighborhoods that high- and low-income children live in might perpetuate income and class gaps in educational attainment, rates of work, and marriage. If children rely on adults in their neighborhood to help them navigate the world of educational and job opportunities, then having less access to economically successful adults might also impede the relative success of children from lower-income families.

The adults with whom children interact in school and through community programs can also have a meaningful impact on their attitudes, behaviors, and life trajectory. Research shows that role models with whom young people identify can positively influence their lives, just as having a teacher of the same gender or race can have a positive causal impact on a student's educational persistence and performance.[16] Furthermore, researchers have found that the single most common factor for children who develop resilience is that they have at least one stable and committed relationship with a supportive parent, caregiver, or other adult.[17]

Nine million at-risk youth report never having an adult mentor of any kind, from any of these domains, in their life.[18] Here begins the work of community-based mentoring programs: to fill this gap and provide youth from socioeconomically disadvantaged backgrounds with positive adult role models and mentors. Evidence suggests that such programs can make a difference.[19] The Big Brothers Big Sisters of America (BBBS) program, launched more than a century ago, is the oldest and largest youth mentoring organization in the United States, pairing mentors and mentees through a rigorous screening process and encouraging these pairs to spend one-on-one time together in settings and activities of their choosing. According to BBBS, there are 240 program agencies operating in all 50 states, and the program has matched nearly two million youth with mentors in the past decade alone—disproportionately serving children from single-parent homes and/or difficult personal situations. Among the nearly 136,000 youth served in 2019, 57% were from single-parent families, 16% had an incarcerated parent, and 79% were from families that received income assistance.[20]

Another randomized controlled trial evaluation conducted in 1995 evaluated whether youth served by the Big Brothers Big Sisters program experienced an improvement in outcomes, relative to similar youth who applied for the program but were not served. The Public/Private Ventures research group that conducted the study focused on 959 10- to 16-year-olds who applied to BBBS programs in 1992 and 1993 across eight cities.[21] They found that BBBS applicants who were matched with a mentor were 46% less likely to begin using illegal drugs during the mentorship period. The results were greatest among boys, who saw a 55% reduction compared to girls' 27% reduction. The reductions in drug initiation were largest among minority boys, at 68%. Assigned mentees were also 27% less likely to begin using alcohol. Results also suggest that mentored students earned higher grades and skipped fewer classes, but the estimated effects on academic outcomes were larger for girls than boys.

The results of this evaluation showed that a caring mentor could have a meaningful impact on the life of a teen from a disadvantaged family background. It also demonstrated the promise of community-based mentoring programs, attracting the attention of policy makers. In January of 2002, President George W. Bush made an official proclamation recognizing January as National Mentoring Month, stating that "mentors play an important role in a child's life, particularly if a parent is absent. A mentor's involvement in the life of a child can brighten that child's future, help maintain healthy families, and help promote more vibrant communities."[22] The BBBS program's website today notes that thousands of girls and boys across the country are waiting to be matched, with more than twice as many boys on their waiting lists as girls.[23] The work of mentoring youth who face adversity at home is ongoing, and the need is great.

Like BBBS, the Becoming a Man (BAM) program is an evidence-backed mentoring program that helps youth, specifically boys, who are facing adversity. BAM began much more recently, in 1999, on the south side of Chicago, and like the early Big Brothers program, it was founded by a young man seeking to help boys who were getting in trouble. Anthony DiVittorio was raised on the southwest side of Chicago by a divorced mother and a largely absent, sometimes violent father. He went on to earn a master's in psychology and was then hired by the Chicago nonprofit Youth Guidance to help kids who had been kicked out of class. DiVittorio drew on both his own understanding of the traumas these kids faced and his expertise in cognitive behavioral therapy to design the program.[24] In 2001, DiVittorio began working with groups of boys for approximately ten weeks at Chicago's Clemente High School, talking about the challenges of manhood and modes of healthy self-expression. His program eventually formally became the Becoming a Man (BAM) program in 2003, organized around six core values: integrity, accountability, positive anger-expression, self-determination, respect for womanhood, and visionary goal setting. Participants engage in role-playing and group exercises that teach them to slow down and apply impulse control, drawing on the techniques of cognitive behavioral therapy.[25]

Researchers at the University of Chicago Crime Lab conducted two waves of randomized control trials to evaluate the impact of BAM on the young men it served. In the first wave, the researchers randomized 2,740 seventh to tenth graders in the 2009–2010 academic year into a control and treatment group for a one-year study; in the second wave, they randomized 2,064 students in the 2013–2015 academic years for a two-year study. Both waves produced consistent findings of positive impacts of BAM participation on student outcomes. Among boys who were randomly assigned to participate in the program, total arrests fell by 28–35%, violent arrests fell by

45–50%, and school engagement improved, as compared to boys in the control group. Follow-up data from the first wave showed that participation in BAM led to a 12–19% increase in the rate at which boys graduated high school.[26]

The program attracted the attention of President Obama, who invited a group of BAM enrollees to the White House in 2013. In 2014, a BAM participant introduced President Obama at the launch of Obama's My Brother's Keeper task force, an effort to promote and scale programs aimed at helping young men and boys of color succeed in school and the workplace.[27] According to the program's 2019 annual report, in that year there were 8,000 BAM students in Chicago, Boston, and Cook County, and plans were underway to expand to additional cities.[28]

BAM and Big Brothers both originate from a belief that children growing up in difficult circumstances, often without a father in their home, are disadvantaged by more than just a lack of financial resources: they need nurturing adults in their lives to help them overcome the myriad adversities and traumas they have experienced in their lives so that they can thrive in school and beyond. Programs like these don't address the underlying challenge of a rise in the share of children growing up without a father figure in their home, but they *do* address some of the consequences of that trend for youth, boys in particular. They can help break the cycle of disadvantage.[29]

Scaling up programs such as Big Brothers Big Sisters and Becoming a Man—programs that have demonstrated success at helping children from disadvantaged family situations—is something that the government and philanthropic groups can (and should) do. Effective programs like these can, after all, help compensate for the disadvantages many children face at home. But these programs are also challenging to operate at a large scale, and they can be expensive. In an ideal world, we would find ways to remove as many of those home-life disadvantages as possible. We would find ways to equip more parents to consistently and reliably provide for their children.

Summary

Too many boys today are struggling. Boys and young men are faring worse than girls and young women on a host of behavioral, educational, and economic dimensions. This gender gap in outcomes has been linked to the heightened disadvantage boys face when growing up without a father figure in their home. Careful scholarship has further documented that it's not just having a dad in the house that is helpful to boys. For Black boys in particular, having a larger share of Black dads present in neighborhood family homes is associated with better lifetime outcomes for Black boys and smaller racial gaps in outcomes.

We cannot give up on dads and stand by as men continue to fall to the margins of economic and family life. For too long, US social policy was aimed almost exclusively at helping single mothers and children, with haphazard efforts to hold fathers responsible for paying child support and essentially no commitment to helping dads address whatever barriers they face in their lives. Recent movements toward a more holistic pro-family approach, one that engages and supports both mothers and fathers in the raising of their children, is promising. But unfortunately, even among fathers who actively want to be more engaged with their children, many face a multitude of barriers that make doing so difficult. Helping children in this country will require helping dads. And helping dads will require addressing the widespread economic and social challenges that hold back millions of adults—challenges including joblessness, mass incarceration, untreated mental illness, and the opioid epidemic, among others.

SEVEN

Declining Births

"Study Finds American Women Delaying Motherhood because the Whole Thing Blows."

The Onion[1]

In January 1996, President Bill Clinton spoke from the White House to address an issue he described as a "moral problem and a personal problem": teen pregnancy. Its incidence peaked in the United States during the baby-boom decade of the 1950s, and after falling steadily in the decades that followed, increased again beginning in the late 1980s. Clinton told reporters that the issue "has reached such proportions that it is a very significant economic and social problem for the United States."[2] He announced a bipartisan effort to bring down rates of teen childbearing in the United States and the launch of the National Campaign to Prevent Teen Pregnancy. In his 1996 State of the Union address, he said, "To strengthen the family we must do everything we can to keep the teen pregnancy rate going down."[3]

Remarkably, the rate of teen childbearing in the US *did* go down, falling by more than 70% since 1996 to the lowest levels ever recorded. What makes this drop in teen pregnancy even more remarkable is that it occurred in the midst of a seemingly opposite trend: the rise in the rate of single-mother families measured over the same time period. This also makes the rise in single-mother families ever more stark, as they became composed of fewer teenage parents over time.

The rise in the share of children living with an unmarried or unpartnered mother also coincided with an overall drop in birth rates—not only among teens, but among Americans overall. Today's trend of American children living with only one parent, then, reflects changes in patterns of marriage, not changes in patterns of births. It has been driven by an increase in the likelihood that a couple that has a child together is not married. It doesn't reflect an increase in births—not overall, and not among groups that have historically had high rates of nonmarital childbearing or single-mother homes.

US birth rates have been falling for more than a decade.

The annual birth rate in the United States has been falling steadily, and sharply, since 2007, a break from a long period of generally stable annual birth rates. For the almost three decades between 1980 and 2007, the US birth rate hovered between 65 and 70 births per 1,000 women ages 15 to 44. The birth rate followed a predictable cyclical pattern: falling during economic downturns and rebounding during economic recoveries. But around the time of the 2007 Great Recession, something changed—the birth rate fell precipitously, as one would expect in a recession, but then it never recovered when the economy improved. Instead, the US birth rate has continued a steady descent. As of 2020, the US birth rate was 55.8 births per 1,000 women between the ages of 15 and 44. (Over this same 40-year period, the number of abortions in the US has also steadily fallen. The recent drop in births reflects a decline in pregnancies, not a rise in abortions.[4])

The decline in the US birth rate has not been driven by any one subpopulation of women, though some demographic groups have had larger declines than others. Teen births, in particular, have plummeted. Figure 7.1 plots birth rates for five different age groups: ages 15–19, 20–24, 25–29, 30–34, and 35 and up. The dramatic decline

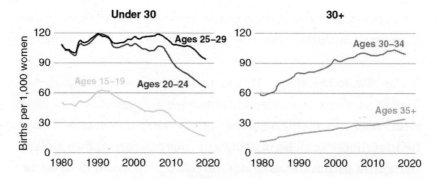

Figure 7.1 Birth rates, by five-year age group: 1980–2019
SOURCE: *Author's calculations using 1980–2019 natality data from the National Center for Health Statistics and the Current Population Survey.*

in teen birth rates since the early 1990s is evident in the figure. The teen birth rate peaked in 1991 at a level of 62.4 births per 1,000 women ages 15 to 19. It has since declined steadily, reaching 40.8 in 2005 and dropping all the way to 16.7 per 1,000 women ages 15–19 in 2019. This reflects a 73% decline over 30 years. As noted above, this is the lowest teen birth rate the United States has seen since the government began collecting such data.

But it isn't just teenagers who are having fewer births. Women in their twenties are also having fewer births than they were in the 1990s. In fact, in looking at births per age group, only women above age 30 are having more births than they were a few decades ago. In terms of what this means for the country's overall birth rates, the additional number of births to women older than 30 is still smaller than the reduced number of births to women below the age of 30, making the overall birth rate lower than in previous decades.

Individual women are also having fewer kids than they used to. The average number of children a US woman is expected to have over her lifetime is now substantially below 2, which is the number required to keep the US population from shrinking (without an increase in immigration). That is a separate issue in terms of the demographic and economic challenges it poses for the country—namely, a shrinking workforce and the challenge of continuing to fiscally support programs like Social Security and Medicare.[5] For all the talk of these programs' challenging finances, their greatest threat may come in the form of fewer people paying into them.

Examining the drop in birth rates among women of different educational backgrounds, the biggest contributor to the drop (by which I mean they're having fewer children, on average) has been women without a high school degree. The birth rate among women without a high school degree has fallen dramatically, especially since 2000, with rates within the group falling from 73.2 per 1,000 women in 1980 to 39.3 in 2019. Much of this decline reflects the drop in teen birth rates. Birth rates among women with a high school degree have not changed much over this same 30-year period, and the birth rate among college-educated women has been in slow overall decline.

If all these changes occurred on their own, without the effects of other concurrent changes in social norms ("with all else held constant," as economists say), then we would expect the huge drops in birth rates among teens and twentysomethings to produce a large decline in the share of children being born outside marriage and raised in a single-parent home. We know, after all, that younger and less educated women are more likely to have a child outside of marriage; if these same women are having fewer kids, then the kids who are being born are probably being born to married parents—right? Alas, no. As we've seen, all else has not remained constant—most relevantly, the incidence of marriage has declined! And thus, even though mothers are older and more educated than in the past, they are also much more likely to be unmarried now.

In terms of trends by race and ethnic group, birth rates have declined the most, by far, among Hispanic women, who previously had the highest birth rates by a wide margin—an astonishing 43% drop since 1990. Non-Hispanic Black and Asian women have also had substantial, albeit slightly less dramatic, drops, with rates that dropped by 24% and 30%, respectively, across the same period. Meanwhile the decline in the birth rate has been the least pronounced among non-Hispanic White women; it fell by just 9% between 1990 and 2019. Given that Hispanic women and Black women have historically had elevated rates of single motherhood, the decline in birth rates among these racial and ethnic groups would, all else held constant, have led us to expect a decrease in the share of children living in a single-mother home. But again, all else was not held constant; namely, the share of births to unmarried women has increased for all racial and ethnic groups.

A brief detour: What explains the recent decline in US births?

All this data is illuminating, but the question remains: why have birth rates been falling? There are a number of potential explanations. First, it is not surprising that birth rates fell in 2007, when the Great Recession hit. We know from economic history that birth rates fall when there is an economic downturn and rebound during a recovery. People tend to avoid having a child during an economic downturn, when their economic situation is less secure. But the puzzling thing here is why the US birth rate didn't recover after 2007. Why have annual birth rates continued to fall?

Explanations that are commonly offered in media and in casual speculation include the rising costs of raising kids, the challenges of increased levels of student debt, and/or women's desire to maintain their careers—basically, a general consensus that today's challenges make life less conducive to the all-encompassing challenge and expense of having a kid. A June 2021 article in the *Onion*, suitably published in the midst of the pandemic, had the facetious headline "Study Finds American Women Delaying Motherhood because the Whole Thing Blows." The article quotes a fictional study by sociologists that found "women have put off having children until much later in life due to the fact that it's completely exhausting, prohibitively expensive, and almost everything about it [expletive] sucks."[6] It's satire, for sure, but is the *Onion* onto something? Are adults today choosing to have fewer children—or remain childless—because they perceive that the whole thing just isn't that great, or at least not better than the alternative?

Evidence points in favor of this explanation. In a 2022 study I published with economists Phil Levine and Luke Pardue, we suggested that "shifting priorities" from one cohort of young adults to the next was the most likely explanation for the recent decline in US births. In studying childbearing for women born between 1970 and 1995, we were studying the experiences of women born and raised in dramatically different eras. A woman who was in her twenties in the 2010s was born in the 1980s; a woman in her twenties in the 1990s was born in the 1970s. Each decade stamped women with a different experience, and our study found that each successive cohort was less inclined toward having children—and not because of economic or policy factors that were in play at the time. In other words, it's not that all of a sudden around 2007, childcare became much more expensive or that highly effective contraception became available. Rather, it seems that the appeal of having kids has declined for more recent cohorts of young adults.

Our analysis investigated the role of changes in public policies and economic conditions on changes in birth rates. Neither of those sets of explanations could explain much of the decline at all. We found that the availability and scale of public assistance benefits affected birth rates some—but not much. Similarly, fluctuations of the labor market and changes to state minimum wages led to modest changes in birth rates, but those changes could statistically account for only minimal amounts of the change in birth rates over this period. The estimated effects of other state-level economic and policy factors— including child-support enforcement expenditures, laws requiring parental notification of abortion for teens, mandatory waiting periods for abortion, regulations requiring private health insurance plans to cover contraceptive costs, Medicaid expansions after the 2010 Affordable Care Act, mandatory sex education, and mandatory contraception instruction—were all statistically indistinguishable from zero. These null results also echoed earlier results in a study of how economic and policy factors affected teen birth rates between 1981 and 2010.[7]

Of course, not all changes in how and when Americans have children are likely traceable to annual changes in policies or the economy. Slower-moving factors, including social changes, would have a big effect, too. The trouble for economists—and for all domains of social science—is that it is challenging, from a statistical perspective, to causally connect changes in these types of factors to changes in the outcome of interest, in this case birth rates. Still, researchers can offer descriptive evidence from explorations of the data, and that's what we did as part of that 2022 study. We augmented the analysis described above with an examination of the potential link between various slower-moving social forces and changes in birth rates over a longer time period: more widespread usage of long-acting reversible contraception (often referred to as LARCs); rising childcare costs; rising housing costs (as measured by rental prices); rising student-debt burdens (which would reduce adults' level of disposable income); improvements in women's economic position (which would increase the opportunity cost of women's time); and declining religious observance (since more-religious people tend to have more children).

To study these dynamics, we cross-referenced data in each of these six domains against birth-rate changes in two time windows, 2004–2008 and 2014–2019. The results were relatively unequivocal: We found no evidence suggesting a meaningful role for any of these individual factors in explaining widespread trends. The data don't support a relationship, for example, between changes in state-level childcare prices, or rental prices, and aggregate-level birth rates. Nor do they give any indication that state-level increases in student debt are related to state-level reductions in birth rates. We didn't find a link between any of the measures of changes in women's economic position and birth rates over this period. This is not to say that the changing roles of women in the economy and the labor market did not lead to changes in birth rates in previous decades. What this study says is that such changes probably did not play a major role in driving down birth rates between 2007 and 2020. And even though measured religiosity has declined over this period, the data do not indicate that states where religiosity declined the most experienced a greater relative decline in birth rates.

Was the US alone in its falling birthrates, or did other countries face them, too? Here the comparison is complicated lightly by the nonstandard measurements of birth statistics across countries. International statistics are available for total fertility rates (TFR), as opposed to the customary statistic in the US, annual birth rates. The TFR is an estimated average of the number of children a woman will have over her lifetime, based on age-specific birth rates at a given point in time. A TFR of 2.0 means that a woman is expected to have two children; 2.1 is generally regarded as the rate required for population replacement (keeping the total number of people roughly equal between births and deaths).

The US total fertility rate was considerably higher than in other high-income countries all through the 1990s and early in the first decade of the 2000s: US women were having more babies, on average, than women in other wealthy nations. US births were at roughly replacement level throughout this period, while the TFR in other high-income countries was generally lower. The substantial decline in US births over the past roughly 15 years, however, has brought the TFR in the US closer to rates in other high-income countries, including the United Kingdom, Canada, and the members of the European Union. Still, even in 2018 (the most recent year for which World Bank statistics are currently available), the US TFR was higher than that in other places, including Scandinavian countries, which have an especially generous system of public support that is often cited for providing greater welfare to citizens than programs in the United States.

In the absence of a historical smoking gun to explain the drop in US birth rates, the body of evidence led us to conclude that the source of decline in US births is likely something more fundamental—a set of shifts in priorities and experiences across successive cohorts of young adults, as opposed to any readily identifiable economic or policy factor that discretely changed in the past 15 years. It certainly seems plausible, even likely, that the generation(s) born after the mid-1980s—the Americans who entered their prime childbearing years around 2005 and later—have different aspirations for their lives (say, with regard to work or leisure time) and expectations about the nature of parenting. Parenting *has* become quite intensive, after all, in terms of both time and financial investments. This intensiveness might understandably deter some people from having as many children as they might have in previous decades, especially if they feel compelled, either by preference or necessity, to spend more time at work or investing in careers.

What explains the sustained decline in US teen childbearing since the mid-1990s?

It seems there has been an attitudinal shift away from the desire to become a mother at a young age, especially as a teen. Given the challenges associated with being a teen mother—for the young mother and for her child—this shift is generally understood to be a good thing. What accounts for it? We know from nationally representative data that teenagers are both having less sex and using more contraception than they were in the early 1990s.[8] The interesting question is what forces are leading them to make these decisions.

In a 2015 study, Phil Levine and I (as you have probably figured out by now, we work together a lot) examined a comprehensive set of potential policy explanations for the rise and fall in teen birth rates from the early 1990s through 2010.[9] We statistically examined the contributory effect of a long list of factors that might have affected teen birth rates, including things like comprehensive sexual education mandates, changes in welfare rules and abortion policies, and others. The only two public policies that were found to have a statistically discernible relationship with teen birth rates were (1) Welfare benefit levels and (2) Expanded access to family planning services through Medicaid. But as with the total birth rate among all women, changes in these factors could not explain much of the overall decline. We calculated that the decline in welfare benefit levels and greater access to family planning services through Medicaid could account for roughly 13% of the observed decline in teen birth rates since 1991.[10] The rest of the decline was unattributable to other, similarly targeted policies.

Rather, the dramatic reduction in teen childbearing since the early 1990s seems to reflect widespread changes in teenagers' attitudes about risky sexual behaviors and the possibility, and perceived perils, of becoming a young parent. A key piece of evidence about the role of teenagers' attitudes toward teen parenting comes from their response to MTV's reality show *16 and Pregnant* and the *Teen Mom* spin-off series.[11]

After Levine and I completed our study of the drivers of the teen birth rate through 2010, the US Centers for Disease Control and Prevention released data showing an unusually large decline in teen births at the end of our study's timeline. Having fallen by between 4% and 6% in each of the previous two years, the teen birth rate fell by a remarkable 10% between 2009 and 2010. Journalists were calling us to ask our expert opinion about the reasons for the excess decline. We couldn't say with any certainty. We knew from our previous work that it couldn't be something as straightforward as expanded sex-ed classes or a sudden, discrete drop in welfare benefits. So, what was new that year?

There was one (unlikely, we thought) novel factor that had been introduced just that year: the new MTV reality series about being 16 and pregnant. A 2010 study for the National Campaign to Prevent Teen and Unplanned Pregnancy—which had updated its name and mission in 2005 to include "unplanned pregnancy"—reported that 82% of teens who watch *16 and Pregnant* indicate that it "helps teens better understand the challenges of pregnancy and parenthood."[12] Only 17% report that it "glamorizes teen pregnancy." Could the show have had an effect?

We bought ratings data on MTV viewership from the Nielson Institute, a media organization that tracks, among other things, which television shows are being watched by which demographics. We obtained access to Google and Twitter data on searches related to the show. And for the next couple years, we worked to connect the data dots. Our main analysis took advantage of geographic variation in MTV viewership rates, comparing changes in teen births after the *16 and Pregnant* show aired across places with different MTV viewership rates beforehand.[13] The analysis found that the introduction of the reality TV show led to a 4.3% total reduction in teen births conceived between June 2009, when the show began, and the end of 2010, which could account for 24% of the total decline in teen births over that period. Ensuing analyses of Google and Twitter data provided evidence suggesting that the airing of episodes led to increased searches for things like "how to get birth control" and tweets along the lines of "Just watched 16 and Pregnant. That show is the best birth control!"

In earlier work, Levine and I had concluded that teens were influenced in their decision to become young mothers by their perceived (or perceived lack of) economic and educational opportunities.[14] I still believe that to be the case. But what we learned from our research on the MTV show is that teenagers also respond to a better understanding of how a pregnancy and birth would affect their life immediately—for example, by making it harder to hang out with friends and do the types of things teens do when they don't have the physical, mental, and financial responsibility of a baby.

Though initially introduced by MTV as pure entertainment, the 16 and Pregnant series' depiction of real teenage girls struggling with pregnancy, childbirth, and the challenges of parenting a baby— including having to tend to a demanding infant in the middle of the night, the expense of diapers and baby food, dealing with a teen father who often isn't very helpful or present—served as a sort of public media campaign that effectively convinced a bunch of teenagers who might otherwise have been ambivalent or even happy about becoming teen parents to think otherwise. This is not to say that MTV is responsible for the sustained decline in teen childbearing over more than two decades. Rather, I describe this study to illustrate the point that things that affect teenagers' attitudes matter— and they can translate into the behavioral changes that lead to lower rates of teen pregnancy and childbearing.

The dramatic reduction in teen childbearing since the early 1990s has been driven, mechanically, by a reduction in sexual activity and an increase in contraceptive use. But these changes ultimately reflect behavioral changes, which are themselves reflections of teenagers' own attitudes and preferences. The declining birth rate, then, is likely a product of changing minds.

The share of births to unmarried mothers has nearly doubled in the past 40 years, despite the declining share of births to younger, less educated women.

As I have described, birth rates have fallen for women below age 30, especially teens. Birth rates have risen for women ages 30 and older. As a result, the age profile of new mothers has shifted upward. In 2019, nearly half of all births in the US were to women 30 or older. Combined with other trends, including the drop in birth rates among the least-educated mothers and the overall rise in the number of people going to college, the educational composition of new mothers has shifted higher, too. In 2019, more than 30% of births were to women with a four-year college degree and only 12% were to mothers with less than a high school degree, as compared to 18% and 24%, respectively, in 1990.

And yet: the share of births to unmarried women has more than doubled between 1980 and 2019! It increased from 18% in 1980 to 33% in 2000 to 40% in 2019. These shares are illustrated in figure 7.2.

The primary explanation for this is pretty straightforward: mothers are less likely to be married now than in previous decades, even though they are older and more educated. Of course, women *in general* are also less likely to be married now than in previous decades. The share of women of childbearing age (between ages 15 and 44) who were married fell from 54% in 1980 to 48% in 2000 to 39% in 2020.

In fact, the share of women who are unmarried at the time of giving birth has increased for women in all major population groups tracked: all five age groups, all three education groups, and all four major racial and ethnic groups. These trends are summarized in figure 7.3. Notice that among women giving birth between the ages of 25 and 29, the share of them who were unmarried at the time of the birth more than doubled between 1980 and 2019, from 18%

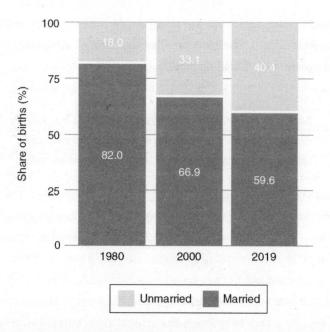

Figure 7.2 Share of births in 1980, 2000, and 2019 to unmarried and married mothers
SOURCE: *Author's calculations using 1980, 2000, and 2019 natality data from the National Center for Health Statistics.*

to 40%. Among women who had a high school degree at the time of giving birth, the unmarried share increased from 25% to 52%. Even among college-educated mothers, the share doubled over this time—from 5% to 11%, though it remains far below the share of mothers without a college degree who are unmarried at the time of giving birth. White women are still far less likely to be unmarried at the time of giving birth than Black women and Hispanic women, but that share increased substantially between 1980 and 2020, rising from 17% to 29%.

In her 2014 book *Generation Unbound*, Isabel Sawhill—a renowned scholar of social policy and founding president of the National Campaign to Prevent Teen Pregnancy—detailed the rising share of births outside a marital union and its association with child poverty. Observing that many births to unmarried mothers are the result of unplanned pregnancies, Sawhill argued that it would be advantageous for children if more parents were "planners," those who delayed parenthood until after marriage, than "drifters," those

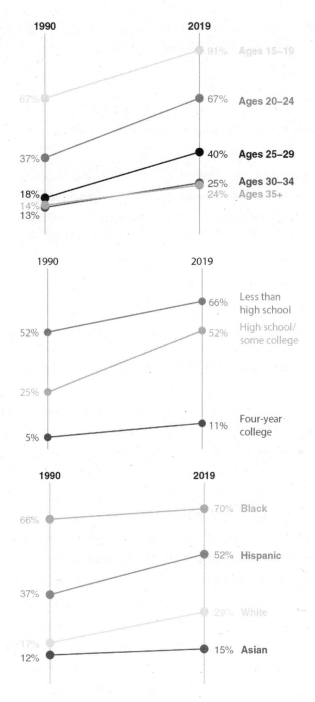

Figure 7.3 Share of births to unmarried women in 1990 and 2019 by age, education level, and race/ethnicity
SOURCE: *Author's calculations using 1990 and 2019 natality data from the National Center for Health Statistics.*

who have unplanned children early and outside of marriage. To do this, she called for expanded access to long-acting reversible contraception (LARCs, including IUDs) and the promotion of social norms that encourage planned pregnancies. Although I share the view that it is important for people to have access to affordable, highly effective contraception, the reason I am not putting more of an emphasis on the issue here is because the primary driver of the high incidence of today's mother-only households is not a lack of access to affordable contraception among young, low-income women. After all, the number of kids being born—including to lower-income moms—is on its way down. More kids are living with just their mom because fewer adults are getting married, including those who have a child together.

What do changes in birth patterns mean for children?

What do these trends in birth rates mean for children's childhood resources? All else equal, the shift in the composition of mothers to older, more educated women would have led to more children being born into more highly resourced homes. But working against these trends have been the decline in marriage, the rise in nonmarital childbearing, and the resulting increase in the share of children living with only their mother. Resources are lower in such households, as can be seen in the poverty gaps between households headed by unmarried mothers and those headed by married couples. In 2020, the likelihood that an infant lived in a household that met the official government threshold of poverty was 46% for those living with an unmarried mother, as compared to 6% for infants living in a married-couple household.

Which brings us back to our earlier discussions about marriage, income, and earnings. As a general matter, two adults have more combined income and overall resources than one adult. This is a big part of the reason why parental marriage is, in general, a good thing for children. Also as a general matter, men—including fathers—who are working and earning more money are more likely to be considered more suitable marriage partners and are more likely to be married. They are also more likely to be engaged with their children and paying child support when they are not married to their child's mother or living with their family. Increasing the share of children born to married parents and strengthening families will require improving the economic situation of many men in this country, especially those without a four-year college degree.

Summary

The increase in the share of American children living without two parents over the past 40 years has happened despite the dramatic decline in teen childbearing and the fact that mothers are older and more educated than they were 40 years ago—trends that, had marriage rates remained constant, would have led to a lower incidence of nonmarital childbearing and single-mother homes. The changing family structure of US children reflects a reduction in the incidence of marriage and a decoupling of marriage from the experience of having and raising children, not an increase in birth rates among demographic groups with historically high rates of single motherhood.

Had all else remained constant, the shift in the composition of mothers toward older, more educated mothers would have led to an increase in childhood resources and economic advantages for children. But all else has not remained constant. The decline in the incidence of marriage between parents has meant that an increasing share of children are being born to an unmarried mother and raised in a home with only their mother present. That tends to mean a less advantageous home environment.

EIGHT

Family Matters

The conventional mores in the United States today are to treat matters of family and family formation with a dedicated agnosticism, avoiding any suggestion that one type of family might be somehow preferable to another family type. As well-meaning as this intention may be, it has given rise to a massive blind spot in how policy observers and many advocates talk about—and indeed, feel *permitted* to talk about—matters related to the home. These sensitivities are particularly acute when the scientific ideas are critical, e.g., when arguing that some household formulations tend to be more beneficial than other formulations.

All of this is to say, I anticipate some measure of backlash from well-meaning people who think it is impolite or impolitic to apply an unforgiving tool like economic analysis on the family. But when I look at the data and evidence that have piled up over decades and across disciplinary fields, I am convinced that it is a conversation people in the US need to have.

What those data say, overwhelmingly, are that children's outcomes in life are profoundly shaped by their family and home experiences. Children who have the benefit of two parents in their home tend to have more highly resourced, enriching, stable childhoods, and they consequently do better in school and have fewer behavioral challenges. These children go on to complete more years of education, earn more in the workforce, and have a greater likelihood of being married. Of course, these are not the only measures of a successful life, but they are useful metrics of achievement and well-being. The data tell a clear story: family matters.

Against this backdrop, the share of American children growing up with the benefit of two parents in their home is at a historic low: in 2019, nearly 40% of American children did not live with married parents. Nearly 20% of American children lived with only their mother, with no second parent figure in the home. These percentages were not proportional across the population. A large family gap, determined by parents' education levels, created a compounding effect on the already stark disadvantages of not having a college degree: children of non-college-educated parents were also less likely to have married parents (and all the benefits married parents bestow).

This family gap contributes to class gaps in childhood resources, experiences, and outcomes. It simultaneously reflects and exacerbates inequality. It undermines social mobility. It perpetuates divisions that are causing fragmentation and fractures in society. And it is part of a cycle that will have to be broken if class gaps are going to shrink and children from all backgrounds are going to have anything close to equal opportunities to get ahead, to thrive, and to live their best life.

Doing so will require talking about issues that are challenging, even uncomfortable. To this end, it is useful to contrast the policy conversation around issues of family structure with the public conversation around who goes to college. College graduates, I've noted several times throughout this book, have greater employment stability and earnings than people without college degrees. We know that from data. Policy makers, journalists, scholars, and advocates do not publicly pretend that those differences don't exist. They don't avoid the issue on the grounds that acknowledging it blames or shames those who haven't gone to college. Rather, our policy conversation around this issue rightly accepts the fact that, in today's economy, a college degree is associated with greater economic security. People push for policies to expand college access and completion, while *also* looking to develop and advance alternative pathways to good jobs for those who do not have a college degree. And at the same time, thought leaders and policy makers look for ways to bolster the economic security of low-wage Americans—through wage subsidies, increases in the minimum wage, and expanded eligibility for public health insurance.

Public and policy conversations could take a similar approach to family structure. Start with an acknowledgment that in most cases, two-parent, stable families are very beneficial for children. With that as a known, we can and should explore ways to boost the prevalence of (healthy) two-parent families. (None of what I write or say on this issue should be misconstrued as arguing in favor of two-parent families regardless of the nature of the relationships involved. I would never, for example, advocate for keeping families together in instances of abuse or violence.) At the same time, we can collectively work to strengthen alternative family structures, so that more children in families in which the parents do not live together have the benefit of positive support and engagement from two parents. And we can also take measures to bolster the childhood experiences of children who, through no fault of their own, are growing up in a disadvantaged home environment.

In summary, here are the things we should do to address the challenges I have laid out in this book:

+ Work to restore and foster a norm of two-parent homes for children
+ Work to improve the economic position of men without a college level of education so they are more reliable marriage partners and fathers
+ Scale up government and community programs that show promise in strengthening families and improving outcomes for parents and children from disadvantaged backgrounds
+ Have a stronger safety net for families, regardless of family structure

Here are some things I do *not* think we should do:

- Accept a new reality where the two-parent family is a thing of the past for less educated, lower-income Americans
- Bemoan the economic independence of women
- Stigmatize single mothers or encourage unhealthy marriages
- Run unsuccessful government marriage programs
- Keep government assistance meager under the mistaken assumption that doing so will incentivize more marriages and two-parent families

Fostering a norm of two-parent homes for children

A few years ago, I was in a cab in Boston and noticed a photo of a young girl that my driver had displayed on his dashboard.

"Is that your daughter?" I asked.

"Yeah," he said with joyful pride. "I have more pictures, want to see?" Of course I did. He handed me his phone and invited me to scroll through his photos. I oohed and aahed over how adorable his four-year-old girl was. We chatted. He told me she lived with her mom.

"You don't live with them?" I asked.

"Nah," he said.

"Could I ask why not?" I continued. I knew this was nosy, so I quickly qualified it. "I'm an economist, and I study families, so I wonder about these kinds of things."

"I don't know." He shrugged. "We talk about it. If we save up some money, we might get married."

I couldn't help myself, and I pressed further. "I don't mean to pry," I said slowly, "but if you guys get along and you both love your daughter, why don't you live together as a family?" He became flustered—not impatient or angry, but genuinely flustered. He missed the exit, looked over his shoulder to get a better look at me, and asked, "Did my mom send you or something?"

This encounter, and a million other domestic arrangements that it describes, prompt an important question: Has the social normalization of raising children outside of a two-parent arrangement led to more children being raised in a one-parent household? I suspect yes. And has this trend served the best interests of children? Based on the evidence, I would say, unequivocally, no. The challenge for society, then, is to find ways to acknowledge the benefits of a two-parent family—including the important role that fathers play in their children's lives—without coming across as shaming or blaming single mothers. By being honest about the benefits that a two-parent family home confers to children, we can break the pattern in which social agnosticism treats all households as the same in terms of the benefits they deliver children.

Children have no say as to how they are brought into this world and raised. They have no say as to whether their parents live together or raise them together. I wonder how many children in one-parent homes would prefer that both of their parents lived with them. As a child growing up in the 1980s, I remember being worried whenever my parents fought that they might get divorced. (Divorce was more prevalent in the '80s than it is now.) My parents might not have always gotten along with each other, but I was always happy to have them both there at home. I realize that's not true for all families and some families would not be better off if the parents were together. But recall the statistics: We are no longer in a situation where children are raised by an unmarried or unpartnered parent only in rare or extenuating circumstances. Only 63% of US children are being raised in a home with married parents. More than one in five children in the US live with a mother who is neither married nor cohabitating. More than half of unpartnered mothers today have never been married.

Could it really be the case that so many children have fathers who would not be positive contributors to the family if they were part of their household? If that is even close to the reality for men in America today, then we really do have a terrible crisis. The decline in the two-parent family relates in part to the struggles of men, which is in turn contributing to the struggles of boys. This cycle is in desperate need of interruption: the US needs to raise boys who are fit to be reliable marriage partners and nurturing, supportive fathers. We need to foster a societal expectation that fathers be present in their children's lives and support them, financially and emotionally.

I have no idea whether that Boston cab driver would be a good dad or husband or long-term cohabitating partner or co-parent. He seemed like a nice guy, and he seemed to really love his daughter and his daughter's mom. Is that enough? No, far from it. But the point is that he and his daughter's mom seemed to believe that the options of cohabitating or living apart were more or less equally good when it came to their daughter's well-being. And that is just not what the data say.

In the formation of social norms and prevailing attitudes, there are a few things scholarly evidence tells us. For one, role models matter. Young people take inspiration and cues from trusted adults in their lives.[1] Children, teens, and young adults will approach their own family formation in ways that are reflective of the examples and lessons they take from the adults around them.

There is also compelling evidence that people's attitudes (and ultimately behaviors) are influenced by media content, even in the complicated sphere of family formation. For instance, economists have documented how the portrayal of family structures in Brazilian *telenovelas* produced changes in the country's family and fertility outcomes—a drop in fertility, a rise in divorce and separation—between 1965 and 1999.[2] Similarly, the depictions of the difficulties associated with being a teen mom as shown on the MTV reality television show *16 and Pregnant* led to a decline in rates of teen childbearing in the US, as I described in chapter 7. Social messaging that comes organically in the form of entertainment and social media can have an impact on how people think and act when it comes to decisions about family and fertility.

My intention here is not to elevate the role that television or media messages has played in driving the observed changes in family structure. Nor am I blaming the media for the paradigm shift away from the prominence of the two-parent family structure among a large segment of US society. But I do suspect—based on evidence that media matters—that current social messaging reinforces the underlying trend toward a decoupling of marriage and raising children.

Social norms are an important contributor to the rise of the single-parent household, but their importance doesn't mean that there aren't many single parents who wouldn't prefer to have a spouse or committed partner. In fact, ethnographic studies confirm as much. In one study of 165 low-income single mothers from urban neighborhoods in Philadelphia, Pennsylvania, and Camden, New Jersey, conducted through interviews early in the first decade of the 2000s, researchers found that many of the women interviewed indicated that they wanted to eventually marry, but that a successful marriage felt out of reach, especially with their child's father.[3] This finding relates to the issue of "marriageable men." If the parent of one's child is unlikely to be an economically and emotionally stable and supportive partner, marriage is not going to be an attractive proposition, even if, in theory, the idea of marriage is appealing.

Relatedly, in her 2019 book, the sociologist Sarah Halpern-Meekin reported on interviews she conducted with 31 low-income, unmarried couples who enrolled in relationship classes through the free "Family Expectations" program—a comprehensive, curriculum-based program designed to help couples strengthen their relationships during and immediately following the birth of a child.[4] She found that the primary motivation many of these couples expressed for taking these classes was to build healthier relationships and a good environment for raising their children. Only one of the 31 couples had experienced a stable, two-parent family growing up, and most reported that they had grown up in a chaotic or abusive family environment. These couples were keenly aware of the impacts of family instability in their lives, and they knew that they struggled with communication and problem solving. Many of the participants also expressed lacking people in their lives whom they felt they could turn to for relationship help and general support—a component of what Halpern-Meekin describes as "social poverty." The finding that these unmarried parents *wanted* their troubled relationships to succeed but didn't have the skills or personal examples to make it happen is an important observation. It is not always, or even often, the case that single-parent households are chosen; sometimes they are the result of impediments and constraints.

The struggles that low-income unmarried couples face relate in large part to economic insecurity and limited opportunities. The behaviors and choices that follow reflect prevailing social norms and economic realities. Addressing underlying economic challenges must be part of any serious attempt to strengthen families in America and increase the share of children being raised in two-parent homes. The challenge is multifaceted, and so must be the response.

Improving the economic position of non-college-educated men so they are more reliable marriage partners and fathers

The decline in the two-parent family for a large segment of the population is not a trend that will be reversed through social messaging alone. Nor will tweaks to the tax code or transfer-program eligibility rules (which currently contain a variety of marriage *dis*incentives) be enough to reverse the trend—although such policy reforms should absolutely be pursued. Such efforts will affect some people on the margin. But the scale of the problem goes way beyond marginal cases at this point. We are now talking about roughly half of children born to non-college-educated parents being born to unmarried parents, most of whom will not stay together. Reversing these trends will require major changes.

The widespread weakening of the economic situation of many American men, especially men without college degrees, has contributed to the decline in marriage and the rise in the share of children living with only their mother. *Fifteen percent* of men between the ages of 25 and 54 are not in the workforce. In the 1960s, 95% of these men worked. That share fell to 88% by the late 1980s and 85% ahead of the COVID pandemic in 2020. A variety of factors have contributed to this trend, including changes that have reduced the labor demand for men without college degrees—factors like increased imports from China and the adoption of industrial automation.[5] A number of other factors have pushed down wages for non-college-educated workers, too, while increasing wages for workers with a four-year college degree—including technological advances that have changed the types of tasks and jobs available to workers with different skill levels, a decline in union representation, and a decline in the real value of the minimum wage.[6]

Studies confirm a causal link between the economic forces that have dampened the employment and earnings of non-college-educated men and a lower married share and a higher share of unmarried childbearing and single-mother homes. Reversing the widespread decline in marriage and the corresponding rise in nonmarital childbearing and single-mother homes will likely require reversing the effects of the seismic economic forces that have disadvantaged non-college-educated men. Addressing these challenges on a large scale will require a tremendous amount of political will and years of time. Or they will just continue to calcify and get worse.

How does a society foster better economic outcomes for working-age adults who lack stable employment or face low earnings? Building skills so that these people can command higher wages is an obvious one. Such an effort starts with improvements to K–12 education, but beyond that, I would endorse a massive infusion of federal resources into the public universities and community colleges that educate and train millions of Americans each year. There are many complementary initiatives that would help more people secure well-paying jobs, such as an expansion of well-designed apprenticeship programs, training programs that lead directly to employment, and well-designed career and technical educational programs. In addition to public and private sector efforts to build skills, there is a strong case to be made for expanded earnings supplements—for example, through an expanded Earned Income Tax Credit. Criminal justice reform and prisoner reentry efforts will also be needed to reduce the number of American men who spend time incarcerated and to help those who do have criminal backgrounds reintegrate into society and the workforce.[7]

I want to be explicit in stating the following: the growth in women's earnings and economic opportunities is a positive social trend, unequivocally. My focus on men's relative economic position should not be interpreted as a lament for the traditions of decades past when too many women were constrained from pursuing educational and economic opportunities and thus had no choice but to marry and depend on a man's earnings. If we wish to promote marriage in the US, we should work to address the reasons why so many men seem to be less than ideal marriage partners—either in their own eyes or those of potential spouses—not attempt to revert to a social and economic paradigm in which many women had essentially no financial choice but to marry and hope that their husbands would provide financially for them.

Promoting and supporting healthy co-parenting and two-parent involvement, regardless of parental marital status or living arrangements

The US also has to find ways to strengthen families as they currently exist. Doing so means encouraging and supporting healthy marriages among parents, as I note above, but also promoting strong and healthy family units in cases where parents cannot, should not, or do not want to be married. When being married or living together is not the right option, the ideal second option is one in which a couple cooperatively co-parents and each parent provides support and nurturing to their child or children. Helping couples achieve this goal might mean providing more institutional or legal support to unmarried parents. It might mean revisiting fatherhood rights and child-support enforcement regimes. I am not prepared to endorse specific changes to these regimes—they are complicated, and oftentimes reforms in one direction lead to unintended consequences elsewhere—but I do think there is a clear need to orient our social policy away from the long-standing, nearly exclusionary focus on single mothers and children, and instead work to strengthen families in a more holistic way.

An obvious way to try to help strengthen families would be to run programs that encourage stable marriages. But such efforts have been tried, and they generally did not work well. Early in the first decade of the 2000s, the federal government took up the cause of trying to encourage healthy, stable marriages by funding community programs with that goal. The Healthy Marriage Initiative, launched by the Bush administration in 2001, provided federal funding for voluntary programs run by local and state governments and community organizations to promote marriage among low-income couples with children. The results of these studies were not very encouraging. The programs appeared to help people in some ways, but they didn't meaningfully increase marital stability among participating couples.[8]

Though such efforts have not been wholly abandoned, there is now a trend toward programming that promotes strong families (not necessarily marriage) and engaged fatherhood. Fatherhood programs are being designed and implemented around the country, as discussed in chapter 6. Some fatherhood programs work with dads on parenting techniques and conflict-management skills. Others additionally work to address personal barriers in the form of unstable employment or previous incarceration. There is still much to be learned about how to design these programs in such a way that they produce meaningful improvements, but it seems clear that building on and experimenting with programs that engage fathers and that work to improve parental cooperation and active co-parenting between mothers and fathers is more likely to be a successful approach than programs that focus on encouraging or sustaining marriage per se. As a purely practical matter, we cannot give up on the many dads who don't live with their children. Bolstering the well-being of children requires recognizing the important role of fathers in children's lives and boosting support to both mothers *and* fathers.

Recall the evidence from chapter 6 about the link between fathers' absences and boys' struggles, or, conversely, the link between fathers' presence and boys' positive outcomes. Boys today are falling behind; they are more likely than girls to get in trouble at school and with the law and they are less likely to go to college. Evidence shows that these outcomes are more likely for boys who don't have a dad in their home. Evidence also shows that Black boys have higher rates of upward mobility when there are more Black dads in their neighborhood. The positive role that dads and men can play in children's lives, even if they don't live with the family, is critical.

Scaling up government and community programs that improve outcomes for parents and children from disadvantaged backgrounds

Thousands of organizations and programs around the country are committed to improving outcomes for families and children in disadvantaged circumstances. These programs include parenting interventions that have been shown to help low-income and resource-constrained parents be better parents. Typically, such interventions take the form of in-home visits: specially trained nurses regularly visiting first-time, low-income moms-to-be, starting early in the pregnancy and continuing through their child's first two years of life.[9] The nurses teach mothers how to safely care for their baby and provide advice on how to set up a safe, stable, secure early-childhood environment for their child. Evidence suggests this program leads to a reduction in rates of childhood neglect and abuse and fewer behavioral and intellectual problems during a child's early years of life. Other programs aim to boost the rate at which low-income parents read with their young children, something that more highly educated, higher-income parents tend to do at higher rates, contributing to class gaps in early-childhood cognitive development and gaps in school readiness.[10] Programs with evidence of cost effectiveness should be scaled up and expanded.

There is also evidence that effective mentoring programs can improve outcomes for children and teens growing up in low-income, single-parent homes, particularly boys. Scaling up programs such as

Big Brothers Big Sisters and Becoming a Man—discussed in chapter 6—that have demonstrated success at helping children who face adversities is something philanthropic groups can and should do. Of course, mentoring is not the only way to address the relative disadvantage of children from single-parent or less resourced homes. Programs that provide lower-income kids with access to after-school enrichment programs, extracurricular activities and sports, enriching summer camps, and the like can potentially go some way toward addressing the gaps in such opportunities between children from higher- and lower-income families.

No single program, however effective, will level the playing field, but moving the needle in a hundred little ways can add up and improve children's lives, and we should do as much of that as we can.

Enhancing public support to low-income and under-resourced families

Whatever choices adults make or barriers they face, children should not be left to suffer the consequences of an under-resourced and unstable home life. It is a losing proposition that is unfair to kids and is decidedly not in the US's best interest. As a matter of federal policy and national spending, I believe the US should do more to provide for the material needs of children—through increased income support, safe housing, adequate health care, nutritious food, and high-quality early-childhood education. Increased spending on children is an investment in their future—and in turn in the country's future—and it would mean that more children would reach their human potential. Evidence shows that income assistance to low-income families leads to better outcomes for kids: they are healthier, do better in school, and have higher earnings and improved health as adults.

This statement is a causal one. Researchers have identified the link between an increase in income to low-income families and the improvement in outcomes for those families' children—and it's significant. When tax laws change such that some families become eligible for larger EITC payments, for example, improvements have been observed in infant and child health as well as improved measures of mother's mental health.[11] There is also evidence that increased EITC benefit amounts lead to improved educational performance and increased educational attainment for children.[12]

Similar evidence has come from a completely different context— tribal casino profit distributions. Studies by economist Randall Akee and coauthors document that children from low-income households benefited in a variety of ways when a tribal casino opened on the Eastern Cherokee reservation in North Carolina in 1998, and the tribal government began distributing casino profit payments on a per-capita basis to adult tribal members.[13] Eligible households saw their annual incomes increase by approximately $3,500 per year, or roughly 15%, on account of these payments. For children living in eligible households, the additional income from the casino payments led to higher rates of high school graduation and a reduced likelihood of being arrested for a crime. The increase in family income led to improvements in measures of children's emotional well-being and behavioral health, as well as increases in positive personality traits, such as conscientiousness and agreeableness. Notably, the researchers also found evidence of improved parental mental health, improved relationships between parents, and improved relationships between parents and children in the affected households.

This evidence speaks directly to the parenting issues discussed in chapter 5: when resources are tight, parents are especially stressed. And when parents are stressed, it's hard to have the emotional bandwidth to engage positively with children. These studies provide causal evidence that relieving some of that income constraint for low-income families leads to a reduction in parental stress, improvements in parental behaviors, improvements in decision-making in the household, and, ultimately, better mental and emotional health for children, along with improved educational outcomes.

For too long, the US has offered scant material assistance to single-mother families out of a fear that if the government made it too "easy" for women to raise children on their own, many mothers would choose to raise their children without a father figure present.

But the evidence on the link between welfare benefit generosity and family formation suggests that more generous welfare benefits have only a small impact on family-formation outcomes, if any at all. To be sure, material support in the form of cash benefits or public health insurance should not be limited to families headed by a single mother, as such programs have been in the past. Doing so creates an explicit disincentive to marry—even if that disincentive is empirically small in practice—and economically struggling families with married parents should also receive income support. But welfare has not been a driving force behind the changes in children's living arrangements that we have witnessed over the past 40 years, and worries about that link should not be a dominant concern guiding policy making. To let children born to low-income families— many of which are headed by single mothers—fall further and further behind out of a misplaced worry that government support will substantially undermine marriage rates would be a terrible mistake.

The evidence is clear: expansions in safety-net programs for low-income families have led to better outcomes for affected children. Studies show that low-income children who had access to food stamps and Medicaid health insurance during their childhood, or for more years of their childhood, have better health, education, and economic outcomes into adulthood, as compared to low-income children who did not.[14] The US system of material support for low-income families should include a meaningful cash allowance or child tax credit for low-income families with children, along with a combination of in-kind support through public health insurance, food assistance, housing assistance, and publicly provided or subsidized high-quality early-childhood education programs. Children from low-income families are done a tremendous disservice by having no entitlement to education until the age of five. Evidence shows that for low-income children, access to public early-childhood education programs can yield large, lasting payoffs in terms of improved educational and labor-market outcomes.[15]

Providing substantial material support to low-income families with children will not equalize childhood resources, nor will it ensure that all children ultimately have the same health, education, or economic outcomes. Even in Denmark, a bastion of public welfare that includes free college tuition, universal access to high-quality health care, universal high-quality pre-K, and a generous childcare and maternity-leave policy, the influence of family background on many child outcomes is about as strong as it is in the US.[16] A recent study shows that despite the generosity of the Danish welfare state, substantial inequality of child outcomes remains across social and economic classes. Parents affect their children's lives and shape their outcomes in ways that government cannot fully make up for. We should be clear-eyed about this reality. Even if the US safety net were much stronger than it is today, children from two-parent, highly re-sourced homes would still be bound to have relative advantages in life. But still, a stronger system of public supports would meaning-fully improve the lives of millions of children from disadvantaged home environments—including many in one-parent homes—and set them off on a better path in life.

» «

The decline in the share of US children living in a two-parent family over the past 40 years has not been good—for children, for families, or for the United States. There has been a massive widening of the family gap, such that a two-parent family has become yet another advantage in life enjoyed disproportionately by the college-educated class. The decline in the two-parent family among parents without a four-year college degree is a demographic trend that should con-cern anyone who cares about the well-being of children and about widespread economic opportunity, inequality, and social mobility in America. The trend both reflects and exacerbates inequality. It has been driven by both economic and social forces and as such, re-versing the trend will require major changes in both economic and social spheres.

If we do not reverse this trend—if millions of American children miss out on the benefits that come from a two-parent home and if the family gap continues to widen—then children will suffer, inequality will continue to widen, and social mobility will erode. We will be a weaker, more fragmented, less prosperous nation as a result. A failure to acknowledge and address these facts is the first step in regrettable inaction.

Acknowledgments

I am deeply grateful to the many scholars, students, friends, and acquaintances who have worked with me and helped me better understand the topics covered in this book. The list of people who have contributed to my understanding of these issues is too numerous to include here, but there are a few people I want to call out by name, who directly contributed to this project:

Victoria Perez-Zetune provided expert research assistance on every aspect of the book. I am so very grateful! Taylor Landon also provided invaluable research assistance with the extensive data work. McCall Pitcher used her data visualization expertise to craft the figures. Dwyer Gunn provided expert editing on the first draft, helping me figure out how to structure and write up the content I wanted to include. Thomas Jesperson helpfully contributed to various elements of the project.

My frequent coauthor Phil Levine has been a wonderful collaborator and friend for over two decades. In the book, I draw on multiple studies that we worked on together. Phil generously read an early draft of the manuscript in its entirety and gave detailed feedback. Rebecca Ryan and Kristin Butcher also gave detailed, extensive feedback on early drafts of every chapter. I benefited greatly from the insights and deep expertise of these wonderful scholars. Chad

Zimmerman of the University of Chicago Press was a superb editor on this project. From our very first conversation, he understood what I wanted to do and what I expressly did *not* want to do. He patiently helped me find a writing voice that wasn't too academic-sounding, while still indulging me in the occasional academic hang-up. My sincere thanks to Chad for believing in this project and for encouraging and guiding me throughout.

Many other scholars, colleagues, seminar participants, and friends provided helpful and constructive feedback. I am indebted to Lisa Dettling, Chanel Dority, Amy Finkelstein, Amanda Loveland, Heather Reynolds, Mark Steinmeyer, and Melanie Wasserman for reading and commenting on early drafts. I also benefited greatly from conversations and exchanges with the following people: David Autor, Lonnie Berger, Leah Brooks, Jeff Denning, Craig Garthwaite, Lisa Gennetian, Jeff Grogger, Sarah Halpern-Meekin, Bradley Harding, Mara Lederman, Orion Martin, Adriana Lleras-Muney, Bruce Meyer, Michael Nutter, Christine Percheski, Valerie Ramey, and Lesley Turner. I acknowledge with gratitude and love the fabulous women in my neighborhood who, over walks and book club meetings, provided me with helpful observations and encouragement, including but not limited to Alicia Abell, Hilary Bednardz, Chrisy Jelen, Brooke Thomas, Jill Pellettieri, and Kathy Stallings.

The final manuscript reflects the tremendously helpful input of four anonymous referees who commented on the first draft I submitted to the Press. Their detailed, thoughtful, critical, and constructive feedback led me to sharpen the narrative of the book.

I also want to thank some of the people who encouraged me to write a book in the first place. I'm not sure I would have taken up this project without their encouragement: Richard Reeves, Belle Sawhill, Sergio Urzua, Jacob Vigdor, and the woman who approached me at a DC think-tank event a few years ago after I had given remarks on social mobility and asked if I had written a book. When I told her I had not, she told me that I should. Not long after that encounter, I was invited to give a keynote address at the Alp-Pop conference hosted by Bocconi University. I put together a talk that, unbeknownst to me at the time, would serve as an initial sketch for what would eventually turn into this book. I thank the organizers of that conference for the invitation.

The University of Maryland granted me a sabbatical semester in the fall of 2020 to work on this project. The pandemic came and my intended sabbatical travel plans gave way to moving between a makeshift desk in our renovated attic space and our kitchen table, but it was very helpful to have the semester to write, instead of scrambling to teach on Zoom. More generally, I am grateful to the University of Maryland, specifically the Economics Department, for providing me with a wonderful place to learn, teach, and work for the past 16 years.

Finally, I express my abiding gratitude to my family—both the one I grew up in and the one I have created with my husband. I am forever grateful to my sisters, Allison, Chrissy, and Vicky, for always being there for me and now my children, with love, support, and laughter. My parents MaryAnne and Lou Schettini are, and have always been, selfless in their parenting and in their commitment to our family. I could never fully express how grateful I am to them for everything. A world of gratitude to my husband Dan, for all his helpful comments on this book project, and much more generally, for all he does for me and our three children. He is everything to us. A big thank you to my in-laws, Gloria and Dan Kearney, for all their love and support. Patricia Quiroz is an angel to our family. I could not have written this book, or more generally kept up my career, if not for her.

And with all my heart, I am grateful to my three children— William, Sophia, and Adelaide—for forgiving my parenting fails and for bringing me joy and love beyond measure. The three of them are my sun, my moon, and my shining stars. There is nothing I am more grateful for in this world than the profound privilege of getting to be their mom. This book is dedicated to them.

Notes

Chapter One

1. I try to make definitions clear throughout the book. I generally include same-sex couples in the definition of married and unmarried parents. As a data matter, households headed by same-sex couples represent a very small fraction of children's households and are not driving overall trends.

2. I wrote this paper in 1999 as my second-year econometrics project in the economics department at the Massachusetts Institute of Technology. It was published in 2004 in the *Journal of Human Resources* under the title "Is There an Effect of Incremental Welfare Benefits on Fertility Behavior? A Look at the Family Cap." (The publication lag in economics is absurdly long.)

3. David Autor, David Dorn, and Gordon Hanson, "When Work Disappears: Manufacturing Decline and the Falling Marriage-Market Value of Men," *American Economic Review Insights* 1, no. 2 (September 2019): 161–78; Ann Case and Angus Deaton, *Deaths of Despair and the Future of Capitalism* (Princeton, NJ: Princeton University Press, 2020).

Chapter Two

1. I define these categories as follows: *Married-parent household*—two parents of any gender are present and married to each other. This category includes biological parents, stepparents, and adoptive parents. *Unmarried couple household*—two parents of any gender are present but are not married to each other. *Unpartnered mother*—a mother is present, but neither a father figure nor a second mother is present. *Unpartnered father*—a father is present, but neither a mother figure nor a second father is present. *No parent present*—neither a mother nor a father is identified in the household of the child. Among children in married-parent households in the 2019 ACS, 99.5% have opposite-sex parents, 0.37% have two mothers, and 0.12% have two fathers.

2. In a 2017 paper I wrote with Phil Levine, we report that data from the 2013 Panel Study

of Income Dynamics (PSID) show that among children born to cohabiting parents (comprising roughly 8% of children born between 1980 and 1999), fewer than half of them were living with both biological parents by the time they were age 14, as compared to 75% of children who had been born to married parents. A 2016 paper by sociologists Susan Brown, Wendy Manning, and Bart Stykes reports on children's family instability using nationally representative data on mothers from the 2006–2010 National Survey of Family Growth (NSFG). They report that children born to unpartnered single mothers or to cohabiting mothers experience an average of 1.7 and 1.4 parental family transitions by age 12, respectively, which is nearly three times the average number of transitions (0.5) that they observe for children born to married mothers. A challenge in interpreting these metrics is that they count transitions into and out of unions symmetrically. From the perspective of resources—which is the perspective on marriage that I emphasize in the next chapter—transitions into and out of unions do not have symmetric effects on a child's household environment. See Susan L. Brown, J. Bart Stykes, and Wendy D. Manning, "Trends in Children's Family Instability, 1995–2010," *Journal of Marriage and Family* 78, no. 5 (2016): 1173–83; Melissa S. Kearney and Philip Levine, "The Economics of Non-Marital Childbearing and the Marriage Premium for Children," *Annual Review of Economics* 9 (2017): 327–52.

3. Andrew Cherlin, "Demographic Trends in the United States: A Review of Research in the 2000s," *Journal of Marriage and Family* 72, no. 3 (June 2010): 403–19.

4. See Marcia Carlson, "Sara McLanahan: Pioneering Scholar Focused on Families and the Wellbeing of Children," a retrospective in *Proceedings of the National Academy of Sciences* 119, no. 16 (April 11, 2022).

5. Sara McLanahan, Irwin Garfinkel, Nancy Reichman, Julien Teitler, Marcia Carlson, and Christina Norland Audigier, *The Fragile Families and Child Wellbeing Study: Baseline National Report* (Princeton, NJ: Bendheim-Thoman Center for Research on Child Wellbeing, March 2003), http://www.fragilefamilies.princeton.edu/documents /nationalreport.pdf.

6. Sara McLanahan and Audrey N. Beck, "Parental Relationships in Fragile Families," *Future of Children* 20, no. 2 (Fall 2010): 17–38.

7. These statistics are from the perspective of the children living with an unpartnered mother. If we instead examine living arrangements from the perspective of the unpartnered mother, we find that 61% of unpartnered mothers live without another adult. The difference in the statistics suggests that unpartnered mothers with multiple children are more likely than unpartnered mothers of only children to live alone, without the support of another adult.

8. Many explanations have been put forward for historical US racial gaps in family structure, including the tragic legacy of separating families during the years of slavery, the historically higher rate of poverty among Black Americans, and persistent systematic discrimination; some scholars have also suggested that some of the racial differences in family structure trace their origin to a greater emphasis on kinship relationships (as opposed to marriage) in Africa as compared to Europe.

9. US Department of Health and Human Services, *Vital Statistics of the United States*

1980: Volume 1—Natality, (Hyattsville, MD: National Center for Health Statistics, 1984): table 1–36, https://www.cdc.gov/nchs/data/vsus/nat80_1acc.pdf; US Department of Health, Education, and Welfare, *Vital Statistics of the United States 1960: Volume 1—Natality* (Washington, DC: US Department of Health, Education, and Welfare, 1963): 1, 12, https://www.cdc.gov/nchs/data/vsus/nat60_1.pdf.

10. Marcia J. Carlson, "Family Structure, Father Involvement, and Adolescent Behavioral Outcomes," *Journal of Marriage and Family* 68, no. 1 (2006): 137–54.

11. Data from the 2018 SIPP show that 40% of children of divorced unpartnered mothers are in households with child-support income, as compared to 19% of children of never-married unpartnered mothers. The shares of children in households receiving child support by maternal divorce or never-married status are 47% versus 29% among the children of college-educated mothers; 39% versus 18% among the children of high school graduates; and 24% versus 15% among the children of mothers with less than a high school degree.

12. Timothy Grall, *Custodial Mothers and Fathers and Their Child Support: 2015*, Current Population Reports P60-262 (Washington, DC: US Census Bureau, January 2018), https://www.census.gov/library/publications/2018/demo/p60-262.html.

13. This data comes from the Luxembourg Income Study and is tabulated in an appendix in a 2017 working paper by Stockholm University sociologist Juho Härkönen: "Diverging Destinies in International Perspective: Education, Single Motherhood, and Child Poverty," LIS Working Paper Series no. 713 (Luxembourg: LIS Cross-National Data Center, August 2017), http://www.lisdatacenter.org/wps/liswps/713.pdf.

Chapter Three

1. Sydney Page, "This 11-Year-Old Sells Cups of Lemonade to Buy Diapers for Single Moms," *Washington Post*, August 21, 2020, https://www.washingtonpost.com/lifestyle/2020/08/21/this-11-year-old-sells-cups-lemonade-buy-diapers-single-moms/.

2. Barack Obama, Father's Day speech, Apostolic Church of God, Chicago, IL, June 15, 2008, https://www.politico.com/story/2008/06/text-of-obamas-fatherhood-speech-011094.

3. US Census Bureau, *Income and Poverty in the United States: 2019*, Current Population Reports P60-270 (Washington, DC: US Census Bureau, September 2020), https://www.census.gov/content/dam/Census/library/publications/2020/demo/p60-270.pdf. Note: the official census poverty threshold in 2019 for a household comprising one parent and two children was $20,598; for a family comprising two parents and two children it was $25,926.

4. Gary S. Becker, *Treatise on the Family* (Cambridge, MA: Harvard University Press, 1981).

5. Irwin Garfinkel and Sara S. McLanahan, *Single Mothers and Their Children: A New American Dilemma* (Washington, DC: Urban Institute Press, 1986).

6. Sara McLanahan and Gary Sandefur, *Growing Up with a Single Parent: What Hurts, What Helps?* (Cambridge, MA: Harvard University Press, 1994).

7. Leonard M. Lopoo and Thomas DeLeire, "Family Structure and the Economic Well-being of Children during Youth and Adulthood," *Social Science Research* 43, no. 1 (2014): 30–44.

8. Jonathan Gruber, "Is Making Divorce Easier Bad for Children? The Long-Run Implications of Unilateral Divorce," *Journal of Labor Economics* 22, no. 4 (2004): 799–833.

9. Economists Betsey Stevenson and Justin Wolfers studied the impact of unilateral divorce laws on rates of domestic violence and female suicide, finding that the introduction of unilateral divorce laws led to a significant decline in domestic violence for both men and women, a decline in the number of women murdered by their partners, and a decline in female suicide. This finding shows clearly that unilateral divorce laws had crucial benefits! Betsey Stevenson and Justin Wolfers, "Bargaining in the Shadow of the Law: Divorce Laws and Family Distress," *Quarterly Journal of Economics* 121, no. 1 (February 2006): 267–88.

10. Elizabeth Ananat and Guy Michaels, "The Effect of Marital Breakup on the Income Distribution of Women with Children," *Journal of Human Resources* 43, no. 3 (2008): 611–29.

11. Adam Blandin and Christopher Herrington, "Family Heterogeneity, Human Capital Investment, and College Attainment," *American Economic Journal: Macroeconomics* 14, no. 4 (2022): 438–78.

12. Carolyn J. Hill, Harry J. Holzer, and Henry Chen, *Against the Tide: Household Structure, Opportunities, and Outcomes among White and Minority Youth*. Kalamazoo, MI: W. E. Upjohn Institute for Employment Research, 2009.

13. Marcia J. Carlson, "Family Structure, Father Involvement, and Adolescent Behavioral Outcomes," *Journal of Marriage and Family* 68, no. 1 (2006): 137–54.

14. Sara McLanahan, Laura Tach, and Daniel Schneider, "The Causal Effects of Father Absence," *Annual Review of Sociology* 39 (2013): 399–427.

15. Melissa S. Kearney and Phillip B. Levine, "The Economics of Nonmarital Childbearing and the Marriage Premium for Children," *Annual Review of Economics* 9, no. 1 (September 2017): 327–52.

16. These statistics come from Kearney and Levine, "Economics of Nonmarital Childbearing," and are based on authors' tabulations of 2013 PSID data. Household income is converted to 2013 dollars for all years using the personal consumption expenditures price index. Income between ages 0 and 16 is the child's annual household income averaged over all available years between those ages, with the median reported. There are 4,983 married mothers and 3,620 unmarried mothers in the analysis sample.

17. Bjorklund-Young reports that data from the Education Longitudinal Survey—a nationally representative sample of students who were high school sophomores in 2002—indicate that among students from the lowest quartile of family income, college completion rates are 14%, as compared to 60% among students from the top quartile of family income; see Alanna Bjorklund-Young, *Family Income and the College Completion Gap* (Baltimore, MD: Johns Hopkins Institute for Education Policy, March 2016), https://jscholarship.library.jhu.edu/bitstream/handle/1774.2/63021/familyincome andcollegegapmastheadfinal.pdf.

18. This data is excerpted from table 5 in Kearney and Levine, "Economics of Nonmarital Childbearing."

19. Christina J. Cross, "Racial/Ethnic Differences in the Association between Family Structure and Children's Education," *Journal of Marriage and Family* 81, no. 2 (2020): 691–712.

20. Anne Case and Christina Paxson, "Mothers and Others: Who Invests in Children's Health?" *Journal of Health Economics* 20, no. 3 (May 2001): 301–28.

21. Carlson, "Family Structure, Father Involvement, and Adolescent Behavioral Outcomes."

22. Paul R. Amato, "The Impact of Family Formation Change on the Cognitive, Social, and Emotional Well-Being of the Next Generation," *Future of Children* 15, no. 2 (2005): 75–96.

23. Wendy D. Manning, Marshall N. Fettro, and Esther Lamidi, "Child Well-Being in Same-Sex Parent Families: Review of Research Prepared for American Sociological Association Amicus Brief," *Population Research Policy Review* 33, no. 4 (2014): 485–502. For a review of the social science evidence on same-sex parenting and family formation, also see Corinne Reczek, "Sexual- and Gender-Minority Families: A 2010 to 2020 Decade in Review," *Journal of Marriage and Family* 82, no. 1 (2020): 300–325; William Meezan and Jonathan Rauch, "Gay Marriage, Same-Sex Parenting, and America's Children," *Future of Children* 15, no. 2 (2005): 97–115; and Dan Black, Seth G. Sanders, and Lowell J. Taylor, "The Economics of Lesbian and Gay Families," *Journal of Economic Perspectives* 21, no. 2 (2007): 53–70.

24. Samuel Norris, Matthew Pecenco, and Jeffrey Weaver, "The Effects of Parental and Sibling Incarceration: Evidence from Ohio," *American Economic Review* 111, no. 9 (2021): 2926–63; Carolina Arteaga, "Parental Incarceration and Children's Educational Attainment," *Review of Economics and Statistics*, published ahead of print, October 15, 2021, https://doi.org/10.1162/rest_a_01129.

Chapter Four

1. Claudia Goldin. "The Quiet Revolution That Transformed Women's Employment, Education, and Family," *American Economic Association Papers and Proceedings* 96, no. 2 (2006): 1–21.

2. "Tenement Apartment Tours," Tenement Museum, accessed November 7, 2022, https://www.tenement.org/apartment-tours/.

3. Published in 2012 by political scientist Charles Murray, the book *Coming Apart: The State of White America 1960–2010* (New York: Crown Forum) describes the cultural divergence of Americans across education and income lines. That book's focus on White Americans emphasizes class differences, as separate from racial differences. Like Murray's book, this book shines a spotlight on the divergence in marriage rates between college-educated and non-college-educated Americans. Unlike Murray's book, this book presents trends in family structure in terms of what they mean for children and the intergenerational transmission of economic advantage or disadvantage.

4. William Julius Wilson, *The Truly Disadvantaged: The Inner City, the Underclass, and Public Policy* (Chicago: University of Chicago Press, 1987).

5. William Raspberry, "The Men Aren't There to Marry," *Washington Post*, May 8, 1985,

https://www.washingtonpost.com/archive/politics/1985/05/08/the-men-arent-there-to-marry/480cfbc7-3ff2-46f8-8a5f-54d4bf18100d/.

6. Kathryn Edin and Maria Kefalas, *Promises I Can Keep: Why Poor Women Put Motherhood before Marriage* (Berkeley: University of California Press, 2005).

7. J. D. Vance, *Hillbilly Elegy: A Memoir of a Family and Culture in Crisis* (New York: Harper, 2016): 144.

8. The stubbornness of this "gender wage gap" is the subject of numerous articles! Suffice it to say there are a variety of explanations for this gap, including women tending to work in lower-paying occupations, women tending to take more time off from work (typically to care for family members), and straight-up discrimination against women, among other factors.

9. Marianne Bertrand, Emir Kamenica, and Jessica Pan, "Gender Identity and Relative Income within Households," *Quarterly Journal of Economics* 130, no. 2 (May 2015): 571–614.

10. David Autor, David Dorn, and Gordon Hanson, "When Work Disappears: Manufacturing Decline and the Falling Marriage-Market Value of Men," *American Economic Review Insights* 1, no. 2 (2019): 161–78.

11. Massimo Anelli, Osea Giuntella, and Luca Stella, "Robots, Marriageable Men, Family, and Fertility," *Journal of Human Resources*, published ahead of print, November 15, 2021, https://doi.org/10.3368/jhr.1020-11223R1.

12. Andrew J. Cherlin, David Ribar, and Suzumi Yasutake, "Nonmarital First Births, Marriage, and Income Inequality," *American Sociological Review* 81, no. 4 (2016): 749–70.

13. Eric Gould, "Torn Apart? The Impact of Manufacturing Employment Decline on Black and White Americans," *Review of Economics and Statistics* 103, no. 4 (2021): 770–85.

14. Kerwin Kofi Charles and Ching-Ming Luoh, "Male Incarceration, the Marriage Market, and Female Outcomes," *Review of Economics and Statistics* 92 (August 2010): 614–27.

15. Gary S. Becker, "A Theory of Marriage," in *Economics of the Family: Marriage, Children, and Human Capital*, edited by Theodore Shultz (Chicago: University of Chicago Press, 1974): 299–351.

16. Martin Browning, Francois Bourguignon, Pierre A. Chiappori, and Valerie Lechene, "Income and Outcomes: A Structural Model of Intrahousehold Allocation," *Journal of Political Economy* 102 (1994): 1067–96.

17. Na'ama Shenhav, "Lowering Standards to Wed? Spouse Quality, Marriage, and Labor Market Responses to the Gender Wage Gap," *Review of Economics and Statistics* 103, no. 2 (2021): 265–79.

18. Melissa S. Kearney and Riley Wilson, "Male Earnings, Marriageable Men, and Non-Marital Fertility: Evidence from the Fracking Boom," *Review of Economics and Statistics* 100, no. 4 (October 2018): 678–90.

19. The local-area unit we use is a census PUMA (Public Use Microdata Areas); these are geographically contiguous, they cover the entire US, and they are defined to contain at least 100,000 people. In the years we study, 611 PUMA in the United States—out of a total of 2,057—had positive fracking production from new wells.

20. For instance, research has shown that increases in housing wealth, driven by aggregate increases in house prices, lead homeowners to have more kids. This correlation is shown in a 2014 research paper written by economist Lisa Dettling and me and a 2013 paper by economists Mike Lovenheim and Kevin Mumford. A 2010 paper by economist Jason Lindo shows that when a husband loses his job, he and his wife subsequently have fewer kids.

21. The astute reader might suspect that the lack of marriage is because many of the men working in fracking jobs were migrants who were not local to the area. The influx of migrant workers to fracking jobs is really a story of North Dakota and nearby areas. We exclude North Dakota from our analysis, because of its unique experience with fracking and migrant workers. Think about fracking in Texas, Oklahoma, Pennsylvania, and Colorado, among other states throughout the country. Here, the fracking boom was not associated with a large influx of migrants, but rather with an increase in jobs and earnings and income for the local population.

22. Dan Black, Natalia Kolesnikova, Seth Sanders, and Lowell J. Taylor, "Are Children 'Normal'?" *Review of Economics and Statistics* 95, no. 1 (2013): 21–33.

23. See James Ziliak. "Temporary Assistance for Needy Families," in *Economics of Means-Tested Transfer Programs*, vol. 1, edited by Robert Moffitt (Chicago: University of Chicago Press, 2015): 303–93.

24. Robert A. Moffitt, "The Effect of Welfare on Marriage and Fertility," In *Welfare, the Family, and Reproductive Behavior: Research Perspectives*, edited by Robert A. Moffitt and National Research Council (US) Committee on Population (Washington, DC: National Academies Press (US), 1998), https://www.ncbi.nlm.nih.gov/books/NBK230345/.

25. Personal Responsibility and Work Opportunity Reconciliation Act of 1996, Pub. L. No. 104-193, 110 Stat. 2105 (1996), https://www.congress.gov/104/plaws/publ193/PLAW -104publ193.pdf.

26. See Ziliak, "Temporary Assistance for Needy Families," for a review of what has happened to AFDC/TANF caseloads between 1970 and 2012.

27. A comprehensive review of the research on the effects of welfare reform, conducted in 2005 by Jeffrey Grogger and Lynn Karoly, does not find compelling evidence in favor of the idea that welfare reform had an appreciable effect on marriage or fertility. See Jeffrey Grogger and Lynn Karoly, *Welfare Reform: Effects of a Decade of Change* (Cambridge, MA: Harvard University Press, 2005).

Chapter Five

1. In this government report, "middle income" is defined as having a before-tax household income between $59,200 and $107,400.

2. More than 80% of single-parent families are in this lower-income group; their per-child expenditures were similar to those of married-parent families in this lower-income group.

3. These estimates are taken from Mark Lino, Kevin Kuczynski, Nestor Rodriguez, and

Rebecca Schap, *Expenditures on Children, by Families, 2015*. Miscellaneous Report no. 1528–2015 (Washington, DC: United States Department of Agriculture, Center for Nutrition Policy and Promotion, January 2017, revised March 2017). The report is based on data from the 2011–15 Consumer Expenditure Survey–Interview (CE), administered by the US Census Bureau and the US Department of Commerce, under contract with the Bureau of Labor Statistics (BLS) at the US Department of Labor. This survey is the most comprehensive source of information on household expenditures available at the national level. The sample consisted of 23,297 married-couple households and 7,030 single-parent households and was weighted to reflect the US population of interest by using BLS weighting methods. The authors of this report allocated household expenditures to children as follows: child-specific expenses were allocated directly to children; food and health care expenses were allocated to children based on findings from federal surveys on children's budget shares; family-related transportation expenses and miscellaneous expenses were allocated by using a per-capita method.

4. Sabino Kornrich and Frank Furstenberg, "Investing in Children: Changes in Parental Spending on Children, 1972–2007," *Demography* 50, no. 1 (2013): 1–23.

5. A 2011 paper by Neeraj Kaushal, Katharine Magnuson, and Jane Waldfogel found a similar result about current period gaps using data from the 1997–2006 years of the Consumer Expenditure Survey. They document that the share of total family expenditures devoted to enrichment rises with each quintile of expenditures. Families in the bottom quintile allocate 3% of their total expenditures to enrichment items while families in the top two quintiles spend 9% on items of child enrichment. The gap in absolute dollars is even wider. See Neeraj Kaushal, Katherine Magnuson, and Jane Waldfogel. "How Is Family Income Related to Investments in Children's Learning?," in *Whither Opportunity? Rising Inequality, Schools, and Children's Life Chances*, eds. G. J. Duncan and R. M. Murnane (New York: Russell Sage Foundation, 2011): 187–206.

6. This survey was conducted among 1,807 US parents with children under age 18. Pew Research Center, *Parenting in America: Outlook, Worries, Aspirations are Strongly Linked to Financial Situation* (Washington, DC: Pew Research Center, 2015), https://assets.pew research.org/wp-content/uploads/sites/3/2015/12/2015-12-17_parenting-in-america _FINAL.pdf.

7. Anamarie A. Whitaker, Garrett Baker, Luke J. Matthews, Jennifer Sloan McCombs, and Mark Barrett, *Who Plays, Who Pays? Funding for and Access to Youth Sports* (Santa Monica, CA: RAND Corporation, 2019), https://www.rand.org/pubs/research_reports/RR2581 .html.

8. Jonathan Guryan, Erik Hurst, and Melissa S. Kearney, "Parental Education and Parental Time with Children," *Journal of Economic Perspectives* 22, no. 3 (2008): 23–46.

9. This gap is shown in the following paper: Ariel Kalil, Rebecca Ryan, and Michael Corey, "Diverging Destinies: Maternal Education and the Development Gradient in Time with Children," *Demography* 49, no. 4 (2012): 1361–83.

10. The analysis sample used for this chapter includes adults between the ages of 21 and 55 with at least one child under age 18, and who had a complete 24-hour time diary.

This nationally representative sample includes 1,552 mothers and 1,187 fathers. "Total childcare" is defined as the sum of four primary time use components. Basic childcare is time spent on the basic needs of children, including breastfeeding, rocking a child to sleep, general feeding, changing diapers, providing medical care (either directly or indirectly), grooming, and so on. (Meal preparation is not counted as childcare, but instead home production.) Educational childcare is time spent reading to children, teaching children, helping children with homework, attending meetings at a child's school, and similar activities. Recreational childcare includes playing games with children, playing outdoors with children, attending a child's sporting event or dance recital, going to the zoo with children, and taking walks with children. Travel childcare is any travel related to any of the three other categories of childcare. For example, driving a child to school, to a doctor, or to dance practice are all included in travel childcare.

11. Ariel Kalil, Rebecca Ryan, and Elise Chor, "Time Investments in Children across Family Structures," *Annals of the American Academy of Political and Social Science* 654, no. 1 (2014): 150–68.

12. Sean F. Reardon, "The Widening Socioeconomic Status Achievement Gap: New Evidence and Possible Explanations," in Duncan and Murnane, eds., *Whither Opportunity?*.

13. Sean F. Reardon and Ximena A. Portilla, "Recent Trends in Income, Racial, and Ethnic School Readiness Gaps at Kindergarten Entry," *AERA Open* 2, no. 3 (July 2016).

14. Joseph Price and Ariel Kalil, "The Effect of Mother-Child Reading Time on Children's Reading Skills: Evidence from Natural Within-Family Variation," *Child Development* 90, no. 6 (2019): 688–702.

15. Mario Fiorini and Michael P. Keane, "How the Allocation of Children's Time Affects Cognitive and Noncognitive Development," *Journal of Labor Economics* 32, no. 4 (2014): 787–836.

16. Annette Lareau, *Unequal Childhoods* (Berkeley: University of California Press, 2003).

17. Garey Ramey and Valerie A. Ramey, "The Rug Rat Race," *Brookings Papers on Economic Activity, Economic Studies Program* 41, no. 1 (Spring 2010): 129–99.

18. Mattias Doepke and Fabrizio Zilibotti, *Love, Money, and Parenting: How Economics Explains the Way We Raise Our Kids* (Princeton, NJ: Princeton University Press, 2019).

19. Eric Dearing, Kathleen McCartney, and Beck A. Taylor, "Within-Child Associations between Family Income and Externalizing and Internalizing Problems," *Developmental Psychology* 42, no. 2 (2006): 237–52.

20. Jason Lindo, Jessamyn Schaller, and Benjamin Hansen, "Caution! Men Not at Work: Gender-Specific Labor Market Conditions and Child Maltreatment," *Journal of Public Economics* 163 (2018): 77–98.

21. Anandi Mani, Sendhil Mullainathan, Eldar Shafir, and Jiaying Zhao, "Poverty Impedes Cognitive Function," *Science* 341, no. 6149 (2013): 976–80.

22. US Department of Health and Human Services, Office of Child Care, "Home Visiting," last updated May 19, 2022, https://www.acf.hhs.gov/occ/home-visiting.

23. Ariel Kalil and Rebecca Ryan, "Parenting Practices and Socioeconomic Gaps in Childhood Outcomes," *Future of Children* 30, no. 1 (Spring 2020): 29–54.

24. Susan Mayer, Ariel Kalil, Philip Oreopoulos, and Sebastian Gallegos, "Using Behavioral Insights to Increase Parental Engagement: The Parents and Children Together Intervention," *Journal of Human Resources* 54, no. 4 (2019): 900–925.

25. William N. Evans and Craig L. Garthwaite, "Giving Mom a Break: The Impact of Higher EITC Payments on Maternal Health," *American Economic Journal: Economic Policy* 6, no. 2 (2014): 258–90.

Chapter Six

1. Barack Obama, Father's Day speech, Apostolic Church of God, Chicago, IL, June 15, 2008, https://www.politico.com/story/2008/06/text-of-obamas-fatherhood-speech -011094.

2. These statistics are obtained from the US Department of Education, Office for Civil Rights, Civil Rights Data Collection, "2013–14 Discipline Estimations by Discipline Type" and "2013–14 Estimations for Enrollment," in National Center for Education Statistics, "Percentage of Students Receiving Selected Disciplinary Actions in Public Elementary and Secondary Schools, by Type of Disciplinary Action, Disability Status, Sex, and Race/Ethnicity: 2013–14," *Digest of Education Statistics*, table 233.28, January 2018, https://nces.ed.gov/programs/digest/d19/tables/dt19_233.28.asp.

3. These statistics were estimated by the author using 2019 American Community Survey data weighted by individual survey weights.

4. Marianne Bertrand and Jessica Pan, "The Trouble with Boys: Social Influences and the Gender Gap in Disruptive Behavior," *American Economic Journal: Applied Economics* 5, no. 1 (2013): 32–64.

5. David Autor, David Figlio, Krzysztof Karbownik, Jeffrey Roth, and Melanie Wasserman, "Family Disadvantage and the Gender Gap in Behavioral and Educational Outcomes," *American Economic Journal: Applied Economics* 11, no. 3 (July 2019): 338–81.

6. Kerwin Kofi Charles and Ming Ching Luoh, "Male Incarceration, the Marriage Market, and Female Outcomes," *Review of Economics and Statistics* 92, no. 3 (August 2010): 614–27.

7. Raj Chetty, Nathaniel Hendren, Maggie R. Jones, and Sonya R. Porter, "Race and Economic Opportunity in the United States: An Intergenerational Perspective," *Quarterly Journal of Economics* 135, no. 2 (May 2020): 711–83.

8. Katie Kindelan, "Dads Form 'Dad's on Duty' Squad to Help Stop Violence at Their Kids' High School," *Good Morning America*, October 27, 2021, https://www.goodmorning america.com/family/story/dads-form-dads-duty-squad-stop-violence-kids-8078 7546.

9. Kindelan, "Dads Form 'Dad's on Duty' Squad."

10. Price V. Fishback, Jessica LaVoice, Allison Shertzer, and Randall Walsh, "The HOLC Maps: How Race and Poverty Influenced Real Estate Professionals' Evaluation of Lending Risk in the 1930s," NBER Working Paper no. 28146 (Cambridge, MA: National Bureau of Economic Research, November 2020), https://www.nber.org/papers/w28146.

11. US Department of Health and Human Services, Office of Family Assistance, "About

Healthy Marriage and Responsible Fatherhood," updated April 8, 2021, https://www.acf.hhs.gov/ofa/programs/healthy-marriage/about.

12. Sarah Avellar, Reginald Covington, Quinn Moore, Ankita Patnaik, and April Wu, *Parents and Children Together: Effects of Four Responsible Fatherhood Programs for Low-Income Fathers*. OPRE report no. 2018–50 (Washington, DC: Office of Planning, Research, and Evaluation, Administration for Children and Families, US Department of Health and Human Services, 2018).

13. Nicholas Eberstadt, *Men without Work* (West Conshohocken, PA: Templeton Press, 2016).

14. Statistics reported in Melissa S. Kearney and Phillip B. Levine, "Role Models, Mentors, and Media Effects," *Future of Children* 30, no. 1 (June 2020): 83–106. We generate these statistics using census-tract-level data from the 2011–15 American Community Survey. We define "low-income" to be having family income below the poverty line and "high-income" as having family income at least five times greater than the federal poverty line. We constructed the "typical" child by taking the population-weighted average of different census-tract characteristics across the country within each income category.

15. Tara Watson, "Inequality and the Measurement of Residential Segregation by Income in American Neighborhoods," *Review of Income and Wealth* 55, no. 3 (2009): 820–44.

16. For a review of this evidence, see Kearney and Levine, "Role Models, Mentors, and Media Effects."

17. For instance, see the "Resilience" guide provided by the Center on the Developing Child, Harvard University: https://developingchild.harvard.edu/science/key-concepts/resilience/, accessed July 20, 2021.

18. Mary Bruce and John Bridgeland, *The Mentoring Effect: Young People's Perspectives on the Outcomes and Availability of Mentoring* (Washington, DC: Civic Enterprises with Hart Research Associates for MENTOR: the National Mentoring Partnership, 2014).

19. For a more thorough review of mentoring programs and evaluations, see Phillip B. Levine, "Designing Effective Mentoring Programs for Disadvantaged Youth," in *Policies to Address Poverty in America*, eds. Melissa S. Kearney and Benjamin Harris (Washington, DC: Hamilton Project, 2014): 47–54.

20. Jessica Mitchell, *2019 Big Brothers Big Sisters of America Annual Impact Report* (Cincinnati, OH: Big Brothers Big Sisters of America, May 2020), https://www.bbbs.org/wp-content/uploads/2019-BBBSA-Annual-Impact-Report-FINAL.pdf.

21. Joseph P. Tierney, Jean B. Grossman, and Nancy L. Resch, *Making a Difference: An Impact Study of Big Brothers/Big Sisters* (Philadelphia, PA: Public/Private Ventures, 1995).

22. George W. Bush, "National Mentoring Month, 2002: A Proclamation by the President of the United States of America," Office of the Press Secretary, January 18, 2002, https://georgewbush-whitehouse.archives.gov/news/releases/2002/01/20020118-3.html.

23. Big Brothers Big Sisters of America, "Get Involved," accessed March 10, 2021, https://www.bbbs.org/get-involved/.

24. See Erick Trickey, "What Works: Group Therapy Is Saving Lives in Chicago," *Politico*, September 21, 2017, https://www.politico.com/magazine/story/2017/09/21/chicago-violence-crime-psychology-cognitive-behavioral-therapy-215633/.

25. Trickey, "What Works: Group Therapy Is Saving Lives in Chicago."

26. Sara B. Heller, Anuj K. Shah, Jonathan Guryan, Jens Ludwig, Sendhil Mullainathan, and Harold A. Pollack, "Thinking, Fast and Slow? Some Field Experiments to Reduce Crime and Dropout in Chicago," *Quarterly Journal of Economics* 132, no. 1 (February 2017): 1–54.

27. Trickey, "What Works: Group Therapy Is Saving Lives in Chicago." In 2017, the My Brother's Keeper (MBK) Alliance became an initiative of the Obama Foundation, per MBK Alliance, "We Are Our Brothers' Keepers," Obama Foundation, accessed April 14, 2021, https://www.obama.org/mbka/.

28. Youth Guidance, *Annual Report 2018–2019* (Chicago: Youth Guidance, 2020), https://www.youth-guidance.org/wp-content/uploads/2022/11/Youth-Guidance-Annual-Report-2018-2019.pdf.

29. The emphasis on boys in the chapter is not intended to obscure or leave unacknowledged the concurrent, albeit different, struggles of girls. Compared to boys today, girls are less likely to exhibit the types of outward-directed behavioral problems that are referred to as externalizing behaviors. This means they are less likely to get in trouble in school or with the law—but it doesn't mean they aren't suffering. Girls are more likely to turn their struggles inward, a tendency that has been acknowledged by a sister program to BAM called Working on Womanhood (WOW). Founded in 2011 in Chicago by a group of female social workers led by WOW director Gail Day, the program is a multifaceted, school-year-long group counseling and clinical mentoring program that aims to improve social-emotional competencies for girls in seventh through twelfth grades who have been exposed to traumatic stressors in high-risk and under-resourced communities. At the time of writing, the University of Chicago Urban Labs is conducting an evaluation of WOW.

Chapter Seven

1. "Study Finds American Women Delaying Motherhood because the Whole Thing Blows," *Onion*, June 18, 2021, https://www.theonion.com/study-finds-american-women-delaying-motherhood-because-1847112786.

2. William Jefferson Clinton, "Statement on Teen Pregnancy," White House Office of the Press Secretary, January 29, 1996, https://clintonwhitehouse4.archives.gov/WH/New/other/preg.html.

3. William Jefferson Clinton, State of the Union address, US Capitol, Washington, DC, January 23, 1996, https://clintonwhitehouse4.archives.gov/WH/New/other/sotu.html.

4. The two main sources of data on abortions in the US (neither of which is complete) both show sizable declines in the US abortion rate. The Guttmacher Institute reports that in 2020 there were 14.4 abortions per 1,000 women ages 15 to 44, down from 29.3 abortions per 1,000 women in 1981. The CDC reports that in 2019, there were 11.4 abortions in the US per 1,000 women ages 15 to 44, down from 25 abortions per 1,000 women in 1980, per Jeff Diamant and Besheer Mohamed, "What the Data Says about Abortion in the U.S.," Pew Research Center, June 24, 2022, https://www.pewresearch.org/fact-tank/2022/06/24/what-the-data-says-about-abortion-in-the-u-s-2/.

5. See Melissa S. Kearney and Phillip B. Levine, "Causes and Consequences of Declining

US Fertility," Aspen Economic Strategy Group, August 13, 2022, https://www.economic strategygroup.org/publication/Kearney_Levine/.

6. "Study Finds American Women Delaying Motherhood because the Whole Thing Blows," *Onion*.

7. Melissa S. Kearney and Phillip B. Levine, "Investigating Recent Trends in the U.S. Teen Birth Rates," *Journal of Health Economics* 41 (2015): 15–29.

8. Joyce C. Abma and Gladys M Martinez, "Sexual Activity and Contraceptive Use among Teenagers in the United States, 2011–2015," *National Health Statistics Report* 104 (June 2017): 1–23, https://pubmed.ncbi.nlm.nih.gov/28696201/.

9. Kearney and Levine, "Investigating Recent Trends in the U.S. Teen Birth Rates."

10. A 2017 paper by Jason Lindo and Annalisa Packham found that Colorado's $23 million Family Planning initiative, launched in 2009, which expanded access to LARCs, led to a 6.4% reduction over five years in teen birth rates in the counties with funded clinics. This study demonstrates that expanded access to LARCs can have a substantial effect on teen birth rates, but large-scale initiatives like this have not occurred in large number around the country and cannot explain a meaningful share of the aggregate trend. See Jason M. Lindo and Analisa Packham, "How Much Can Expanding Access to Long-Acting Reversible Contraceptives Reduce Teen Birth Rates?" *American Economic Journal: Economic Policy* 9, no. 3 (2017): 348–76.

11. Melissa S. Kearney and Phillip B. Levine, "Media Influences on Social Outcomes: The Impact of MTV's *16 and Pregnant* on Teen Childbearing," *American Economic Review* 105, no. 12 (2015): 3597–632.

12. Bill Albert, *With One Voice 2010: America's Adults and Teens Sound Off about Teen Pregnancy* (Washington, DC: National Campaign to Prevent Teen and Unplanned Pregnancy, 2010).

13. To address the possibility that the appeal of a show about teen pregnancy might be correlated with teen birth-rate trends, we implemented what econometrics refer to as an instrumental variables (IV) strategy, predicting *16 and Pregnant* ratings with a broad measure of MTV ratings from a previous period. The identifying assumption of this econometric approach is that MTV ratings in the period before the show aired would be unrelated to subsequent trends in teen childbearing, but for the introduction of the *16 and Pregnant* content.

14. See, for instance, Melissa S. Kearney and Phillip Levine, "Income Inequality and Early, Non-Marital Childbearing," *Journal of Human Resources* 49 (Winter 2014): 1–31.

Chapter Eight

1. For a review of the evidence on this claim, see Melissa S. Kearney and Phillip Levine, "Role Models, Mentors, and Media Influences," *Future of Children* 30 (June 2020): 83–106.

2. Eliana La Ferrara, Alberto Chong, and Suzanne Duryea, "Soap Operas and Fertility: Evidence from Brazil," *American Economic Journal: Applied Economics* 4, no. 4 (2012): 1–31; and Alberto Chong and Eliana La Ferrara, "Television and Divorce: Evidence from Brazilian *Novelas*," *Journal of the European Economic Association* 7 (2009): 458–68.

3. Kathryn Edin and Maria Kefalas, *Promises I Can Keep: Why Poor Women Put Motherhood before Marriage* (Berkeley: University of California Press, 2005).

4. Sarah Halpern-Meekin, *Social Poverty: Low-Income Parents and the Struggle for Family and Community Ties* (New York: New York University Press, 2019).

5. See Katharine Abraham and Melissa S. Kearney, "Explaining the Decline in the U.S. Employment-to-Population Ratio: A Review of the Evidence," *Journal of Economic Literature* 58, no. 3 (September 2020): 585–643.

6. See, for example, Daron Acemoglu and David Autor, "Skills, Tasks and Technologies: Implications for Employment and Earnings," *Handbook of Labor Economics* 4 (2011): 1043–171; Nicole M. Fortin, Thomas Lemieux, and Neil Lloyd, "Labor Market Institutions and the Distribution of Wages: The Role of Spillover Effects," *Journal of Labor Economics* 39, no. S2 (2021): S369–S412; Henry S. Farber, Daniel Herbst, Ilyana Kuziemko, and Suresh Naidu, "Unions and Inequality over the Twentieth Century: New Evidence from Survey Data," *Quarterly Journal of Economics* 136, no. 3 (2021): 1325–85.

7. The 2019 Aspen Economic Strategy Group annual policy volume contains policy proposals along these various lines. See Melissa S. Kearney and Amy Ganz, eds., *Expanding Economic Opportunity for More Americans: Bipartisan Policies to Increase Work, Wages, and Skills* (Aspen, CO: Aspen Institute Economic Strategy Group, February 2019), https://www.economicstrategygroup.org/publication/expanding-economic-opportunity-for-more-americans-copy/.

8. Researchers at MDRC conducted an RCT evaluation beginning in 2003 of the Supporting Healthy Marriage (SHM) program in eight locations around the country. The SHM program was a voluntary, yearlong program consisting primarily of a series of relationship- and marriage-education workshops, which provided a total of 24–30 hours of established curriculum lessons. Workshop topics included strategies for managing conflict, communicating effectively, increasing supportive behaviors, and building closeness, among others. The SHM program also offered supplementary social and educational events, as well as family support services that paired couples with a specialized staff member who maintained contact with them and connected participants with other services as needed. The RCT evaluation revealed that two years after program initiation, couples who stayed together reported higher levels of marital happiness and lower levels of marital distress. Women who attended the program reported having reduced feelings of sadness and anxiety. But couples who were randomly assigned to participate in the SHM program did not stay together at a higher rate than couples in the control group: 18% of the couples were no longer married or in a committed relationship at the 30-month follow-up, in both the treatment and control groups. See Erika Lundquist, JoAnn Hsueh, Amy E. Lowenstein, Kristen Faucetta, Daniel Gubits, Charles Michalopoulos, and Virginia Knox, *A Family-Strengthening Program for Low-Income Families: Final Impacts from the Supporting Healthy Marriage Evaluation*, OPRE report 2014–09A (Washington, DC: Office of Planning, Research and Evaluation, Administration for Children and Families, US Department of Health and Human Services, 2014).

9. For more information about the program's model, implementation, and mixed evidence of success across studies and implementation settings, see US Department of Health

and Human Services, Administration for Children and Families, "Home Visiting Evidence of Effectiveness," accessed November 15, 2022, https://homvee.acf.hhs.gov.

10. See the study of one such program by Susan E. Mayer, Ariel Kalil, Philip Oreopoulos, and Sebastian Gallegos, "Using Behavioral Insights to Increase Parental Engagement," *Journal of Human Resources* 54, no. 4 (2019): 900–925.

11. Hilary Hoynes, Doug Miller, and David Simon, "Income, the Earned Income Tax Credit, and Infant Health," *American Journal of Economics* 7, no. 1 (2015): 172–211; William N. Evans and Craig L. Garthwaite, "Giving Mom a Break: The Impact of Higher EITC Payments on Maternal Health," *American Economic Journal: Economic Policy* 6, no. 2 (2014): 258–90.

12. A 2012 study by Dahl and Lochner looked at what happened when changes in the EITC formula led to some families getting more income in a year. The researchers found that a $1,000 increase in household income due to an EITC change raised standardized math and reading test scores by 6% of a standard deviation, with the largest gains for children from more disadvantaged families, younger children, and boys. See Gordon B. Dahl and Lance Lochner, "The Impact of Family Income on Child Achievement: Evidence from the Earned Income Tax Credit," *American Economic Review* 102, no. 5 (August 2012): 1927–56. A 2019 study by Manoli and Turner found that children from low-income families who received additional EITC income during the spring of their senior year of high school (because of peculiarities in the tax credit formula) were more likely to enroll in college. It seems that the extra cash on hand enabled some families who would not have otherwise been able to afford to send their child to college to do so. See Day Manoli and Nicholas Turner, "Cash-On-Hand and College Enrollment: Evidence from Population Tax Data and the Earned Income Tax Credit," *American Economic Journal: Economic Policy* 10, no. 2 (2018): 242–71.

13. Randall Akee, William E. Copeland, Gordon Keeler, Adrian Angold, and E. Jane Costello, "Parents' Incomes and Children's Outcomes: A Quasi-Experiment Using Transfer Payments from Casino Profits," *American Economic Journal: Applied Economics* 2, no. 1 (January 2010): 86–115; Randall Akee, William Copeland, E. Jane Costello, and Emilia Simeonova, "How Does Household Income Affect Child Personality Traits and Behaviors?" *American Economic Review* 108, no. 3 (2018): 775–827.

14. For instance, see Hilary Hoynes, Diane Whitmore Schanzenbach, and Douglas Almond, "Long-Run Impacts of Childhood Access to the Safety Net," *American Economic Review* 106, no. 4 (2016): 903–34; Martha J. Bailey, Hilary W. Hoynes, Maya Rossin-Slater, and Reed Walker, "Is the Social Safety Net a Long-Term Investment? Large-Scale Evidence from the Food Stamps Program," NBER Working Paper no. 26942 (Cambridge, MA: National Bureau of Economic Research, April 2020), https://www.nber.org/papers /w26942; Sarah Miller and Laura R. Wherry, "The Long-Term Effects of Early Life Medicaid Coverage," *Journal of Human Resources* 54, no. 3 (2019): 785–824; David Brown, Amanda Kowalski, and Itahai Lurie, "Long-Term Impacts of Childhood Medicaid Expansions on Outcomes in Adulthood," *Review of Economic Studies* 87, no. 2 (March 2020): 792–821.

15. See, for instance, Jens Ludwig and Douglas L. Miller, "Does Head Start Improve

Children's Life Chances? Evidence from a Regression Discontinuity Design," *Quarterly Journal of Economics* 122, no. 1 (2007): 159–208; Rucker Johnson and C. Kirabo Jackson, "Reducing Inequality through Dynamic Complementarity: Evidence from Head Start and Public School Spending," *American Economic Journal: Economic Policy* 11, no. 4 (2019): 310–49; Owen Thompson, "Head Start's Long-Run Impact: Evidence from the Program's Introduction," *Journal of Human Resources* 53, no. 4 (2018): 1100–1139.

16. James Heckman and Rasmus Landersø, "Lessons for Americans from Denmark about Inequality and Social Mobility," *Labour Economics* 77 (August 2022).

References

Abma, Joyce C., and Gladys M. Martinez. "Sexual Activity and Contraceptive Use among Teenagers in the United States, 2011–2015." *National Health Statistics Report* 104 (June 2017): 1–23. https://pubmed.ncbi.nlm.nih.gov/28696201/.

Abraham, Katharine, and Melissa S. Kearney. "Explaining the Decline in the U.S. Employment-to-Population Ratio: A Review of the Evidence." *Journal of Economic Literature* 58, no. 3 (September 2020): 585–643.

Acemoglu, Daron, and David Autor. "Skills, Tasks and Technologies: Implications for Employment and Earnings." *Handbook of Labor Economics* 4 (2011): 1043–171.

Akee, Randall, William Copeland, E. Jane Costello, and Emilia Simeonova. "How Does Household Income Affect Child Personality Traits and Behaviors?" *American Economic Review* 108, no. 3 (2018): 775–827.

Akee, Randall, William E. Copeland, Gordon Keeler, Adrian Angold, and E. Jane Costello. "Parents' Incomes and Children's Outcomes: A Quasi-Experiment Using Transfer Payments from Casino Profits." *American Economic Journal: Applied Economics* 2, no. 1 (January 2010): 86–115.

Albert, Bill. *With One Voice 2010: America's Adults and Teens Sound Off about Teen Pregnancy*. Washington, DC: National Campaign to Prevent Teen and Unplanned Pregnancy, 2010.

Amato, Paul R. "The Impact of Family Formation Change on the Cognitive, Social, and Emotional Well-Being of the Next Generation." *Future of Children* 15, no. 2 (2005): 75–96.

Ananat, Elizabeth, and Guy Michaels. "The Effect of Marital Breakup on the Income Distribution of Women with Children." *Journal of Human Resources* 43, no. 3 (2008): 611–29.

Anelli, Massimo, Osea Giuntella, and Luca Stella. "Robots, Marriageable Men, Family, and Fertility." *Journal of Human Resources*. Published ahead of print, November 15, 2021. https://doi.org/10.3368/jhr.1020-11223R1.

Arteaga, Carolina. "Parental Incarceration and Children's Educational Attainment." *Review of Economics and Statistics*. Published ahead of print, October 15, 2021. https://doi.org /10.1162/rest_a_01129.

Autor, David, David Dorn, and Gordon Hanson. "When Work Disappears: Manufacturing Decline and the Falling Marriage-Market Value of Men." *American Economic Review Insights* 1, no. 2 (September 2019): 161–78.

Autor, David, David Figlio, Krzysztof Karbownik, Jeffrey Roth, and Melanie Wasserman. "Family Disadvantage and the Gender Gap in Behavioral and Educational Outcomes." *American Economic Journal: Applied Economics* 11, no. 3 (July 2019): 338–81.

Avellar, Sarah, Reginald Covington, Quinn Moore, Ankita Patnaik, and April Wu. *Parents and Children Together: Effects of Four Responsible Fatherhood Programs for Low-Income Fathers*. OPRE report no. 2018–50. Washington, DC: Office of Planning, Research, and Evaluation, Administration for Children and Families, US Department of Health and Human Services, 2018.

Bailey, Martha J., Hilary W. Hoynes, Maya Rossin-Slater, and Reed Walker. "Is the Social Safety Net a Long-Term Investment? Large-Scale Evidence from the Food Stamps Program." NBER Working Paper no. 26942. Cambridge, MA: National Bureau of Economic Research, April 2020. https://www.nber.org/papers/w26942.

Becker, Gary S. "A Theory of Marriage." In *Economics of the Family: Marriage, Children, and Human Capital*, edited by Theodore Shultz, 299–351. Chicago: University of Chicago Press, 1974.

Becker, Gary S. *A Treatise on the Family*. Cambridge, MA: Harvard University Press, 1981.

Bertrand, Marianne, Emir Kamenica, and Jessica Pan. "Gender Identity and Relative Income within Households." *Quarterly Journal of Economics* 130, no. 2 (May 2015): 571–614.

Bertrand, Marianne, and Jessica Pan. "The Trouble with Boys: Social Influences and the Gender Gap in Disruptive Behavior." *American Economic Journal: Applied Economics* 5, no. 1 (2013): 32–64.

Big Brothers Big Sisters of America. "Get Involved." Accessed March 10, 2021. https://www .bbbs.org/get-involved/.

Bjorklund-Young, Alanna. *Family Income and the College Completion Gap*. Baltimore, MD: Johns Hopkins Institute for Education Policy, March 2016. https://jscholarship.library .jhu.edu/bitstream/handle/1774.2/63021/familyincomeandcollegegapmastheadfinal .pdf.

Black, Dan A., Natalia Kolesnikova, Seth Sanders, and Lowell J. Taylor. "Are Children 'Normal'?" *Review of Economics and Statistics* 95, no. 1 (2013): 21–33.

Black, Dan A., Seth G. Sanders, and Lowell J. Taylor. "The Economics of Lesbian and Gay Families." *Journal of Economic Perspectives* 21, no. 2 (2007): 53–70.

Blandin, Adam, and Christopher Herrington. "Family Heterogeneity, Human Capital Investment, and College Attainment." *American Economic Journal: Macroeconomics* 14, no. 4 (2022): 438–78.

Brown, David, Amanda Kowalski, and Ithai Lurie. "Long-Term Impacts of Childhood Medicaid Expansions on Outcomes in Adulthood." *Review of Economic Studies* 87, no. 2 (March 2020): 792–821.

Brown, Susan L., J. Bart Stykes, and Wendy D. Manning. "Trends in Children's Family Instability, 1995–2010." *Journal of Marriage and Family* 78, no. 5 (2016): 1173–83.

Browning, Martin, Francois Bourguignon, Pierre A. Chiappori, and Valerie Lechene. "Income and Outcomes: A Structural Model of Intrahousehold Allocation." *Journal of Political Economy* 102, no. 6 (1994): 1067–96.

Bruce, Mary, and John Bridgeland. *The Mentoring Effect: Young People's Perspectives on the Outcomes and Availability of Mentoring.* Washington, DC: Civic Enterprises with Hart Research Associates for MENTOR: the National Mentoring Partnership, 2014.

Bush, George W. "National Mentoring Month, 2002: A Proclamation by the President of the United States of America." Office of the Press Secretary, January 18, 2002. https:// georgewbush-whitehouse.archives.gov/news/releases/2002/01/20020118-3.html.

Carlson, Marcia. "Family Structure, Father Involvement, and Adolescent Behavioral Outcomes." *Journal of Marriage and Family* 68, no. 1 (2006): 137–54.

Carlson, Marcia. "Sara McLanahan: Pioneering Scholar Focused on Families and the Wellbeing of Children." *Proceedings of the National Academy of Sciences* 119, no. 16 (April 11, 2022).

Case, Ann, and Angus Deaton. *Deaths of Despair and the Future of Capitalism.* Princeton, NJ: Princeton University Press, 2020.

Case, Anne, and Christina Paxson. "Mothers and Others: Who Invests in Children's Health?" *Journal of Health Economics* 20, no. 3 (May 2001): 301–28.

Charles, Kerwin Kofi, and Ching-Ming Luoh. "Male Incarceration, the Marriage Market, and Female Outcomes." *Review of Economics and Statistics* 92, no. 3 (August 2010): 614–27.

Cherlin, Andrew. "Demographic Trends in the United States: A Review of Research in the 2000s." *Journal of Marriage and Family* 72, no. 3 (June 2010): 403–19.

Cherlin, Andrew J., David Ribar, and Suzumi Yasutake. "Nonmarital First Births, Marriage, and Income Inequality." *American Sociological Review* 81, no. 4 (August 2016): 749–70.

Chetty, Raj, Nathaniel Hendren, Maggie R. Jones, and Sonya R. Porter. "Race and Economic Opportunity in the United States: An Intergenerational Perspective." *Quarterly Journal of Economics* 135, no. 2 (May 2020): 711–83.

Chong, Alberto, and Eliana La Ferrara. "Television and Divorce: Evidence from Brazilian *Novelas.*" *Journal of the European Economic Association* 7 (2009): 458–68.

Clinton, William Jefferson. "Statement on Teen Pregnancy." White House Office of the Press Secretary, January 29, 1996. https://clintonwhitehouse4.archives.gov/WH/New /other/preg.html.

Clinton, William Jefferson. State of the Union address. US Capitol, Washington, DC, January 23, 1996. https://clintonwhitehouse4.archives.gov/WH/New/other/sotu.html.

Cross, Christina J. "Racial/Ethnic Differences in the Association between Family Structure and Children's Education." *Journal of Marriage and Family* 81, no. 2 (2020): 691–712.

Dahl, Gordon B., and Lance Lochner. "The Impact of Family Income on Child Achievement: Evidence from the Earned Income Tax Credit." *American Economic Review* 102, no. 5 (August 2012): 1927–56.

Dearing, Eric, Kathleen McCartney, and Beck A. Taylor. "Within-Child Associations between Family Income and Externalizing and Internalizing Problems." *Developmental Psychology* 42, no. 2 (2006): 237–52.

Dettling, Lisa, and Melissa S. Kearney. "House Prices and Birth Rates: The Impact of the Real Estate Market on the Decision to Have a Baby." *Journal of Public Economics* 110 (2014): 82–100.

Diamant, Jeff, and Besheer Mohamed. "What the Data Says about Abortion in the U.S." Pew Research Center, June 24, 2022. https://www.pewresearch.org/fact-tank/2022/06/24 /what-the-data-says-about-abortion-in-the-u-s-2/.

Doepke, Matthias, and Fabrizio Zilibotti. *Love, Money, and Parenting: How Economics Explains the Way We Raise Our Kids*. Princeton, NJ: Princeton University Press, 2019.

Eberstadt, Nicholas. *Men without Work*. West Conshohocken, PA: Templeton Press, 2016.

Edin, Kathryn, and Maria Kefalas. *Promises I Can Keep: Why Poor Women Put Motherhood before Marriage*. Berkeley: University of California Press, 2005.

Edin, Kathryn, and Timothy J. Nelson. *Doing the Best I Can: Fatherhood in the Inner City*. Berkeley: University of California Press, 2013.

Evans, William N., and Craig L. Garthwaite. "Giving Mom a Break: The Impact of Higher EITC Payments on Maternal Health." *American Economic Journal: Economic Policy* 6, no. 2 (2014): 258–90.

Farber, Henry S., Daniel Herbst, Ilyana Kuziemko, and Suresh Naidu. "Unions and Inequality over the Twentieth Century: New Evidence from Survey Data." *Quarterly Journal of Economics* 136, no. 3 (2021): 1325–85.

Fiorini, Mario, and Michael P. Keane. "How the Allocation of Children's Time Affects Cognitive and Noncognitive Development." *Journal of Labor Economics* 32, no.4 (2014): 787–836.

Fishback, Price V., Jessica LaVoice, Allison Shertzer, and Randall Walsh. "The HOLC Maps: How Race and Poverty Influenced Real Estate Professionals' Evaluation of Lending Risk in the 1930s." NBER Working Paper no. 28146. Cambridge, MA: National Bureau of Economic Research, November 2020. https://www.nber.org/papers/w28146.

Fortin, Nicole M., Thomas Lemieux, and Neil Lloyd. "Labor Market Institutions and the Distribution of Wages: The Role of Spillover Effects." *Journal of Labor Economics* 39, no. S2 (2021): S369–S412.

Garfinkel, Irwin, and Sara S. McLanahan. *Single Mothers and Their Children: A New American Dilemma*. Washington, DC: Urban Institute Press, 1986.

Goldin, Claudia. "The Quiet Revolution That Transformed Women's Employment, Education, and Family." *American Economic Review* 96, no. 2 (2006): 1–21.

Gould, Eric. "Torn Apart? The Impact of Manufacturing Employment Decline on Black and White Americans." *Review of Economics and Statistics* 103, no. 4 (2021): 770–85.

Grall, Timothy. *Custodial Mothers and Fathers and Their Child Support: 2015*. Current Population Reports P60-262. Washington, DC: US Census Bureau, January 2018. https:// www.census.gov/library/publications/2018/demo/p60-262.html.

Grogger, Jeffrey, and Lynn A. Karoly. *Welfare Reform: Effects of a Decade of Change*. Cambridge, MA: Harvard University Press, 2005.

Gruber, Jonathan. "Is Making Divorce Easier Bad for Children? The Long-Run Implications of Unilateral Divorce." *Journal of Labor Economics* 22, no. 4 (2004): 799–833.

Guryan, Jonathan, Erik Hurst, and Melissa S. Kearney. "Parental Education and Parental Time with Children." *Journal of Economic Perspectives* 22, no. 3 (2008): 23–46.

Halpern-Meekin, Sarah. *Social Poverty: Low-Income Parents and the Struggle for Family and Community Ties*. New York: New York University Press, 2019.

Härkönen, Juho. "Diverging Destinies in International Perspective: Education, Single Motherhood, and Child Poverty." LIS Working Paper Series no. 713. Luxembourg: LIS Cross-National Data Center, August 2017. http://www.lisdatacenter.org/wps/liswps/713.pdf.

Heckman, James, and Rasmus Landersø. "Lessons for Americans from Denmark about Inequality and Social Mobility." *Labour Economics* 77 (August 2022).

Heller, Sara B., Anuj K. Shah, Jonathan Guryan, Jens Ludwig, Sendhil Mullainathan, and Harold A. Pollack. "Thinking, Fast and Slow? Some Field Experiments to Reduce Crime and Dropout in Chicago." *Quarterly Journal of Economics* 132, no. 1 (February 2017): 1–54.

Hill, Carolyn J., Harry J. Holzer, and Henry Chen. *Against the Tide: Household Structure, Opportunities, and Outcomes among White and Minority Youth*. Kalamazoo, MI: W. E. Upjohn Institute for Employment Research, 2009.

Hoynes, Hilary, Doug Miller, and David Simon. "Income, the Earned Income Tax Credit, and Infant Health." *American Journal of Economics* 7, no. 1 (2015): 172–211.

Hoynes, Hilary, Diane Whitmore Schanzenbach, and Douglas Almond. "Long-Run Impacts of Childhood Access to the Safety Net." *American Economic Review* 106, no. 4 (2016): 903–34.

Johnson, Rucker, and C. Kirabo Jackson. "Reducing Inequality through Dynamic Complementarity: Evidence from Head Start and Public School Spending." *American Economic Journal: Economic Policy* 11, no. 4 (2019): 310–49.

Kalil, Ariel, and Rebecca Ryan. "Parenting Practices and Socioeconomic Gaps in Childhood Outcomes." *Future of Children* 30, no. 1 (Spring 2020): 29–54.

Kalil, Ariel, Rebecca Ryan, and Elise Chor. "Time Investments in Children across Family Structures." *Annals of the American Academy of Political and Social Science* 654, no. 1 (2014): 150–68.

Kalil, Ariel, Rebecca Ryan, and Michael Corey. "Diverging Destinies: Maternal Education and the Development Gradient in Time with Children." *Demography* 49, no. 4 (2012): 1361–83.

Kaushal, Neeraj, Katherine Magnuson, and Jane Waldfogel. "How Is Family Income Related to Investments in Children's Learning?" In *Whither Opportunity? Rising Inequality, Schools, and Children's Life Chances*, edited by G. J. Duncan and R. M. Murnane, 187–206. New York: Russell Sage Foundation, 2011.

Kearney, Melissa S. "Is There an Effect of Incremental Welfare Benefits on Fertility Behavior? A Look at the Family Cap." *Journal of Human Resources* 39, no. 2 (2004): 295–325.

Kearney, Melissa S., and Amy Ganz, eds. *Expanding Economic Opportunity for More Americans:*

Bipartisan Policies to Increase Work, Wages, and Skills. Aspen, CO: Aspen Institute Economic Strategy Group, February 2019. https://www.economicstrategygroup.org /publication/expanding-economic-opportunity-for-more-americans-copy/.

Kearney, Melissa S., and Phillip B. Levine. "Causes and Consequences of Declining US Fertility." Aspen Economic Strategy Group, August 13, 2022. https://www .economicstrategygroup.org/publication/Kearney_Levine/.

Kearney, Melissa S., and Philip B. Levine. "The Economics of Non-Marital Childbearing and the Marriage Premium for Children." *Annual Review of Economics* 9 (2017): 327–52.

Kearney, Melissa S., and Phillip B. Levine. "Income Inequality and Early, Non-Marital Childbearing." *Journal of Human Resources* 49 (Winter 2014): 1–31.

Kearney, Melissa S., and Phillip B. Levine. "Investigating Recent Trends in the U.S. Teen Birth Rates." *Journal of Health Economics* 41 (2015): 15–29.

Kearney, Melissa S., and Phillip B. Levine. "Media Influences on Social Outcomes: The Impact of MTV's *16 and Pregnant* on Teen Childbearing." *American Economic Review* 105, no. 12 (2015): 3597–632.

Kearney, Melissa S., and Phillip B. Levine. "Role Models, Mentors, and Media Effects." *Future of Children* 30, no. 1 (June 2020): 83–106.

Kearney, Melissa S., and Phillip B. Levine. "Subsidized Contraception, Fertility, and Sexual Behavior." *Review of Economics and Statistics* 91, no. 1 (2009): 137–51.

Kearney, Melissa S., and Phillip B. Levine. "Why Is the Teen Birth Rate in the United States So High and Why Does It Matter?" *Journal of Economic Perspectives* 26, no. 2 (2012): 141–66.

Kearney, Melissa S., and Phillip B. Levine. "Will Births in the US Rebound? Probably Not." Brookings Institution (blog), May 24, 2021. https://www.brookings.edu/blog/up-front /2021/05/24/will-births-in-the-us-rebound-probably-not/.

Kearney, Melissa S., and Riley Wilson. "Male Earnings, Marriageable Men, and Non-Marital Fertility: Evidence from the Fracking Boom." *Review of Economics and Statistics* 100, no. 4 (October 2018): 678–90.

Keene, Elodie, dir. *The Wire.* Season 2, episode 3, "Hot Shots." Aired June 15, 2003, on HBO.

Kindelan, Katie. "Dads Form 'Dad's on Duty' Squad to Help Stop Violence at Their Kids' High School." *Good Morning America*, October 27, 2021. https://www.goodmorningamerica .com/family/story/dads-form-dads-duty-squad-stop-violence-kids-80787546.

Kornrich, Sabino, and Frank Furstenberg. "Investing in Children: Changes in Parental Spending on Children, 1972–2007." *Demography* 50, no. 1 (2013): 1–23.

La Ferrara, Eliana, Alberto Chong, and Suzanne Duryea. "Soap Operas and Fertility: Evidence from Brazil." *American Economic Journal: Applied Economics* 4, no. 4 (2012): 1–31.

Lareau, Annette. *Unequal Childhoods.* Berkeley: University of California Press, 2003.

Levine, Phillip B. "Designing Effective Mentoring Programs for Disadvantaged Youth." In *Policies to Address Poverty in America*, edited by Melissa S. Kearney and Benjamin Harris, 47–54. Washington, DC: Hamilton Project, 2014.

Lindo, Jason M. "Are Children Really Inferior Goods? Evidence from Displacement Driven Income Shocks." *Journal of Human Resources* 45, no. 2 (2010): 301–27.

Lindo, Jason M., and Analisa Packham. "How Much Can Expanding Access to Long-Acting

Reversible Contraceptives Reduce Teen Birth Rates?" *American Economic Journal: Economic Policy* 9, no. 3 (2017): 348–76.

Lindo, Jason M., Jessamyn Schaller, and Benjamin Hansen. "Caution! Men Not at Work: Gender-Specific Labor Market Conditions and Child Maltreatment." *Journal of Public Economics* 163 (2018): 77–98.

Lino, Mark, Kevin Kuczynski, Nestor Rodriguez, and Rebecca Schap. *Expenditures on Children, by Families, 2015.* Miscellaneous Report no. 1528–2015. Washington, DC: United States Department of Agriculture, Center for Nutrition Policy and Promotion, January 2017, revised March 2017.

Lopoo, Leonard M., and Thomas DeLeire. "Family Structure and the Economic Wellbeing of Children during Youth and Adulthood." *Social Science Research* 43, no. 1 (2014): 30–44.

Lovenheim, Michael, and Kevin Mumford. "Do Family Wealth Shocks Affect Fertility Choices? Evidence from the Housing Market." *Review of Economics and Statistics* 95, no. 2 (2013): 464–75.

Ludwig, Jens, and Douglas L. Miller. "Does Head Start Improve Children's Life Chances? Evidence from a Regression Discontinuity Design." *Quarterly Journal of Economics* 122, no. 1 (2007): 159–208.

Lundquist, Erika, JoAnn Hsueh, Amy E. Lowenstein, Kristen Faucetta, Daniel Gubits, Charles Michalopoulos, and Virginia Knox. *A Family-Strengthening Program for Low-Income Families: Final Impacts from the Supporting Healthy Marriage Evaluation.* OPRE report 2014–09A. Washington, DC: Office of Planning, Research and Evaluation, Administration for Children and Families, US Department of Health and Human Services, 2014.

Mancuso, Gail, dir. *Modern Family.* Season 4, episode 7, "Arrested." Aired November 7, 2012, on ABC.

Mani, Anandi, Sendhil Mullainathan, Eldar Shafir, and Jiaying Zhao. "Poverty Impedes Cognitive Function." *Science* 341, no. 6149 (2013): 976–80.

Manning, Wendy D., Marshall N. Fettro, and Esther Lamidi. "Child Well-Being in Same-Sex Parent Families: Review of Research Prepared for American Sociological Association Amicus Brief." *Population Research Policy Review* 33, no. 4 (2014): 485–502.

Manoli, Day, and Nicholas Turner. "Cash-On-Hand and College Enrollment: Evidence from Population Tax Data and the Earned Income Tax Credit." *American Economic Journal: Economic Policy* 10, no. 2 (2018): 242–71.

Mayer, Susan, Ariel Kalil, Philip Oreopoulos, and Sebastian Gallegos. "Using Behavioral Insights to Increase Parental Engagement: The Parents and Children Together Intervention." *Journal of Human Resources* 54, no. 4 (2019): 900–925.

MBK Alliance. "We Are Our Brothers' Keepers." Obama Foundation, accessed April 14, 2021. https://www.obama.org/mbka/.

McLanahan, Sara, and Audrey N. Beck. "Parental Relationships in Fragile Families." *Future of Children* 20, no. 2 (Fall 2010): 17–38.

McLanahan, Sara, Irwin Garfinkel, Nancy Reichman, Julien Teitler, Marcia Carlson, and Christina Norland Audigier. *The Fragile Families and Child Wellbeing Study: Baseline National Report.* Princeton, NJ: Bendheim-Thoman Center for Research on Child Wellbeing,

March 2003. http://www.fragilefamilies.princeton.edu/documents/nationalreport.pdf.

McLanahan, Sara, and Gary Sandefur. *Growing Up with a Single Parent: What Hurts, What Helps?* Cambridge, MA: Harvard University Press, 1994.

McLanahan, Sara, Laura Tach, and Daniel Schneider, "The Causal Effects of Father Absence." *Annual Review of Sociology* 39 (2013): 399–427.

Meezan, William, and Jonathan Rauch. "Gay Marriage, Same-Sex Parenting, and America's Children." *Future of Children* 15, no. 2 (2005): 97–115.

Miller, Sarah, and Laura R. Wherry. "The Long-Term Effects of Early Life Medicaid Coverage." *Journal of Human Resources* 54, no. 3 (2019): 785–824.

Mitchell, Jessica. 2019 Big Brothers Big Sisters of America Annual Impact Report. Cincinnati, OH: Big Brothers Big Sisters of America, May 2020. https://www.bbbs.org/wp-content/uploads/2019-BBBSA-Annual-Impact-Report-FINAL.pdf.

Moffitt, Robert A. "The Effect of Welfare on Marriage and Fertility." In *Welfare, the Family, and Reproductive Behavior: Research Perspectives*, edited by Robert A. Moffitt and National Research Council (US) Committee on Population. Washington, DC: National Academies Press (US), 1998. https://www.ncbi.nlm.nih.gov/books/NBK230345/.

Murray, Charles. *Coming Apart: The State of White America 1960–2010*. New York: Crown Forum, 2012.

Norris, Samuel, Matthew Pecenco, and Jeffrey Weaver. "The Effects of Parental and Sibling Incarceration: Evidence from Ohio." *American Economic Review* 111, no. 9 (2021): 2926–63.

Obama, Barack. Father's Day speech. Apostolic Church of God, Chicago, IL, June 15, 2008. https://www.politico.com/story/2008/06/text-of-obamas-fatherhood-speech-011094.

Okun, Arthur M. *Equality and Efficiency: The Big Tradeoff*. Washington, DC: Brookings Institution, 1975.

Page, Sydney. "This 11-Year-Old Sells Cups of Lemonade to Buy Diapers for Single Moms." *Washington Post*, August 21, 2020. https://www.washingtonpost.com/lifestyle/2020/08/21/this-11-year-old-sells-cups-lemonade-buy-diapers-single-moms/.

Personal Responsibility and Work Opportunity Reconciliation Act of 1996. Pub. L. No. 104-193, 110 Stat. 2105 (1996). https://www.congress.gov/104/plaws/publ193/PLAW-104publ193.pdf.

Pew Research Center. *Parenting in America: Outlook, Worries, Aspirations Are Strongly Linked to Financial Situation*. Washington, DC: Pew Research Center, 2015. https://assets.pewresearch.org/wp-content/uploads/sites/3/2015/12/2015-12-17_parenting-in-america_FINAL.pdf.

Pew Research Center. "Religion and Living Arrangements around the World." Pew Research Center, December 12, 2019. https://www.pewforum.org/2019/12/12/religion-and-living-arrangements-around-the-world/.

Price, Joseph, and Ariel Kalil. "The Effect of Mother-Child Reading Time on Children's Reading Skills: Evidence from Natural Within-Family Variation." *Child Development* 90, no. 6 (2019): 688–702.

Ramey, Garey, and Valerie A. Ramey. "The Rug Rat Race." *Brookings Papers on Economic Activity, Economic Studies Program* 41, no. 1 (Spring 2010): 129–99.

Raspberry, William. "The Men Aren't There to Marry." *Washington Post*, May 8, 1985. https://www.washingtonpost.com/archive/politics/1985/05/08/the-men-arent-there -to-marry/480cfbc7-3ff2-46f8-8a5f-54d4bf18100d/.

Reardon, Sean F. "The Widening Socioeconomic Status Achievement Gap: New Evidence and Possible Explanations." In *Whither Opportunity? Rising Inequality and the Uncertain Life Chances of Low-Income Children*, edited by R. J. Murnane and G. J. Duncan, 91–116. New York: Russell Sage Foundation, 2011.

Reardon, Sean F., and Ximena A. Portilla. "Recent Trends in Income, Racial, and Ethnic School Readiness Gaps at Kindergarten Entry." *AERA Open* 2, no. 3 (July 2016).

Reczek, Corinne. "Sexual- and Gender-Minority Families: A 2010 to 2020 Decade in Review." *Journal of Marriage and Family* 82, no. 1 (2020): 300–325.

"Resilience." Center on the Developing Child, Harvard University, accessed July 20, 2021. https://developingchild.harvard.edu/science/key-concepts/resilience/.

Sawhill, Isabel. *Generation Unbound: Drifting into Sex and Parenthood without Marriage.* Washington, DC: Brookings Institution Press, 2014.

Shenhav, Na'ama. "Lowering Standards to Wed? Spouse Quality, Marriage, and Labor Market Responses to the Gender Wage Gap." *Review of Economics and Statistics* 103, no. 2 (2021): 265–79.

Stevenson, Betsey, and Justin Wolfers. "Bargaining in the Shadow of the Law: Divorce Laws and Family Distress." *Quarterly Journal of Economics* 121, no. 1 (February 2006): 267–288.

"Study Finds American Women Delaying Motherhood because the Whole Thing Blows." *Onion*, June 18, 2021. https://www.theonion.com/study-finds-american-women -delaying-motherhood-because-1847112786.

"Tenement Apartment Tours." Tenement Museum, accessed November 7, 2022. https:// www.tenement.org/apartment-tours/.

Thompson, Owen. "Head Start's Long-Run Impact: Evidence from the Program's Introduction." *Journal of Human Resources* 53, no. 4 (2018): 1100–1139.

Tierney, Joseph P., Jean B. Grossman, and Nancy L. Resch. *Making a Difference: An Impact Study of Big Brothers/Big Sisters.* Philadelphia, PA: Public/Private Ventures, 1995.

Trickey, Erick. "What Works: Group Therapy Is Saving Lives in Chicago." *Politico*, September 21, 2017. https://www.politico.com/magazine/story/2017/09/21/chicago-violence -crime-psychology-cognitive-behavioral-therapy-215633/.

US Census Bureau. *Income and Poverty in the United States: 2019.* Current Population Reports P60-270. Washington, DC: United States Census Bureau, September 2020. https://www .census.gov/content/dam/Census/library/publications/2020/demo/p60-270.pdf.

US Department of Education, Office for Civil Rights, Civil Rights Data Collection. "2013– 14 Discipline Estimations by Discipline Type" and "2013–14 Estimations for Enrollment." In National Center for Education Statistics, "Percentage of Students Receiving Selected Disciplinary Actions in Public Elementary and Secondary Schools, by Type of Disciplinary Action, Disability Status, Sex, and Race/Ethnicity: 2013–14." *Digest of*

Education Statistics, table 233.28, January 2018. https://nces.ed.gov/programs/digest
/d19/tables/dt19_233.28.asp.

US Department of Health and Human Services. *Vital Statistics of the United States 1980: Volume 1—Natality*. Hyattsville, MD: National Center for Health Statistics, 1984. https://www.cdc.gov/nchs/data/vsus/nat80_1acc.pdf.

US Department of Health and Human Services, Administration for Children and Families. "Home Visiting Evidence of Effectiveness." Accessed November 15, 2022. https://homvee.acf.hhs.gov/.

US Department of Health and Human Services, Office of Child Care. "Home Visiting." Last updated May 19, 2022. https://www.acf.hhs.gov/occ/home-visiting.

US Department of Health and Human Services, Office of Family Assistance. "About Healthy Marriage and Responsible Fatherhood." Updated April 8, 2021. https://www.acf.hhs.gov/ofa/programs/healthy-marriage/about.

US Department of Health, Education, and Welfare. *Vital Statistics of the United States 1960: Volume 1—Natality*. Washington, DC: US Department of Health, Education, and Welfare, 1963. https://www.cdc.gov/nchs/data/vsus/nat60_1.pdf.

Vance, J. D. *Hillbilly Elegy: A Memoir of a Family and Culture in Crisis*. New York: Harper, 2016.

Watson, Tara. "Inequality and the Measurement of Residential Segregation by Income in American Neighborhoods." *Review of Income and Wealth* 55, no. 3 (2009): 820–44.

Whitaker, Anamarie A., Garrett Baker, Luke J. Matthews, Jennifer Sloan McCombs, and Mark Barrett. *Who Plays, Who Pays? Funding for and Access to Youth Sports*. Santa Monica, CA: RAND Corporation, 2019. https://www.rand.org/pubs/research_reports/RR2581.html.

Wilson, William Julius. *The Truly Disadvantaged: The Inner City, the Underclass, and Public Policy*. Chicago: University of Chicago Press, 1987.

Youth Guidance. *Annual Report 2018–2019*. Chicago: Youth Guidance, 2020. https://www.youth-guidance.org/wp-content/uploads/2022/11/Youth-Guidance-Annual-Report-2018-2019.pdf.

Ziliak, James. "Temporary Assistance for Needy Families." In *Economics of Means-Tested Transfer Programs*, vol. 1, edited by Robert Moffitt, 303–93. Chicago: University of Chicago Press, 2015.

Index

Page numbers in italics indicate figures and tables.